The Ethics of Terminal Care

Orchestrating the End of Life

The Ethics of Terminal Care

Orchestrating the End of Life

Erich H. Loewy and Roberta Springer Loewy

University of California, Davis
Sacramento, California

Kluwer Academic / Plenum Publishers
New York, Boston, Dordrecht, London, Moscow

Library of Congress Cataloging-in-Publication Data

Loewy, Erich H.
    The ethics of terminal care: orchestrating the end of life/Erich H. Loewy and Roberta
Springer Loewy.
        p. cm.
    Includes bibliographical references (p.   ) and index.
        ISBN 0-306-46435-7 (alk. paper)
        1. Terminal care—Moral and ethical aspects.   2. Terminal care.   I. Loewy, Roberta
Springer. II. Title.

R726 .L59 2000
174'.24—dc21

                                                                            00-041588

ISBN 0-306-46435-7

©2000 Kluwer Academic / Plenum Publishers, New York
233 Spring Street, New York, New York 10013

http://www.wkap.nl/

10 9 8 7 6 5 4 3 2 1

A C.I.P. record for this book is available from the Library of Congress

To those who lack fair access to those things
that make a life with dignity possible.

Oh Herr, gib jedem seinen eigenen Tod.
Das Sterben, das aus einem Leben geht,
Darin er Liebe hatte, Sinn und Not.

   Rainer Maria Rilke, *Die Gedichte*

Oh, Lord, give each their own death.
A dying which emerges from a life
Composed of Love and Sense and Suffering.

   Translation by Erich H. Loewy

Preface

All living things die. Unless they die suddenly, all living things go through a period of decline that can, at least in retrospect, be called "the end of life." The artwork we call our life is not one that we shape in splendid isolation. It is one that is crafted in the context and developed within the framework of the possibilities our community offers. Thus, while much about a life is biologically determined, much else is determined by the social circumstances surrounding it. One need think only of the way Tolstoy's Ivan Illych died or the way that Betty Higden experienced her evident transient ischemic episodes and eventually died in Dickens' "Our Mutual Friend" to be convinced of this. In our own Western culture how we die is a product of biological, psychological and social factors and circumstances.

In this book we examine some of the medical, social and psychological conditions which affect the way we die. How we will die is partially, but only partially, beyond our control. Today we have more control over how we live and how we die than we have ever had before. This fact has produced many ethical problems but has also offered us some wonderful opportunities. Unfortunately (at least in the view of the authors) we have spent altogether too little energy in dealing with the social and psychological factors within which the medical (i.e., biological) are imbedded and which, to a large measure, determine them.

We are a wealthy nation and have many of the world's leading medical and nursing colleges. We do not need to have over forty million uninsured who have, at best, only capricious access to health care. We do not need to have an increase in distance between the grindingly poor and the enormously (some of us would say obscenely) wealthy. We do, however, need to educate physicians and nurses who remain ill equipped to deal with issues of pain, suffering and loneliness. The fact that we do have these uninsured, these poor and these abandoned is a national shame. It is well within our ability to change these factors, and until we do, speaking about ethical problems at the end of life is only speaking about the ethical problems of those of us who are already too well off. For that reason we have chosen to reiterate such factors repeatedly in our discussion.

In addition, we must realize that such a topic is one that, for the greater populace of this world, is meaningless. Far more people live in what we have chosen to call "third world" or "underdeveloped nations" than the minority who have had the enormous luck to be born into our western society. Thus, these concerns are as meaningless to the majority of people outside of this country as they, unfortunately, often are for the poor in the United States. Bertolt Brecht long ago remarked, "Erst kommt das Fressen, dann kommt die Moral" ("First one must eat, then one can worry about ethics.").

Parenthetically, we have assumed a number of issues as currently being rather more, than less, settled in the end-of-life discussion. We assume, for example, that there is no significant ethical (or legal, for that matter) difference between supplying artificial fluid and nutrition and other forms of medical intervention. We also assume that there is no significant ethical (or legal) difference between withholding and terminating life support. These are issues that, because of the now wide consensus among persons in the medical, ethical and legal professions, we have chosen not to discuss in order to allow us to focus our energies elsewhere.

Our hope is that this book will spark not only professional debate but public debate as well. Since the end of life is an eventuality for us all, we should all have an opportunity to participate in that debate.

Acknowledgments

The authors wish to thank a number of people whose contributions have made this book a reality. Our thanks go first of all to Dr. Faith Fitzgerald at UC Davis who invariably asked challenging questions and often suggested provocative points of view. Likewise our thanks go to the Dean of the Medical School at the University of California, Davis, who was instrumental in creating the kind of atmosphere which made this work possible and encouraged it all along the way. Dr. Fred Meyers, the chairperson of internal medicine and an oncologist who has always had a keen and constructive interest in end-of-life issues, was likewise helpful in creating a conducive work environment. Dr. Ben Rich, formerly of the University of Colorado and now our colleague here, deserves special thanks for his interest and help.

Among the many people who gave constructive criticism for our work in progress and to whom we owe a great deal is Dr. Perry Pugno, former head of the alumni association and now in charge of the educational efforts of the American Academy of Family Physicians, and Dr. Anita Tarzian of Baltimore. Both of them read and commented most helpfully on parts of this manuscript. Special thanks also go to the Medical Alumni Association of the University of California, Davis, for their interest, encouragement and creative support.

Special thanks go to our friend and colleague Dr. Thomas Frühwald of Vienna, Austria, a geriatrician with an innovative approach to geriatric as well as palliative care and a keen sense of decency and justice. Together with his former chief Dr. Christian Zembaty, he created an institutional setting—now for political reasons no longer extant—from which we learned a great deal and from which this book profited.

It has been said that we stand on the shoulders of giants and, to an extent, this is true. The insights we develop are nurtured by many of the great thinkers who have made our own thinking possible. But with even more reason we need to be aware of the many shoulders of colleagues, friends, associates and, above all, students upon which we stand. Without their comments, questions and stimulation our work would have been not only impoverished but, indeed, impossible.

Contents

Contents

Chapter 1

Introduction

This book deals with ethical issues at the end of life—and in particular with what we shall call orchestrating this stage of our existence. The perception not only of what it is to die but also of what it is to live has changed over the ages. To live (in the sense of conscious living) as we understand it in our culture today, is to have individual life plans and expectations, individual hopes and fears. Such a concept of what it is to be alive is one prevalent in our industrialized western society. It is not necessarily a point of view shared (or at least seen in the same way and to the same extent) by other cultures and often not even by particular cultural and religious enclaves within our own American culture. Thus, any book (and any reader) attempting to grapple with such life issues—and especially with ethical issues at the end of life—must understand and be sensitive to this fact.

In considering such issues we need to see what experience can teach us. Our ethical problems need to be attuned to pertinent historical, social, cultural and economic conditions. Therefore, the way such problems are confronted in the United States, will differ somewhat from the way they are confronted in France, Germany or Austria. And yet we must not over-emphasize these differences. People—no matter who they are or what they are, no matter what their cultural or religious heritage and beliefs—have more in common that unites them than they have differences that divide them. Two of the things they have in common and both of which in all cultures are in many ways looked upon as mysterious are birth and death. We come, as it were, from the unknown and to the unknown we eventually depart.

We live longer today than we ever have before. Under normal circumstances—barring violence or sudden catastrophic illness—there is an increasingly longer period between the time when we stop being employed and the time when we eventually die. In many ways this lengthening of time is

analogous to the shortening of the average workday in this century: both
have left an increase of leisure time; both can be perceived as a boon or
grudgingly accepted as a curse.

One of the achievements of modern medicine is the creation of chronic
illness—and we do not mean this sarcastically. For without modern medicine
many persons with birth defects, many diabetics, many arthritics, many patients with heart disease, many cancer patients and many patients with a host
of other maladies would not be alive. The fact that we live longer—and increasingly with the burden of some chronic disease—has inevitably shaped
the way in which we tend to view the end of life. And, it has greatly increased the costs of health care.

It has been said that the cost of dying is enormous. We tend to spend an
enormous percentage of our medical resources during the last few weeks of
life—though some dispute the figures on which this is based.[1] With the
graying of the West there is an ever greater anxiety about the resources
needed to maintain persons who are no longer gainfully employed. Such a
fear, of course, rests in part on a societal attitude towards the elderly. Many
societies and cultures view members of the older generation as assets to be
cherished. By and large our culture in the United States does not. Rather, we
tend to view the elderly as burdensome obligations to be grudgingly supported. Our attitude towards the elderly and the health-costs expended on the
elderly rides piggyback on such a view.

In this book we hope to speak not only about the way individuals end
their lives in our culture today but also about the culture itself. To speak of
dealing well with the end of life is to acknowledge the value of life and of
living at all stages. Ethical problems do not exist in some sort of theoretical
outer space; they are issues we confront in our daily existences. Thus, they
must, if they are to be properly recognized, analyzed and confronted be attentive to context. Individuals do not and, in fact, cannot exist outside of a
social nexus which shapes all their thoughts and activities. If we hope to create an atmosphere in which our last few days, weeks, months or years form
an integral part of our life, we must be attentive to the social conditions
which shape such living.

In the view expressed here personal morality may very well be derivable
from religion, tradition, culture or one's conscience; ethics is not.[2] Ethics is
basically a question of "authority," but an "authority" which we can point to
when discussing different courses of action and expect others to accept. Our
particular religion, tradition or cultural mores (and our conscience, to a large
part formed by these) may and probably is a quite different one than is the
religion, tradition or culture of the person with whom we are in dialogue.
Ethics seeks to find a link connecting these various religiously, culturally
and traditionally derived but quite different points of view. As a result, ethics

must inevitably resort to logic and a common framework of inevitable human capacities and experiences in order to establish its authority. Given that all humans (and to some extent all higher animals) share such a framework and sense of logic, it should come as no surprise that all religions and all ethical systems share very similar ground rules. For example, they all prohibit murder, theft and lying, and they all recommend helping, rather than hindering, one's neighbour.[3]

Why should we bother ourselves about ethical problems to begin with? An ethical problem comes up whenever our contemplated action or rule affects another—something that in life and especially in medicine is inevitably the case. The problem presupposes the ability to execute the contemplated action or enforce a contemplated rule, but once that is established (once we know that we can do something) the ethical question, "Ought I to do what I know (or think) I can do?" presents itself. If our sense of self and self-preservation were to be the only primitive drive we have, this "ought" question would be answerable purely by one's self interest—but in fact it is not. Human beings (and probably all higher animals) do care about the answer to such a question—they care because all such beings are endowed with a sense of compassion that balances self-interest.[4] It is what Schopenhauer has rightfully termed "the driving spring of ethics."[5] Equipped with a sense of compassion and united as humans by common capacities and basic experiences we can craft an ethical framework within which we can live, express and appreciate our cultural differences.[6]

The authors have both had the experience of having seen many people die. We have been at the bedside and have had to deal with many and varied vexing ethical issues. What has impressed us most is how badly the end of life is, in fact, handled compared to how well it could be. Likewise we have been impressed that the end of life is a period which is not separable from the rest of that life—that it represents the final stages in a patient's work of art. The last symphony, concerto or song written by a composer does not stand alone. It is integrally connected to what has gone before. That is, it derives its strength and its individual expression from what has gone before. Just as in the entire *oeuvre* of a composer, the last work derives its strengths and weaknesses from what has gone before, so the last chapter in the life of each of us is indivisibly part and parcel, of what has gone before. In this text the authors carefully examine our society's current attitudes towards this last chapter (as well as material conditions that seem to render it more problematic than necessary) and suggest an alternative to the reactive and piecemeal manner in which it is so often confronted today.

ENDNOTES AND REFERENCES

1. There is a question whether the last six months of life are an important factor in escalating health care costs. Among a plethora of papers see, S. Felder, "Cost of Dying: Alternatives to Rationing," *Health Policy* 1997; 39(2): 167-176 and E.J. Emanuel, L.L. Emanuel, "The Economics of Dying: The Illusion of Cost Savings at the End of Life," *New England Journal of Medicine*, 94; 330(8): 540-544.

2. D.C. Thomasma and E.H. Loewy, "Exploring the Role of Religion in Medical Ethics," *Cambridge Quarterly of Healthcare Ethics*, 1996; 5: 257-268.

3. E.H. Loewy, *Moral Strangers, Moral Acquaintance and Moral Friends: Connectedness and Its Conditions* (Albany, NY: State University of New York Press), 1997.

4. The importance of compassion as a natural trait with which all sentient beings are endowed is emphasized throughout Rousseau's work. See especially, J.J. Rousseau, *The Social Contract and the Discourses*, edited and translated by G.D.H. Cole (NY: Everyman's Library), 1993.

A. Schopenhauer, "Preisschrift über die Grundlagen der Moral," *Arthur Schopenhauer: Kleinere Schriften*, Band III: *Arthur Schopenhauer's sämtliche Werke*, edited by Wolfgand Frhr. von Löhneisen (Frankfrut a/M, Deutschland: Suhrkamp Tachenbuch, 1986), p 742.

5. E.H. Loewy, *Moral Strangers, Moral Acquaintance and Moral Friends: Connectedness and Its Conditions* (Albany, NY: State University of New York Press), 1997.

Chapter 2

Dying, Death and Attitudes

1.   INTRODUCTION

Thinking about the end of life inevitably conjures up visions of death and these visions may blight or enrich what life remains. That we are bound to die is a truism to which we pay lip service—even if, as Freud claimed, we really don't believe it. In many ways one can compare one's life to a great symphony or to some other work of art. The comparison is, of course, a comparison and not an analogy—we have experiences before we hear the music and we will continue to have experiences after the music ends. But insofar as a symphony has a beginning, a middle and an end and has themes, exposition and development, it has an inescapable similarity to life. When we come to the last movement of Beethoven's 9th symphony we realize that we are approaching the end of something awe-inspiring, filled with beauty and thoroughly enjoyable in the way only great art can be. But this knowledge that we are nearing the end does not sadden us. It neither dampens our spirit nor detracts from our appreciation and enjoyment of that great last movement. As much as the first movement, the last belongs to the totality of a work that, to be truly appreciated, must be understood as a whole.

The last movement of Beethoven's ninth is truly meaningful only in the context of the entire symphony. If the preceding movements had been less majestic, if they had failed to prepare the ground properly, our perception of the last movement would have been quite different. If the first three movements had been boring or distasteful, the last would have hardly been much appreciated. A work of art—or its performance—has a completeness about it without which any of its integral parts loses beauty and meaning.

5

The ninth Beethoven or its performance, furthermore, does not take place in a vacuum. It occurs in a social, historical and cultural setting that can serve to heighten or to lessen our ability to appreciate the work. Heard in a great concert hall it is a different work than when heard in our living room while sipping a good glass of wine. Heard while huddling on the doorstep of a great symphony hall, while hungry, cold and with no place to go will modify or even nullify our ability to hear and to appreciate it. Heard emanating from a Berlin symphony hall while going down the streets of Berlin wearing rags and a yellow star or hearing the music from a radio while being driven into a gas chamber by one's enemies—will change the way we hear the music. In dealing with issues at the end of life, then, we cannot take that life out of the context of its history, of its social setting or its existential being.

The end of life can be arbitrarily defined—but such a definition is rarely useful. There are times when the end of life can only be defined arbitrarily, as when a patient dies relatively suddenly or as the result of an unexpected or generally remediable illness. Often in western society today months or years of waning capacity and strength herald that end, which is frequently (but by no means always) associated with old age. Whenever and however it comes, it cannot be understood or managed well outside an understanding of the context of the entire life preceding it. Helping to shape the end of life or, to use our language, "to orchestrate it," then, requires one to be mindful of the entire life and its opportunities (or lack thereof).

2.   THE SOCIAL CONTEXT IN AMERICA TODAY

In discussing the way we shape the end of our life we need to be very aware of what a luxury it is even to think about being able to do so. Throughout history and down to the present a large number of people (probably a majority) did not have this luxury and still do not have it today—the death of many (perhaps most) people was and continues to be violent, harried and surrounded by indifference or even hatred. Their lives as well as their deaths seem almost as unfortunate accidents. Wars, genocides and other acts of terror as well as famines, poverty, and homelessness have sealed and today continue to seal, the fate of many if not a majority of the earth's population. People starving, worked to death or gassed in concentration camps, persons hacked to death in Rwanda or those ground up in the ever-recurring Yugoslav tragedy have not had the opportunity to worry about, shape or modulate their dying. The poor, homeless, hungry and those without ready access to adequate medical care dying in America today should be ever present reminders that one does not need to live in an overtly terrorized or terrorizing situation or nation to meet a similar fate. We in the western world who happen to be well off (as compared to those in the rest of the world and those in our midst who are poor) are a small minority of very fortunate people. We would submit that such undeserved fortune obligates us to be concerned about the fate of the many who are less well positioned.

The end of life is no different from the beginning or middle insofar as it occurs in, and is conditioned by, the social context in which it occurs. However, just as in the last movement of a symphony the music is heard in a given location which affects the way in which it is heard and felt, the end of life is inevitably shaped by and can be understood only in terms of what has gone before. The end of life occurs in a particular locus (home, hospital or other institution) and thus critically affects the way it is experienced. A person's life is inevitably shaped by and understood in terms of that person's personal story, within the context of a particular social framework. This social framework, in turn, exists within the embrace of a particular society. The social context in which the last phase of living occurs, is not made up only of family and friends but includes the entire social situation in which individuals and their families find themselves. Hopefully, the end of life or "dying" (like living) takes place in the midst of our friends, our family and of others who are intimately connected with the way we understand ourselves. When circumstances allow this to be the case, our family and our other close associations condition, if not in fact determine, the way in which our living and dying will occur. The individual members of our family are, however, not only enmeshed in a relationship with us but a host of other relationships each peculiar to each. To see families as being isolated from the larger society is to miss such wider connections. Our family exists in the midst of others, in community that conditions and/or determines the very structure of the family itself and which is intimately associated with its ability to flourish or decay. A focus on individuals to the exclusion of their complex social nexus is, therefore, much too narrow a focus.

To understand how we die—or better said how we live the last part of our lives—is to try to understand not only how we have lived but also to understand the social context in which our lives are pursued and the end of our lives will occur. Our attitudes towards life (and, therefore, our attitude towards death), our hopes, aspirations and expectations are molded and shaped by the kind of life which we have lived and continue to live. The end of life is neither separate nor separable. All of our life takes place in and is a response to a particular culture and its particular social conditions. We shall, therefore, begin by sketching the wider and more general social context of this discussion.

The United States today is, in many respects, a land of extremes. Nowhere in the industrialized world are the differences between the highest and the lowest wage earner within any given field as great. Nowhere in the western world are the differences between the "haves" and the "have-nots" as marked. Our schools vary from the few superb to the many incredibly bad. Our health care system is, simultaneously, one of the most technically advanced and one of the most socially deplorable. No other western society has as much private charity—or needs it. No other western society claims to be as religiously oriented yet remains callous to the fate of its poor, weak and disadvantaged as ours.

A large percentage of the population in the United States lives below the poverty line. Many of these individuals are not unemployed: they are considered the "working poor." Working full time at a minimum wage still leaves many—at times whole families–in poverty. While the percentage of all persons below the poverty line has fallen from 1970 to 1995, the number of black persons in the same category has decreased only slightly. During the period from 1980 to 1995 the number of all children below the poverty level has gone from 17.9% to 20%; and while the percentage of black children in the same category has remained stable at a staggering 41.5%, that of Hispanics has increased from 33% to 39.3%.[1] Above all and most importantly: the way it is defined has pushed what is considered to be the poverty line unrealistically low. To quote:

> Because the cost of basic necessities at the minimum standard rose more rapidly than the general price index...the official poverty line fell ever further behind economic reality over the years....If government officials had simply re-applied the same formula for measuring the cost of necessities that was used to calculate the original poverty line, they would have discovered that a family of four needed at least 50% more than that.[2]

This means that the a poverty line set at $10,000.00 would, in real terms, have to be $15,000 and one of $15,000 would be $ 22,500.00 In effect this makes the so-called "decrease" in poverty a shameful deceit.

Thanks to the way that our insurance and pension systems are organized and managed, the affluent can well afford to build up a substantial retirement portfolio whereas the poor cannot. As a result, the growing spread between the very wealthy and the very poor greatly affects access to health care among the elderly as well as among other age groups.[3]

Everyone will agree that a death with dignity (or an end of life with dignity) is something they would wish for themselves. Most will agree that an end of life with dignity should be available for everyone. And many will agree that, to the extent that this is possible, a decent community would do everything to provide this for all its members. A decent community, it has been argued, is one that avoids humiliating its members.[4] Yet, what can it mean to be provided with the means to a dignified end of life when life prior to that end was bereft of that opportunity? The end of life must, in all of its aspects, be integrated into the totality of a particular life. Medical care—whether it is medical care aimed at cure, prolongation or palliation and whether it concerns itself with the purely "medical" or with the psychosocial as well—takes place within a social nexus which determines what can be done as well as the shape of what is done.

In former times, physicians and hospitals generally cared for the poor regardless of their ability to pay. It was relatively simple: the well to do and wealthy were charged more so that the poor could be adequately cared for. Those days (wherein what was called the "Robin Hood Principle" balanced the books) are gone. While the costs of medical care have increased astronomically, third party payers are not concerned with providing health care to those not insured by them. If they are "for profit" their main obligation is to maximize profit for their stockholders and if they are "not-for-profit" their obligation is to maximize care only to the people actually enrolled in their plan. Increasingly managed care organizations and other "third parties" are determining not only who will be treated but the kind of diagnostic and therapeutic procedures a physician is "allowed" to do, including the length of time a physician spends with each particular patient. Furthermore, physicians are far from being free agents who can dispose of their time and skills according to their own lights. Many of the ethical problems today are, in reality, "system errors." A system error is a problem whose just solution is, if not entirely prevented, at least critically conditioned by the system within which it is located. This fact alone should make it evident that health care professionals who truly care about their patients must do more than merely "do the best for their patients within the confines of the system" (and here and there "game the system"). They must begin to take an active part in reshaping the system itself. One cannot practice truly ethical medicine in an unethical institution.

Health-care professionals are primarily concerned with the physical and psychological welfare of their particular patients and properly so. And, yet, while they concede the importance of the prior medical history, the prior social history is too often given short shrift. Health care professionals are largely dedicated to the issues of here and now. They may realize that their patients have lived an altogether unfulfilled life and they know that they cannot alter the past social history of their individual patients. Undoubtedly past history cannot be changed; but equally undoubtedly what happens today becomes history tomorrow and what happens tomorrow is history the day after. Unless we work towards changing the system in which we are forced to operate, our tomorrows will be beyond our control and most likely worse (for doctors as well as patients). Social conditions, unlike earthquakes or droughts, are subject to willful manipulation. Society as we know it today is something we have constructed and something we—and especially we who live in a democracy—are able to change. Health care professionals frequently try to separate themselves and their practice from the social circumstances in which their professional activity takes place and fail to partake of the common and inevitably ongoing task of reconstructing society. As experts in the field of health care who know full well the role that social conditions play not only in the genesis of illness but likewise in the way in which such illness will be perceived and managed, health care professionals can (and we feel must) play an important political role.

Beyond this, health, disease, being born and dying takes place within a society, which shapes them. The way we live (whether we are well nourished, have a warm or a cooled home, have ready access to basic health care and so forth) not only determines sickness and health but shapes the illness and the understanding of that illness for the rich and poor alike. Infectious diseases which may occur in patients who lack access to health care, spreads to those who do have access. Tuberculosis—a not inconsiderable problem today—readily spreads to those who live well and have good health coverage. The pneumonia a patient on chemotherapy contacts may very well be one he or she would not have contacted had their neighbor without health insurance been adequately treated. The problems physicians encounter in their daily practice cannot be isolated from the context in which they occur and which has shaped them. Thus in order to have a positive effect on the particular institution or system within which they treat their particular patients, physicians must trouble themselves about the problems of the society in which these systems and institutions are located. As experts in health care they are particularly well placed to see the effects of social conditions on the health of their patients as well as on the nature of their institutions. Not only can one not practice truly ethical medicine in an unethical institution, one cannot hope to create just institutions in the context of an unjust and uncaring society.

Our social context is not only one in which terrible poverty and inequity happens to occur, it is one in which such poverty and inequity is accepted as part of an individualistic world view. Such a world-view has to lead to estrangement from one another as well as to a lack of solidarity within the community. Poverty and inequity are not necessary conditions of existence, but part of a social construct. The point of view that we are (unless for our own convenience we choose to be otherwise) essentially free standing isolated individuals whose social connection with others is purely voluntary and tenuous is, at best, what Jonathan Moreno has so aptly termed the "myth of the asocial individual."[5] It is a myth of convenience, a world view very congenial to a crass and exploitive form of capitalism, one that allows us to view the suffering of others in our community with only passing and superficial interest, if at all. We focus on our own problems or on those of people similar to us. It can be no great wonder that with such a lack of solidarity the United States lacks a unified (let alone an even approachably equitable) health care system.[6]

Our most common relationships within our society tend to be superficial. People, for example, readily call each other by their first names but know little of substance about one another—and generally do not care to. Despite (and some will argue because of) our ready ability to communicate with one another (telephone, e-mail, etc.) we have become progressively more estranged. Why should the end of life in a context in which the fullness of life is so empty be suddenly different? Living in a society in which our relationships with others are a peculiar combination of superficiality and formality has been one of the factors promoting such institutions as nursing homes and in-patient hospices. Of course, there are other reasons for such institutions: in many families all of the adults work and can afford little time to care for dependent others—especially not for many months or for the round-the-clock care which end of life situations often demand. Still, most persons in the United States wish to die at home and a greater number now in fact do compared to the number in the past few decades. Some—because families genuinely and most understandably find themselves incapable of giving round the clock home care—will be sent to nursing homes and a few to the occasional in-bed hospice facility.

Hospice care can be most helpful. However, most hospices in the United States (see the chapter on hospice care) have rather explicit requirements, such as the presence of some sort of regular and dependable caregiver in the patient's home. For this reason, too, some people—especially the elderly, the senile or the totally incapacitated—are sent to nursing homes. While those nursing homes in which patients are cared for with Medicaid or other support dollars in the United States tend to be rather terrible, even those that cater to patients who can afford to pay out of pocket leave much to be desired. It is no wonder that patients so often feel that nursing home admission is a fate worse than death.

3.   WHAT WE THINK DYING AND BEING DEAD IS LIKE

People may be afraid of dying or afraid of being dead—those are quite different things to be afraid of. Our attitudes, both towards dying and towards what it means to be dead, have undergone marked changes throughout time and are different in the context of different cultures and different religious beliefs today. When we deal with people at the end of life it is well to understand not only their specific and explicit attitudes but also their cultural and religious background beliefs. The personal attitudes and beliefs a person has at any particular time may differ radically from the attitudes and beliefs of the culture or religion in which that person was reared or currently belongs. Although a person may well have abandoned the attitudes and beliefs with which they were brought up, these attitudes and beliefs nevertheless form an important part of the person's later attitudes and beliefs—if only as a reaction by the current towards the former. Likewise, persons may have—by choice or otherwise—changed their culture and may, in many if not indeed in all respects, have apparently adapted to and adopted the culture of their new abode. Nevertheless what they are at any one time is inevitably conditioned by what they were in the past. During crisis situations or as life is beginning to come to its end, such religious or cultural attitudes or beliefs may once again begin to manifest themselves in subtle (or perhaps not so subtle) ways. Dealing with persons at these points in life entails sensitivity to such issues.

The way people have viewed what being dead is like—and what persons may consider a fate which, contrasted with being dead, is "worse"—has greatly affected the way we deal with the whole notion of death today. When patients wish for death, it is often this picture of what being dead is like which serves as a contrast to their present existence. There are, as Carrick has pointed out, basically four ways of conceptualizing the state of being dead:[7]

1. In the Homeric tradition (in Egypt as well as Greece) and in what has been called the chthonic (from under the ground) religions, death was seen as an unconquerable and strange twilight condition. Little of interest happened. The dead were conceived as shadows wandering morosely through the underworld. In this tradition the immortal person was an eternal pale and spiritless wanderer:

   > Oh shining Odysseus, never try to console me for dying. I would rather follow the plow as a thrall to another man—one with no land allotted to him and not much to live on—than be a king over the perished dead.[8]

2. The Orphic-Pythagorean view espoused by Socrates and Plato (and which later gave rise to the various Christian ways of looking at what being dead is like) is that of the immortality of the soul.
3. The genetic survival (Carrick calls it "species survival") concept espoused by Aristotle holds that we live on through our offspring and fellow creatures.
4. The Stoic view of personal extinction considers death to be the true end of existence. There are, of course, variations on this theme: a

view of personal extinction and a belief in the immortality of the soul would not, for example, be inconsistent with a simultaneous belief that our genes or our works survive us.

Except for the chthonic view, which is not prevalent today, these basic views of what being dead is like continue to influence us. These differing conceptions of what being dead is like may produce feelings ranging from extremes of fear, revulsion or even envy. Understanding the function of these concepts in our everyday lives and attitudes as well as understanding the linguistic and conceptual symbolism of these ideas, is critical if we are to understand some of the ethical problems and deal with some of the choices which people wish to make.

The ancient Greek and Pythagorean model sees the disposition of the soul as an uninterrupted continuum. It was a view of the soul accepted by Socrates and Plato. In their view and in the view of some Christian churches today, the soul—freed from the body—continues on uninterrupted in another existence. This view may, for example, affect the way we feel about persons who are brain dead or permanently vegetative—it is the belief that even with the physical substrate gone, consciousness of some sort persists. On the other hand, many Christian traditions see the body and soul dying together (or, at least, the soul lying in a dormant stage) until, at a later time, (on the Day of Judgement) the soul (and in some beliefs the body) is resurrected. The fear or other emotions persons feel at the thought of death may be intimately connected with the way in which they envision the continuity of their souls. In a sense it is similar to the fear of general anesthesia: when I have surgery under local, "I" am still continually here; when I am under general anesthesia I rely on someone else to reawaken me. No matter how much I may trust, there is always that lingering doubt!

Depending on the particular tradition, Christianity today has varied (and, at times, no set) views of immortality. Hebrew thought is likewise neither clear nor uniform on these issues. Hebrew thought sees the relationship of man and God as one of covenant in which each has a part to play and each can call the other to account. In the traditional Hebrew viewpoint, life here on this earth is to be valued above all else and is, therefore, to be preserved at all costs. Until fairly recent times (and in the belief of most Jews) a belief in an afterlife played no great role in Judaism. Judaism today is split into many factions. Much of modern orthodox Jewish belief can be traced back to the Ghettos of Eastern Europe and the influence of Russian Orthodoxy. Judaic beliefs vary, ranging from the Hasidim through the Orthodox and Conservative to the Reformed, and they vary greatly among the individuals within these factions. Even though the definition of what constitutes life may vary, if there is any one point of agreement, it is that life is precious and merits the highest consideration and respect.

Islam has a set belief in the afterlife and Mohammedans believe in resurrection and heavenly judgment. Many eastern religions, moreover, subscribe to some form of reincarnation—for some, a reincarnation that continues until perfection is attained. There are great variations in the various cultural and religious belief systems of the East. Those who are concerned with helping persons in the last phase of life are well advised to familiarize themselves thoroughly with the religious and cultural beliefs and attitudes of the particular religion and culture their patients may embrace. Beyond this (and this cannot be stressed enough), the fact that a given individual comes from a particular culture and belongs to a particular religion does not necessarily predict how such a person will feel about any particular issue. It is important to understand the background culture and beliefs of the persons involved. However, it is also equally important not to assume that persons who come from a given culture or belief system necessarily share those beliefs.

The belief in personal extinction is rooted in the Stoic and Epicurean belief. Many persons, even when ostensibly sharing such a belief, find it hard to imagine that their ability to feel, think and participate will be no more. We can—even if at times with difficulty—imagine a world in which we did not exist but we find it most difficult (if not indeed repellent) to imagine a world in which those we know act without our participation. In part this is because we find it hard to believe that those we feel emotionally tied to (whether by bonds of love or hatred) are distinct from our emotions and not, in some way, contingent upon them. Our deep seated Cartesian dualism—which allows our body as the *res extensa* to perish—makes it difficult for us to perceive that our knowing self, our *res cogitans*, will vanish.

Beliefs of personal extinction are bereft of personal satisfaction except in the negative sense: If no personal "I" persists, then the "I" can no longer know or feel and, therefore, no further evil (or good) can befall it. What matters, the Epicureans, Stoics and those who share their belief today agree, is to live honorably and well. In this belief one lives well not because one is driven by fears of punishment or hope of reward, but because, as a human being and as a member of a community one shares a set of values and obligations with others. Life, then, is viewed as a necessary condition for experience and not as a freestanding value. When the possibility of positive experience seems to have irrevocably vanished and the future holds only negative experiences, ending life no longer seems an immoral or an impossible choice.

Many people say that they are not afraid of being dead but are very much afraid of dying. This seems unrelated to their belief or disbelief in a personal extinction or immortality. It is curious (and there seem to be no disciplined studies to confirm or refute what we are about to say), but many physicians we've asked have agreed—and none disagreed—that the impact which death seems to have on those remaining behind and to a lesser extent the behavior of people who are dying does not seem related to the presence or absence of religious beliefs. People who are dying face a loss in many respects more grievous than those who mourn a death. Even when a person who has been central to one's own life dies, it is the death of a single—even if, at times, a key—person. It is a loss buffered by a series of other relationships. The person who is dying faces a loss of all that they have ever known—not just one person or even many persons but a whole social nexus and, in fact, a whole world. It is little wonder that the stage of grieving by the dying person can be profound.

The way that we want to die has changed radically. In contrast to the predominant wish for a sudden death prevalent in western culture today, sudden death was greatly feared in early Christian times. To die suddenly was to be prevented from going through the required rituals—from performing the socially necessary tasks of taking one's leave, from receiving the sacraments and from not having done a host of other things deemed necessary by western culture at that time.[9] Thus, people prayed to be spared a sudden death. The early church had rules against burying in hallowed ground those who died suddenly—even those who had been victims of murder. In contrast, most people today see a "good death" as being one which comes suddenly, at an advanced age but still in the fullness of one's functions. The horror of dying suddenly has changed to a horror of dying with one's powers abating and dependent.

In the earlier parts of the Christian era there was a great deal of familiarity and far less dread of death. Dying, like much else, was public—the family and others naturally partook of this final event, children were present. The ceremony of death was far more important and public than the funeral that followed. People knew that death was their destiny and they accepted it. According to Ariés there is an echo of the chthonic belief—there was a belief in a continuity after death, albeit a "deadened and weakened one".[10] It is not surprising that persons died in this way since the idea of individual destiny and personality had not yet developed as fully as it has developed in today. We take for granted that persons always felt as individuals whose individual destiny and personality was clear and distinct. But that is not the case. It is only with the emergence of the later middle ages that individuality, as we know it, began to emerge. With this developed a more personal and a less communal feeling towards death—a "passion for being, an anxiety at not sufficiently being."[11] As time went on, death began to be seen differently: more dramatic and more distant and finally displaced from the consciousness of many people. Dying, as we know it today, is no longer a dying in the midst of family and friends, is no longer surrounded by social ritual.

Ritual has been displaced and the ritual of the funeral (especially in America) has replaced the ritual of dying.

Part of this change may simply be due to the increased ability of modern medicine to keep people alive far beyond the time when reasonable improvement or return of acceptable function can be expected. But that is not the only answer for attitudes changed already well before modern medicine's "success" in this regard. Pneumonia—until quite recent times, very much beyond medical control—carried the knickname, "old man's friend," because of the large number of elderly who succumbed to it in former times. Antibiotics only developed after the Second World War and intensive care units and most of the paraphernalia capable of prolonging life was unknown forty years ago. And yet people in the 1800's already hoped for a rapid rather than a more lingering death. After all: the ability to care for one's elderly at home depends not as much on individual circumstance as it does on social and communal support. In some countries family caregivers are allowed a leave from their job and paid a stipend by the community to take care of family members. Even then, however, factors other than the financial are operative. In the western world and especially in the United States today, families are spread far apart and while they may meet at stipulated times they are often far apart in much more than geography. The bonds of obligation tacitly assumed in times when people lived together are different than are these same bonds of obligation today.

Symbols at the end of life have also greatly changed. As the influence of religion has diminished and as the world has grown ever more secular the need for symbols—a need which seems a rather fundamental need in most cultures—has often remained unfulfilled and thus has left an important void. In many respects cardio-pulmonary-resuscitation has, we believe, assumed symbolic importance. Formerly and especially in the Roman Catholic world, what was called "last rites" and what is now called "sacrament of the sick" was an important rite and had immense symbolic significance. One did not necessarily need to believe in its utility to grasp its social symbolism. As cardio-pulmonary-resuscitation spread increasingly from its original intent of restarting a heart temporarily disabled by a myocardial infarction to becoming the standard of care whenever cardiac action or respiration stopped, it became to be accepted as the standard "last effort." It began to assume symbolic significance beyond its actual utility in a given case. Passing 300 joules of energy across a chest in some important ways and for many people seems to have supplanted earlier rituals. Here, however, it is a ritual which is hardly harmless and which, furthermore, requires an immense input of resources. The symbolic value of cardio-pulmonary-resuscitation however does point out the immense importance of rituals and people's needs for them.

In the western world there are great similarities as well as considerable differences in the way the last stage of life and dying are perceived. Not surprisingly, perhaps, the similarities are greater than the differences. Aging, likewise, is perceived in different ways and the status of the elderly varies from culture to culture and from nation to nation. As cultures interpenetrate and as an ever greater number of people live in cultures other than their own native ones, those who care for patients in their last stages of life need to be sensitive to this. This does not imply that health care professionals need to understand all cultures or all social conventions. It means that they must be ready to ask patients and families about such differences, that they be willing to learn from their patients and their families and that they refrain from condescending to other cultures or practices.

4.   PHYSICIANS' OBLIGATIONS

The way the end of life is handled in today's medical setting has much to do with what health-professionals consider to be their obligation—not only what such obligations are but also to whom they are owed. The thorough medicalization of the end of life is a rather modern wrinkle. True—physicians and their allied professionals have dealt with the end of life since time immemorial. But, as we have mentioned earlier, in former days dying was a much more social affair. It took place in the embrace of one's family, entailed certain prescribed rituals, and may or may not have been attended by a physician. Dying today, whether it takes place in the home or in institutions, is most often attended by a physician. When it is not—as when someone is found dead in their own bed or collapses on the street—it is medicalized in retrospect: it becomes a coroner's case and will generally be subject to a medical autopsy.

Obligations of physicians have changed through the ages. In all cultures and historical epochs, however, physicians have a relationship with their patients that had its roots in an evolving tradition as well as in the expectations of a particular culture. Expectations do not necessarily translate into obligations—but expectations that are repeatedly met over time become more and more justified and are, eventually, perceived as obligations. In western culture physicians did not see themselves as obligated to prolong life until relatively recent times. In ancient times, the physician's obligations entailed ameliorating suffering, helping nature regain balance and refraining from treating those who were (probably) beyond treatment. Medicine since the 16th century has dropped the obligation of refraining to treat those believed to be beyond treatment and substituted the obligation to save and if possible, to prolong life. As our technical ability to do so has greatly improved the obligation to prolong life has, in many cases, become an obsession.[12] Today, in the light of current practices and experience, we are re-examining this issue. Almost no one who dies in a hospital today, dies precisely when they would have to: almost always there is "something" that one can do to prolong life for a few minutes, hours, days or weeks. Somewhere along the line a decision that "enough is enough" is made. Such decisions are often (and in some cases justifiably) made tacitly or in an ad hoc manner. Calling off resuscitative attempts and not starting yet another pressor are two such examples. Too often these ad hoc decisions are made by clinicians in the press of a frustrating moment with emotions running high. Planning ahead, setting goals and defining limits with patients and families can avoid such ad hoc decisions. Such decisions, because they are insightful and forward looking rather than simply reactive, have a greater tendency to result in greater overall control over both the situation and the means by which dying is orchestrated.

5.   THE CENTRALITY OF SUFFERING

One of the central features in any consideration dealing with decision making in ethics and in any discussion about orchestrating the end of life relates to the capacity to suffer. Orchestrating the end of life, as we shall see later in this book, has two interrelated functions: to maximize the positive content of life, to make it enjoyable and worthwhile and to minimize the suffering so commonly experienced during that phase of life. Suffering is a complex bio/psycho/social occurrence. It requires the integrity of some neural structures and connections and it is modulated by personal history and social circumstances. In past works one of the authors (EHL) has suggested that the capacity to suffer can play a critical role in ethical theory. When we ask what makes an entity a worthy subject of ethical inquiry, the answer must include the capacity to suffer—a role more critical, this author has argued, than the capacity for rational thought.[13] We care about those unable to think rationally for the very reason that they can—reason or not—suffer.

When we speak of suffering we mean far more than pain. Suffering may be (and in the medical setting often is) the result of pain. But pain can exist without real suffering and suffering most certainly does not presuppose (physical) pain. Freud claimed that suffering comes to us from three sources: 1) "from our own body which is doomed to decay and dissolution"; 2) by external threats "raging against us;" and 3) and to Freud most importantly, "from our relations to other men."[14] The conditions which provoke suffering, then, are all around us and all are or can be operative at the end of life. At the end of our life, our body assuredly is decaying—instead of supporting us it has turned against us. External threats are many—not least of which are the threats exemplified by the very establishment to which the patient must turn for help. It is here that understanding, appreciating and acknowledging a patient's fears can be most helpful. And, perhaps most importantly Freud was right: suffering is produced from the relationships of the patient with others, from fears of abandonment and from the knowledge of loss. For we who lose a loved one, it is one person among a cluster of others; the patient who dies loses all. Grieving is part of that suffering and only the closeness and warmth of human relationships can help to alleviate it. An additional insight, this time from Viktor Frankl, may sharpen our understanding. According to Frankl, suffering is suffering only when it is bereft of meaning.[15] In other words, when we can find meaning in our suffering we may be left with pain—but it is pain with, as it were, a "light (instead of utter darkness) at the end of the tunnel." One of the functions of orchestrating the end of life is helping patients and families find meaning in this phase of life.

Health-care professionals must be careful not to reduce suffering to physical pain and to reach the conclusion that when pain is adequately controlled suffering no longer exists. The assumption that when pain has been controlled suffering is at an end, is one of the most destructive fallacies we can cling to in managing the end of life. We want to be very clear: pain control is essential.[16] It is, perhaps, the necessary condition for all else. But pain control alone can not, by itself, abolish suffering; much more is needed. Indeed, unskilled attempts at controlling pain can very much increase the suffering of patients. It can do so not only because of some of the devastating side-effects which these drugs may have, but also because these drugs tend to immobilize patients and prevent them from engaging in activities they find meaningful. While patients fear pain at the end of life, while pain must be controlled as well as that is possible, and while pain-control as it is practiced today leaves much to be desired, patients who wish to end their life fear other things more than they fear pain. They fear loss of decisional capacity, loss of autonomy and abandonment much more than they fear pain.[17]

Skilled pain control can add much to the management of patients at the end of life or, for that matter, at any time of their life; unskilled and thoughtless pain control can easily compound the problem. If we take the patients fear of losing decisional capacity and autonomy seriously, than we are obligated to do all in our power to preserve decisional capacity and autonomy. The degree to which patients wish to have their pain controlled—which is sometimes but not necessarily bought at the price of some desired activity or capacity—is a matter of personal choice. Persons skilled in the discipline can often manage to control pain without interfering greatly with desired activities or capacities—indeed, removing pain may, if done skillfully, enhance the patients' capacity to engage in activities and hence abolish or at least greatly attenuate their suffering. Likewise, controlling pain adequately and well may help restore some measure of lost autonomy.

Suffering is closely related to despair—exemplified as we have seen by a loss of hope. Despair has been termed a mortal sin because classically it means forsaking a belief (or a hope in) the mercy of God. Today despair, in secular parlance, is still about losing all hope. Hope is closely allied to meaning—when we can see meaning in an occurrence we have, in a sense, hope. To find meaning means to envision a goal. When we can see no meaning in what is happening to us and are powerless to control it, we lose hope and suffer.

The concept of hope becomes critical at the end of life. The problem, as is so often the case, starts with the problem of definition. Hope has been defined as a "desire accompanied by the expectation or belief in fulfillment."[18] The definition thus has two parts: hope implies that what is hoped for is desirable to the person hoping and hope implies that the person believes that what he or she hopes for can, in fact, be realized. Religious hopes are beyond the scope of this book. Nonetheless, in illness hope must be maintained—but it is not necessarily a hope that cure can be effected or life significantly prolonged.

Often relatives, physicians and other health-professionals will hesitate to inform patients about the nature or gravity of their illness. Often the reason given is that it is improper "to remove hope." Sometimes this excuse is simply a way of evading a responsibility which relatives, physicians and other health care professionals find painful; sometimes it is heartfelt; often it is a mixture of both. But patients at the end of life may (and usually in fact do) know full well that their end is near. At the end of life, when realistic hope of cure or even of significant meaningful prolongation of life has vanished, patients can very well hope for other things. They can, with justification, hope that what remains of their life can be made more rather than less meaningful. They can (and when well handled can legitimately) hope that they will not suffer greatly. They can hope for deeper relationships with loved ones and they can have realistic faith in the fulfillment of many of their desires. Rather than delude patients, rather than attempt to mislead patients most of whom are quite aware of what is happening, it is far better to deal forthrightly with the particular situation, supporting their justified hopes and gently speaking about their unfulfillable hopes. Dealing with patients honestly enables them to make the most of their expectations, to fulfill many of their desires and to find satisfaction in what can be achieved rather than frustration in what cannot.

ENDNOTES AND REFERENCES

1. "Statistical Abstracts of the United States," Washington, DC: GPO, 1997, p. 475.
2. From material quoted in D.S. Eitzen and M.B. Zinn, *Social Problems,* 7th ed. (Boston, MA: Allyn and Bacon, 1997), p. 186; but originally published by J.E. Schwarz and T.J. Volgy, in "Above the poverty line—but poor," *The Nation* (February 15, 1993, p 191-192.
3. For an extensive review of today's access to health care for three age groups, see G. Simpson, et al: "Access to Health Care, Part 1: Children," *Vital and Health Statistics, Series 10: Data from National Health Survey,* 1997, (196): 1-30; B. Bloom: "Access to Health Care, Part 2: Working-age Adults," *Vital and Health Statistics, Series 10: Data from National Health Survey,* 1997, (197): 1-31; R.A. Cohen, et al: "Access to Health Care, Part 3: Older Adults," *Vital and Health Statistics, Series 10: Data from National Health Survey,* 1997, (198): 1-14.
4. Avishai Margolis has argued that how decent a society is can be measured by the extent to which it prevents humiliation for and to its members. In many respects "dignity" presupposes a lack of humiliation.
5. J. Moreno, "The Social Individual in Clinical Ethics." *Journal of Clinical Ethics* 1992, 3(1): 53-55.
6. V. Navarro, "Why Some Countries Have National Health Insurance, Others Have a National Health Service and the US Has Neither," *Social Science and Medicine,* 1989; 28(9): 887-898.
7. The discussion of what being dead was conceived to be owes much to the excellent book by Paul Carrick, *Medical Ethics in Antiquity* (Dordrecht, the Netherlands: D. Reidel), 1985.
8. R. Lattimore, (trans) *The Odyssey of Homer* (NY: Harper & Row), 1967
9. The way death has been viewed and the social rituals which surround death are beautifully described in what has come to be the standard work on the subject: P. Ariés, *The Hour of Our Death,* trans. by Helen Weaver, (NY: Oxford University Press), 1991. A much shorter, much less detailed but highly readable version is P. Ariés, *Western Attitudes Towards Death,* trans. by Patricia Ranum, (Baltimore, MD: The Johns Hopkins University Press), 1974.
10. P. Ariés, *Western Attitudes towards Death*, trans. by Patricia Ranum (Baltimore, MD: The Johns Hopkins University Press, 1974), p. 104.
11. P. Ariés, *Western Attitudes towards Death*, trans. Patricia Ranum (Baltimore, MD: The Johns Hopkins University Press, 1974), p. 105.
12. D.W. Amundsen, "The Physician's Obligation to Prolong Life: A Medical Duty without Classical Roots," *Hastings Center Report* 1978, 8(4): 23-31.
13. For a discussion of suffering two sources are recommended. The centrality of suffering at the bedside and in clinical medicine was emphasized prominently by Eric Cassell. See, for example, *The Nature of Suffering and the Goals of Medicine* (NY: Oxford University Press), 1994; "The Nature of Suffering and the Goals of Medicine," *NEJM,* 1982, 306(11): 639-645; and "Recognizing Suffering," *Hastings Center Report,* 1991, 21(3): 24-31. For a discussion of the neurological substrate needed as well as the relevance of the capacity to suffer to ethical theory, see E.H. Loewy, *Suffering and the Beneficent Community* (NY: SUNY Publishers), 1991; and E.H. Loewy, *Freedom and Community: The Ethics of Interdependence* (NY: SUNY Publishers). 1993.
14. S. Freud, *Civilization and Its Discontents*, trans. by James Strachey (NY: W.W. Norton: 1961), p. 24
15. V. Frankl, *Man's Search for Meaning* (NY: Simon & Schuster), 1963.

16. There are excellent books that speak to the basic pharmacology and the clinical methods of controlling pain. Such considerations are not only beyond the scope of this book but entirely outside the ability of the authors. The reader is referred, among others, to M.A. Ashburn and L.J. Rice, *The Management of Pain* (NY: Churchill-Livingston), 1998.
17. For an excellent discussion of this issue and its multiple dimensions see A.L. Back, J.I. Wallace, H.E. Starks and R.A. Pearlman, "Physician-assisted Suicide in Washington State: Patient Requests and Physician Responses". *JAMA* 1996, 275(12): 919-923.
18. Merriam Webster's Collegiate Dictionary.

Chapter 3

Questions, Methods and the Problem of Autonomy

1. A BRIEF WORD ABOUT THEORY

Before we go on to speak about some of the ethical problems at the end of life, we need to come to grips with some of the questions, concepts, language and methods in ethics. The questions we ask and the way we ask them help to determine the answers we will find. The concepts we use and the way we understand these concepts go a far way towards understanding the way we address these questions. The language we use shapes the way we phrase the questions and understand the concepts; and the methods we apply to help "solve" the question asked, in turn, shape the way we understand the concepts and use the language.

We want, first of all, to say something about ways of looking at ethics. There are, essentially, two major ways of conceiving the "truth," whether what we are speaking about is a scientific or an ethical moral truth.[1] One way of understanding truth is as the end product of a quest of discovery: somewhere, out there is Truth—Truth with a capital "T." Such a Truth is something that, once "discovered" is true now and forever more (amen!). Generally, such a Truth is considered to be absolute and contextless—it holds for all times, for all contexts and in all situations. One can easily find examples from both science and ethics. In science the belief that the shortest distance between two points necessarily is a straight line and in morals the belief that one must never, whatever the circumstances, lie are just two examples of such an understanding of truth. However, in real life such beliefs simply do not invariably prove to be true. Although we believed for millennia that the shortest distance between two points was a straight line this bit of Euclidean revealed truth was seen to be context dependent. Although one can claim that lying is ethically wrong, one soon—in life and in medical practice—is confronted with situations which make the application of an invariable "truth" (and, therefore, the truth) problematic.

The other way of conceiving truth understands it to be neither discoverable nor absolute: we in the human condition, in the light of our experience, prior insights and given context, craft and/or stipulate such tentative truths. The point of view that truth is neither discoverable nor absolute can, in turn, be expressed in two ways. Some will claim not only that an absolute Truth has never been convincingly discovered but that an absolute Truth does not exist at all. The other will admit that the belief that no Truth exists is as inherently unproven a way of looking at things as is the belief that it does. In either case, however, we as humans are destined to develop our own insights and craft our own (limited) truths. In this work we subscribe to the latter view (viz., that truth is crafted instead of discovered) and, claim, in addition, that such crafting must occur within a community of interactive participants.

Here is not the place for a comprehensive review of ethical theory. However, it is necessary to point out yet another division within ethical theory which has conditioned our thinking.[2] Some theorists hold that the merit of an action lies solely in the consequences it produces. Others hold that consequences are ephemeral and, therefore, not the proper way of judging an act. Presumably, what matters is that one intends to act consistent with one's principles. The former point of view is fundamental to consequentialism and is exemplified by utilitarianism. However, such a view is problematic for a number of reasons. It fails to provide an adequate explanation for the following facts:

1. that consequences are so often largely beyond our control
2. that what is a "good" consequence is often the very point at issue
3. that when one speaks of consequences it is unclear whether one refers to immediate or to remote effects
4. that our intuitions caution us that a good produced by evil means is suspect

And yet, the view that consequences are an ephemeral and illicit way of judging an act, and that what matters is that one intends to follow—and does the best one can to follow—one's principles (referred to as deontology and exemplified by Kant) has it's difficulties as well: it can all too easily slip into rigid and mechanical rule-following. Within this view, personal relations tend to become lost, consequences neglected and context ignored.

However, there is an alternative approach (one most congenial to the authors of this book) that is largely exemplified by the method of John Dewey. According to Dewey, what raises a question (be it a question of ethics or science) is a "hitch" in the way we go about our usual tasks. Something just doesn't work out as anticipated. This is as true in technical medical practice as it is when it comes to questions of ethics. That is, our treatment did not have quite the excellent results we expected every time we used it; the solution to our moral quandary allowed us to act but left us with the feeling that things still were not quite right. Such a failure to work out as expected (Dewey's "hitch") causes us to re-examine our "solutions" and to examine our habitual activities. To do this we use our prior concepts, employ our understanding of language and bring to bear insights we have gained from prior ways of going about dealing with similar issues. Our principles, our traditions and our own intuitions all play an important role in the way we deal with such problems—they are the information antecedent to hypothesis-development. The method we use to deal with questions of ethics differs from the scientific method only in the material with which it deals. It basically remains a method of postulating and then testing hypotheses—a testing which is first carefully subjected to thought experiments and only then tested in actual practice.

The result is a new way of going about dealing with a particular problem. We have, to use the language of Dewey, changed an indeterminate situation to one that is more (but not fully) determinate. To use the language of one of the authors [EHL] we have created a situation of lesser indeterminacy. This new way of going about things is not an answer in a final or ultimate sense—it is tentative but sound enough to act upon. By acting we begin to fully appreciate what we have done; we see not only the way we now deal better with a given situation but also see new actual or potential hitches. This might, in turn, suggest that we need further work, leading us to continue improving and shaping the "answers" we have developed. Such a process is one of evolution and learning. It is a dynamic process in which we, as actors, are fully involved. It is one through which we not only affect the answer but are ourselves shaped and changed by it.[3]

Such an approach is not one congenial to many people—it cannot deliver a set of prescriptions to follow or a set of rules to be blindly and mindlessly applied (nor does it try to). Instead, it forces us to consider the shape and context of individual problems in a way that "sucks us into their resolution". Such an approach is not relativistic, for it uses past insights, traditions, rules and ethical theories (be they deontological or utilitarian) as critical antecedent information and as critical guidelines. But it does not use past insights, traditions, rules or theories as straightjackets which predetermine what we should do. Such an alternative approach is one most useful in the myriad problems of daily life and especially useful in health care ethics with its complex situations and contexts. It is essentially the one used throughout this book.

2. CONCEPTS OF LIFE AND ART

The way we use and understand certain words conditions the way we will decide and act. Often our words carry within them more than one meaning. One such word, important in all of health care ethics, is the word "life." This one word, in English, German or French covers two rather different meanings. In Greek, there are two different words each conveying a somewhat different concept of life: "zoe" and "bios." "Zoe" denotes a biological concept; "bios" a more subjective, biographical one.[4] The biological concept of "being alive" ("zoe") denotes that an entity is capable of doing those things by which we differentiate living from dead or from inanimate states: viz., it metabolizes, excretes and, in higher organisms, circulates blood. The other concept ("bios") denotes "having a life," being the subject of a life: the capacity to have a history, to have hopes, fears, pains and joy. It is not equivalent to "quality of life"—rather it is the prior necessary condition for the possibility of being able to entertain the concepts connected to "quality of life" issues.

Being alive is the necessary condition for having a life—without being alive (except in a religious sense, which does not concern us here), we cannot enjoy or despair of our life. It is, basically, why patients with a serious illness consult their physicians: they hope that their lives will be saved or extended so that they can continue to live with all that living implies for them. Conscious patients at the end of life still have both "zoe" and "bios." That is, they not only *are alive*, they *have lives*. This phase of life, however, not only places being alive in jeopardy (which it now by definition is) but likewise jeopardizes their ability to have those experiences they treasure and value in the course of having a life. Being alive usually underwrites a living that is composed of hopes and joys, pains and fears. When being alive underwrites a life from which all positive aspects (including all hope for their return) have vanished and only pain, suffering and fear remains, being alive may well be something persons are no longer anxious to preserve.

Our having a life is, for each of us, a unique experience. No one's life is quite like another. No one's history is the same, no one's tastes, values and attitudes are quite like that of any other person. We see our world and experience our history through our genetic predispositions as well as through the accumulation of our past experiences. Importantly these experiences include others—others whose identity is likewise uniquely composed and shaped by genetic as well as by a multitude of relational factors. Such experiences, moreover, occur in a larger community of interconnected others which enables, shapes and modulates the relationships and experiences individuals have and the way we see and understand such experiences and relationships.

Eric Cassell some time ago suggested the analogy of life to a work of art.[5] We are engaged in composing our own symphony or painting our own portrait at least from the time that we began to differentiate ourselves as particular entities from all that is around us. Our own work of art is unique—it can be created best and most authentically by those whose life it is. Others cannot hope to compose or to paint quite in our style. Imagine Schubert's Unfinished symphony finished by Mahler or imagine a Rembrandt self-portrait completed by Van Gogh—they all are wonderful artists but they each have their own distinctive styles. If they had to finish each other's work of art, the best we could hope for is that Mahler would try to steep himself in Schubert's style of composition or that Van Gogh would try to understand Rembrandt's style of painting. Such efforts may produce acceptable works of art but it will, perforce lack the genuineness which only the artists themselves could have given it. When patients have lost their decisional capacity and others must act for them and help them finish their work of art, we, therefore, try to choose persons who have known the patients well and who are willing to compose or paint as they truly think the patient might have. Such a process can go a long way towards helping us make decisions, but it will never be quite as satisfying as having patients speak for themselves.

One's particular work of art is created within a community that has shaped one's artistic ability and often determined its dimensions. People in poverty whose lives are truncated by their social and material conditions have a work of art which, like a tree desperately trying to cling to life on barren rocks, will be stunted and misshapen. And persons facing the last phase of life often—and often prematurely—come from that very class. In examining issues at the end of life, it behooves us to be ever mindful that what we, who concern ourselves with such issues, generally come from a class which does not have such worries. We often forget those whose voices are not heard. Those many voiceless in our midst in the United States and in some of the other less fortunate, countries have an end of life which is perforce quite different from that which we who mainly concern ourselves and write about such issues are privileged to have. Truly, their lives are nasty, brutish and short—and often they are solitary, in the sense that we who are well off neither see nor hear them. If we truly wish to consider the ethics of end of life care (and act ethically), we cannot merely pay lip service to their existence or simply forget them.

3. IDENTIFIED AND UNIDENTIFIED LIVES AT THE END OF LIFE

In dealing with issues in health care ethics we make two types of judgments: the one deals with identified (or "known") and the other with unidentified (or "statistical") lives. Identified lives are the lives of people we know either directly or at least know about through others. They may be patients, friends, acquaintances or even enemies—but they engage our emotions in a very direct sense. Unidentified or statistical lives, on the other hand, are lives personally unknown to us but nevertheless lives which (when we make decisions, articulate protocols or set criteria) will be affected by our actions. We must be fully aware that the term "unidentified" or "statistical" lives is indeed a misnomer: these are not, in truth, unidentified lives but lives which we personally happen not to know and, therefore, have not "identified." They are, nevertheless, very real lives.

Making judgments about identified lives is what physicians and other health care professionals customarily do at the bedside: a judgment about how to care for a particular patient at the end of life, for example. Judgments about unidentified or statistical lives are judgments made remote from the people ultimately involved. They are made in boardrooms or in other settings in which decisions about groups of people must be made. An example might be what services to provide patients at the end of life. Such a differentiation between judgments made about identified and unidentified lives is not peculiar to ethics. When physicians choose a given treatment for a given patient they are dealing with identified lives; when they write books or articles and make recommendations for the treatment of a particular condition or a particular population group, they are making these recommendations for unidentified lives. Nor is this differentiation peculiar to health care: when judges judge the accused they deal with identified lives; when legislators make laws they deal with unidentified lives.

When we deal with "identified lives" (persons we know or about whom we know) our emotion is the first thing to be aroused. That emotion is likely to be compassion (the capacity to feel "with" someone his/her joys or woes) but may, if that person is an enemy, be the converse. It is here that reason must interpose between our emotion and our action. Acting on emotion alone may cause us to do quite destructive things: physicians may, because they feel uncontrolled compassion for a patient in pain, fail to do an essential but very painful task; persons may, acting from uncontrolled emotion, do some very unjust things to their enemies. This tempering of compassion by reason is what, one of the authors (EHL) has in prior works, called "rational compassion." On the other hand, when we deal with statistical or "unidentified" lives (persons we do not know or have no personal knowledge of or when we deal with future persons), we tend to deal with their problems using reason alone. When that happens, rather inhumane decisions can result. For example, hospice patients may suddenly be deprived of benefits. Aliens may be deprived of certain benefits and, therefore, thrown into abject poverty in their old age. Brutal rationing decisions can be made that negatively affect many persons who lack recourse. There are many more examples we could cite. It is here that reason must be modified by compassion—what one of the authors (EHL) has called "compassionate rationality." Here, as in the former case, curiosity and imagination serve to connect the two.[6]

When it comes to "rational compassion" (or, if you will, emotion controlled or modulated by reason) curiosity impels us to overcome our initial impulse and to further inquire into the situation and into the contemplated action. Imagination then offers us several hypotheses about what is the case as well as about contemplated courses of action which reason, then, allows us to test. Thus a physician may decide to inflict pain on her patient so as to save his life; or, on the other hand, one may decide not to harm an enemy one hates or to deal compassionately with an obnoxious patient even when one's emotions would have us do them harm. When it comes to "compassionate rationality" (or, if you will, emotion directed by reason) curiosity and compassion mediate. When it comes to unidentified lives, curiosity and imagination work together: curiosity to ask the question "what would it be like to be in the shoes of that person" and imagination to go at least a bit of the way towards finding an answer. Curiosity and imagination allow us to realize that unidentified or statistical lives are not unidentified or merely statistical but that they are very real (past, present or future) lives, which we personally simply have not identified. If we were to make judgments—either about identified or unidentified lives—purely guided by either reason or emotion, rather unfortunate results would occur.

At the end of life, health care professionals will be involved in making decisions for both lives they know and lives which are unknown to them. These are decisions are interconnected. As health care professionals deal with their patients, their overall understanding of the problem is enhanced. As health care professionals help in determining the allocation of resources and crafting rules and setting criteria for end of life care they must draw on this understanding. As they engage in such resource allocation and as they help craft the rules, this activity in turn will help them better understand and deal with some of the problems at the bedside.

4. AUTONOMY, COMPETENCY AND DECISIONAL CAPACITY

Ethical problems at the bedside often relate to questions of autonomy. The concept of autonomy is a relatively recent acquisition. Up to and well into the middle ages persons saw themselves as necessarily far more embedded in and interconnected with their community than is the case today. A large number of factors are responsible for bringing about this change. Furthermore, cultural attitudes towards individual identity differ greatly: in the United States, individuals tend to see themselves as isolated entities; elsewhere, they often see themselves more as connected with and defined by their community.

In its original Kantian formulation autonomy refers to the capacity that persons have for formulating their own rules and determining their own destiny. It is necessary to distinguish between two senses of freedom. Kant distinguished between freedom of acting and freedom of willing.[7] Within the limits of reason we ordinarily take our ability to translate our willing into our acting for granted. I wish to eat a pizza and (provided I have the resources to procure it) I do so; I wish to consult my physician and (provided I am lucky enough to have health insurance) I consult him or her. Already here we can see some barriers that separate our will from our possible actions. Such limitations are, however, artifacts of the culture in which we live and not internal to the patient—were food or medical care free, no barrier would exist. In the medical setting the barrier can be one internal to the patient. When confused, severely inebriated or psychotic patients are brought to the emergency room their minds are clouded and their "willing" cannot be said to be free; yet their actions are very much free and may result in their having to be (chemically or physically) tied down. At the end of life, the opposite is often true—patients evidently have the capacity to make decisions but are unable to carry such decisions into action: severe weakness, immobility, inability to swallow or a host of other physical problems may separate freedom of willing from freedom of acting.

As persons have become better educated and as Christianity (and especially Protestantism) began to emphasize individual salvation, persons increasingly began to see themselves as free agents.[8] Politically, socially and economically this idea developed in different and often contradictory directions. The idea that personal fate matters and that we can do things to change it underwrites the notion of democracy (a political system) as well as socialism (an economic system); it also (in a crasser form) spawned capitalism. Socially, persons began to insist not only on their political rights but likewise upon the right as individuals to chart their own lives and, therefore, medical destinies. As we have seen in the previous chapter, the last phase of life, including dying, have become much more isolated and lonely events.

In some cultures individual decision making is either a communal or a family activity. Until fairly recently and in some cultures yet today, physicians made decisions about medical care—often with little or no input from patients or families. In the United States the pendulum has tended to swing the other way—not rarely physicians feel that their task is to present a patient with options, allow the patient to choose and then do as the patient (or designated surrogate) wishes. There is no question that patients must be informed and must then consent to whatever is or is not done to them. However, patients may be abandoned, as it were, to their own autonomy.

There is, it would seem, a middle way between the crass paternalism health care professionals (or health care institutions) used to practice and the abandonment of patients to their own autonomy. Most patients go to consult health care professionals not only because these professionals have more knowledge about illness and health than they do but also because they wish to hear the advice of such experts. It is, of course, ethically necessary to present patients with all of the options and with the probable results of following various courses of action. But the job does not end there! Patients may understand what they have been told—but that understanding is tempered by fear and, above all, is not seasoned by experience. Patients generally expect to be told the clinical "facts" and, in addition, are entitled to hear their physician's advice. Patients are entitled to enunciate their own goals—no one can do this as well as the person whose goals they are. Physicians and other health care professionals need to advise patients as to the feasibility and means of attaining such goals. Often the choices are not clear cut and it is especially at such times that patients may wish to put their trust in their physician's judgment. Physicians are, in our view, obligated not only to present "facts" and delineate options but are also obligated to advise patients about particular courses of action. After all: when we go to our favorite restaurant, we not only want to be handed a menu but also would like to be informed what "is good today". When all is said and done, we may not follow the waiter's advice—but we do want to hear it and chances are good might follow it.

That being said, patients with decisional capacity must be allowed to make their own choices. When patients lack decisional capacity, physicians must be guided by advance directives or by the appropriate surrogates. In all these cases, however, the obligation of physicians not simply to present options. Rather, to advise and guide is also part of their fiduciary obligation as it exists today. This obligation is rooted in historical tradition and in repeatedly fulfilled patient expectations.

In clinical practice as in daily life we are apt to use the terms "competency" and "decisional capacity" interchangeably. Even though they are at times related these two terms are neither identical nor interchangeable. Issues of decisional capacity as well as of competency are critical at any time in medical practice and are often crucial when dealing with the end of life. Patients in the last stages of their illness may lose the capacity to choose for themselves. Often such an eventuality can be and ought to be foreseen (preferably long before the patient is truly at the end of life) and arrangements can be made (see section on advance directives). Whether such provisions have been made or not, it is essential to determine a patient's decision making capacity (a) in order to know when such instruments should be in effect—i.e., they have no power while patients maintain decision making capacity—or (b) to determine when others must be asked to speak for the patient.

When a patient reaches maturity, he or she is considered to be competent. Competency is a legal term—unless a judge in a formal procedure has ruled otherwise, every person of adult years is assumed to be competent. It is a decision for a duly appointed judge to make not a health care professional. Patients who are ruled "incompetent" have a court appointed guardian who may or may not be a relative and if there is no one else available an agency of the state (variably termed but often called a "guardianship commission") is appointed. The problem with the latter arrangement is that, like most such agencies (the child or adult protective agencies are examples), these agencies are generally terribly understaffed. What often happens is that the particular case worker assigned knows little about each case and assumes a "default" mode: discontinuing life-sustaining treatment will only rarely be allowed. Here ethics consultants and ethics committees can play a crucial role (see the section on ethics committees later in this chapter).

It is, however, not necessarily the case that patients who have been ruled incompetent by a judge are also unable to make reasonable and acceptable decisions about medical treatment. The capacity to make decisions concerning one's own treatment is not necessarily ethically or legally related to competency. Patients who are competent (that is, those who have not been ruled incompetent by a judge) may or may not have decisional capacity. Persons who are incompetent (i.e., who have been ruled incompetent by a judge) likewise may or may not have decisional capacity.[9] The more common case is the "competent" patient who lacks decisional capacity—the patient may be in coma, may be confused, demented or heavily sedated. Decisions need to be made about such patients—physicians have judged that such patients lack decisional capacity although no judge has ruled on their competency. In such cases, physicians decide in concert with relatives or others close to the patient or, when these exist, utilize formal advance directives to attempt to approximate the patient's presumed wishes. Such cases are an everyday occurrence. More rarely, patients who have been judged to be incompetent and who, therefore, are under some type of guardianship may still have decisional capacity when it comes to their treatment. The courts have so ruled in a number of such cases.

Determining decisional capacity is something health care professionals do on a daily basis. It should include:

1. Making sure that the patient understands the issue—i.e., that the patient knows, in layman's terms, what the disease is and how it will develop.

2. Ascertaining that the patient understands the various treatment options, what these options entail and what the outcome of various forms of treatment (including non-treatment) are likely to be.

3. Obtaining from patients a choice as to what they wish done— under some circumstances the choice may be *not* to choose, i.e., to leave the choice in the hands of a next of kin or of the physician. It is clear that the freely made decision not to choose is a decision that must be respected. It is a decision that is often related to the patient's particular culture.

4. Ascertaining that the patient's reasons for the choice is one that can—in terms of the patient's and not the health-professional's value system—be logically defended. Thus patients are entitled to make decisions which a majority of us might consider to be foolish—refuse a transfusion, for example, because their particular faith prohibits it.

Determining decisional capacity, then, is quite similar to determining whether a decision has been autonomously made. Classically, autonomous decisions must be:

1. Informed—persons must have sufficient information to understand the problem.

2. Deliberated upon—persons must have time to consider the issue, ask questions and think.

3. Free of coercion—such can be external (someone else imposing his/her will by force or guile) or internal (hypoxia, hysteria, extreme fear, etc. are frequent examples in the medical setting)

4. Authentic—that is, they should be consistent with the patient's prior world-view. A decision that startles those who know the patient well may be suspected to be inauthentic. That does not mean that persons cannot change their minds or that surprising decisions may not be valid. But it does mean that when decisions are made which appear to be contrary to a sustained prior world view, they should be re-examined: was the person really informed, have time to think or is he or she, in some way, being coerced?

When we speak of decision making, we must differentiate between two types of decisions: the first is a decision concerning goals. Such a decision depends upon the way a particular patient sees his or her work of art. It concerns such things as the decision that life under certain circumstances is or is not still worthwhile. Some patients, for example, would (even if not gladly) be willing to tolerate a reduction in the ability to concentrate, read, think or study so long as their capacity to enjoy other things (raspberry sherbet, sunlight or a visit from their family) persisted. Others would find such a reduced life intolerable and not commensurate with their work of art. These are decisions which others—especially strangers—cannot make for patients. The other decision is a more technical one. It takes the patient's goals as a given and inquires, first, into the feasibility of attaining these goals. Secondly, it inquires into the appropriate means for doing so. Such decisions are clearly decisions that professionals must make; once made, physicians must inform and advise their patients accordingly.

The emphasis on autonomy is carried to its logical extreme by the libertarians who, basing their view on the earlier works of Hobbes, would see humans as isolated entities whose only obligation to others is strictly to leave them alone and to be left alone. In their language and unless we belong to a particular circumscribed moral community, we are (especially when we come from differing cultures, traditions or belief systems) "moral strangers"—persons whose only obligation to one another is mutual non-harm. Libertarians see persons as unconnected socially except as they freely choose to be connected within a particular moral enclave (for example, a church community). It follows that communities are but loosely knit entities whose only function is peace keeping within and security without. In such communities, individuals who must deal with one another (physicians and patients, for example) are contractually related but have no obligations beyond the explicit terms of their contract.[10] This sort of philosophy cannot be irrelevant to us. It necessarily translates into a physician-patient relationship that is far from the one that has been historically accepted and it easily leads to social isolation of patients. Furthermore, the notion that mutual obligations can be reduced to respecting each other's freedom and mutual non-harm easily leads to abandonment of persons who are poor, weak and powerless. Our social conditions (briefly discussed in the last chapter) exemplify the political results of such a point of view. The tendency to isolate patients at the end of life shows its social ramifications.

We shall assume and not long argue that patients of sound mind have the legal as well as ethical right to make their own choices when it comes to a range of legitimate treatment options. This right, like all other rights, is conditional: that is, it is not absolute but is hedged by such things as non-harm to others, social as well as professional acceptability and communal needs. The extent of such a "right" then (like the right itself) is something articulated, limited and safeguarded by the particular community in which such a "right" exists. Furthermore, the way such a right is understood and the way it is expressed will depend upon the culture in which it is said to exist. That such a right is understood and, therefore, expressed differently in different cultures is critical for our understanding of end of life issues. In some cultures (e.g., rural Mediterranean or some Oriental areas) decisions are commonly not made by the individual concerned but by the family.

The "right" to make one's own decisions rides piggy-back on another right: the right to be fully informed. This seems obvious; persons cannot be expected to make wise choices or choices appropriate to the way they understand their work of art unless full information has been given. But here a few by no means insignificant barriers (linguistic, emotional, conceptual and cultural) exist. First of all, informing people requires that people understand what is being said. And that means more than understanding the words and their definitions. Understanding implies not only "knowledge" of a given thing but some experiential familiarity with that thing. It is one of the critical problems with informing people. Telling someone unfamiliar with the medical setting that the mortality rate of a given procedure is 5% has a quite different emotive effect than telling the same thing to a health care professional who deals with such a procedure on a daily basis. Understanding, moreover, is very much connected to and with the emotions or aesthetic perceptions present in the person receiving (as well as in the person giving) the information and, likewise, depends upon the impact which receiving such information has on that person. Informing people therefore already has intrinsic and inevitable experiential, emotive and aesthetic barriers.

Linguistic barriers—especially in fields such as medicine—can be severe. Physicians who in general tend to communicate with other health care professionals are generally quite sure that the person to whom they are talking will understand their language. This is by no means necessarily or even generally the case. Ordinary mortals are not born with an intrinsic understanding of the workings of their body and they are, unfortunately, taught little about it in the course of their ordinary schooling. It is, therefore, important for health care professionals not only to avoid medical jargon but also to make sure that they have conveyed more than merely words. Informing a person that they have an oat cell cancer of the left upper lobe of the lung with metastases to the cerebellum is—in general—not conveying meaningful information. And yet it can be done—telling people that there is a tumor in their lung and that it has spread to their brain will quite suffice for their purpose. Telling someone that their kidneys have failed is meaningless if that person does not understand the function of the kidney in the overall economy of the body. Provided patients have near-normal intelligence it is possible to adequately get across all the medical facts needed for patients or relatives to make informed choices. Even patients who are somewhat below

average can, if one is patient, be adequately informed. Incidentally: education must not be conflated with intelligence—some highly intelligent people
have (and that for many reasons) not enjoyed a good education and most
regrettably some rather educated people seem to lack basic intelligence.
More than lack of education or intelligence, staunchly though unreflectively
held opinions may stand in the way of functional understanding—that is to
say understanding not only the "facts" but likewise appreciating the options.
Such unreflectively and staunchly held beliefs and opinions are a form of
superstition that may be cultural, religious or idiosyncratic—but it is a barrier not only to decision but often also to being informed. It can manifest
itself as rejecting either information or option. Once information has been
conveyed in language the patient can understand, health care professionals
are well advised to test the understanding of their patient.

Often patients and relatives are unable to understand the significance of
what is being said because of language, education or superstition. And frequently they are not "ready" to hear and therefore either block out what has
been said or transform what has been said into what was either most hoped
for or feared. Conveying information, therefore, is best done over time and
best led by patients' or relatives' questions. This process has been aptly described as a *pas de deux,* a process in which informer and the persons to be
informed interact or "dance" with one another and feel each other out.[11]
Shoving "the truth" down the throats of patients and families who are not yet
ready or unwilling to hear it or being insensitive to the implied or explicit
wishes of patients or families is no more moral than withholding the truth
from persons ready or at least willing to hear it. Human understanding and
empathy, rather than technical knowledge, are what is necessary. Physicians
have to "size up" patients. They have to deliver a judgment as to the patient's (or the family's) desire and capacity for the truth.[12] It is important to
speak to patients in a way which seeks to level the playing field, enlists them
as partners and re-affirms the common humanity of the professional and the
patients (or relatives). Such a process is greatly helped along by the setting
in which it takes place. We have personally found that talking over a cup of
tea or coffee can be most helpful: sharing food and drink together has a
symbolic significance that is the same in all cultures and throughout history.
Furthermore, humor is virtually always helpful—the kind of humor that allows people to regain perspective, to smile and which causes them to feel a
bond with the health care team. It is the kind of humor that implicitly conveys caring.

There are conceptual barriers. Such a barrier can be either the physician's
in transmitting or the patient's (or relatives) in receiving information. By
conceptual barrier we mean a different understanding of facts, options and/or
their implication. Patients and physicians, relatives among one another or in

their conversation with health care professionals may mean quite different things when they use the same language. The concepts "death" and "being dead" are (as we have seen in the first chapter) often conceptual stumbling blocks. When we assume that our partner conceives the same thing we do when we speak of a "poor prognosis" (or "outlook") or when we speak of "living in a nursing home" or of "having little pain" we may be seriously in error. When physicians say that they can, for example, relieve pain they often assume that the concept of pain-relief is understood by the patient often to entail some distinct functional costs. The concept "hope" presents such a barrier. Health-care professionals generally define "hope" in somatic terms—when no realistic chance for a cure or for prolongation of life exists, they will often hesitate to convey this information for fear that they would "remove all hope." But there are many more things that patients can and do hope for than merely cure or prolongation of life. Fear, in many respects, is the flip side of hope. Patients at the end of life appear to fear many things more than death.[13] When no hope for cure or meaningful prolongation of life exists, patients may hope for an eternal life. If they are like many of the rest of us, they may have some legitimate and very realistic hopes for the life that remains. The fear of not being in charge, of being left to the mercy of health care providers can be countered by assuring and showing them that they are still very much in charge. Helping to affirm a person's autonomy is, as Eric Cassell long ago pointed out,[14] one of the most important functions of good medical practice. It is essential that patients who are clear-minded (even when weak or physically disabled) continue to be consulted and given the very clear message that they are in ultimate charge. In such patients just as in the elderly there is an unfortunate tendency to turn progressively more to family and friends and away from the patient in making decisions. Such decisions tend to be made for instead of with patients. Another fear that patients have is the not unrealistic fear of social abandonment. Orchestration, in part, is aimed at dealing with fears common to most patients and with other fears specific for the patient and/or the situation as well as at providing realistic hope: hope for such things as control of symptoms, maintenance of autonomy and continuing meaningful social connectedness.

Cultural barriers are sometimes very real. One often hears that the basic urban western principle—that patients decide for themselves—is not one subscribed to in many other cultures. In many Eastern cultures, in much of rural Africa and in the more rural parts of the Mediterranean world, specific information about diagnosis and prognosis are not given to individual patients. In fact, individual patients rarely make specific treatment decisions. Such decisions are often family matters or, in some instances, are made by husbands for wives.[15] In such cultures, however, individuals see themselves quite differently from how we see ourselves—they see themselves far more

as an integral part of their family and society and far less as lone disconnected individuals than we do. Often the very notion of "making a decision
for oneself" is an alien one. It is not quite true to say that individuals in such
cultures do not decide for themselves: it is more correct to state that individuals see themselves differently and that they therefore see such decisions
as properly being social.

The decision not to decide is as much of a decision—and, at times, need
to be as much respected, as is the decision to decide for oneself. Often it is
argued that the decision not to decide is the product of social forces that have
conditioned patients to choose in this way. There is no doubt that this is
true—but a decision to decide for oneself is no less the product of social
conditioning! Contrary to the belief that we are asocial and free standing
beings stands the fact that "our" decisions are very much the decisions we
are conditioned to make by our social setting as well as by our "personal"
experience, an experience which, itself, is unavoidably conditioned by the
social context.

The problem comes up when different cultures live together and different
beliefs and ways of going about things come into conflict. Consider: a patient from the Abbruzi region of rural Italy who has lived in the United
States for perhaps thirty years is seen by her physician. A lump in her breast
is diagnosed and is eventually biopsied. A cancer is found and a modified
radical mastectomy is recommended. The patient has lived in a largely Ital-
ian community, has continued to speak the language and in most other ways
has lived as she would have lived in her native land. Her husband of thirty-
five years insists that her physician not tell her of the diagnosis or prognosis.
He tells the physician that he wishes to be informed and he, together with the
rest of the family, will decide for his wife. This presents a distinct problem
for the health care team. Not to inform the patient, but to allow the husband
to receive the information and to make, with the family, the decision forces
an American physician to practice in a way foreign to his or her own culture.
However, to sweep the husband's desires aside and to confront the patient
directly smacks of an imperialism that is both ethically and culturally inde-
fensible. In such a contingency (and it is one which, in different guises
comes up frequently) the physician would be well advised to go to the patient's bedside and say something like the following to her: "Mrs. Garibaldi,
I have a real problem. In our culture we generally inform all patients of their
diagnosis and patients usually make their own choices. Your husband tells
me that in your culture such problems are not handled that way but that he
and the family are informed and will make the choices. I am willing to do it
whichever way you like—if you wish, we shall do as Mr. Garibaldi has suggested; if you would rather be informed and choose for yourself, that too can
be done. Let me know how you would like me to handle this." It is not un-

likely that the patient will wish her husband and her family to receive the information and to choose. It is not impossible that she might wish to be informed and to choose for herself; and it is possible that she may want to be informed but leave the choices up to her family. In any of these cases, the patient has ultimately chosen.[16] We have linked informing and choosing as two sides of the same coin. Unless one is informed as completely as possible, one can make no meaningful choice. Some patients, however, may choose to be informed but will leave the choice of what to do to others—to family, physicians or some other person close to them. In such cases physicians should make clear that, should patients change their minds and wish to be informed or to choose for themselves, the door is open. Such a move maximally protects the integrity of the patient, the family and the health care team.

In our society today we have generally subscribed to a rather asocial view of autonomy—to what Jonathan Moreno has so aptly called the "myth of the asocial individual."[17] Such a viewpoint has some rather practical consequences for the patient-physician relationship. Physicians tend to view themselves as businessmen or as employees of a face-less organization and they view patients as persons to whom they are merely contractually related. The language shift from physician to provider and from patient to consumer betrays such an attitude. However, especially when it comes to dealing with problems at the end of life patients, more than ever, need inclusion into rather than exclusion from the human community. A crassly asocial idea of autonomy tends to lead to distrust towards health care professionals by patients and to abandoning patients to a rather thin and meager notion of autonomy on the part of physicians and other health care providers. Physicians are apt to offer patients a plethora of options, they may tell them about the expected consequences of particular courses of action but they have become more and more loath to strongly recommend.

5.   EXTENDED AUTONOMY AND ADVANCE DIRECTIVES

When patients have decisional capacity it clearly is ultimately the patient who (within a framework of social and institutional acceptability) must have the final say in what is to be done—or to have the final say as to who is to decide what is to be done. Physicians and other health care professionals have the obligation to inform patients of the choices and, furthermore, are (at least in the view we are expressing here) ethically remiss if they do not strongly advise patients. And, being moral agents just as are patients, health care professionals are not obligated to do as the patient wishes when doing so contravenes their own professional or personal moral code. Patients are neither the property of physicians, nor are physicians merely their patients' employees. Both must have respect for each other's moral agency. Patients as well as physicians must, when conflicts are irreconcilable, be willing to sever the relationships. Physicians are obligated to help the patient find another competent physician more attune to the patient's world-view and patients cannot expect their physicians to violate their own moral beliefs. Such a move should rarely be necessary if patients and physicians have placed a high value on communication throughout their association. As we have previously suggested, formulating advance directives can further such a dialogue.

Advance directives (or AD's) are legal instruments that are intended to give persons the chance to determine their own fates in advance of the loss of their power to decide. For that reason advance directives have properly been referred to as "extended autonomy." They are legal and legally enforceable in all fifty of the United States, and they are beginning to be introduced into some of the states of the European community as well. In German these are called "Patiententestamente"—that is, testaments (or wills) made by patients. A general will takes effect once a patient has died and once such a will has been duly probated; an advance directive takes effect not when the patient has physically died but when the patient's capacity to make choices has vanished. It differs from a general will in that the loss of decisional capacity may not (like death) necessarily be permanent and in that it need not be probated. There is some vagueness—an advance directive is certainly not in force while a patient undergoes general anesthesia or is briefly unconscious. But it might well take effect when patients have been unconscious for some time and when there is a serious question whether further treatment might or might not restore consciousness with or without a possible return of decisional capacity.

The whole question of advance directives, of course, raises the question of personal identity. Is the gentleman in a nursing home, quietly vegetating in the sunshine while being fed raspberry sherbet still the same sturdy professorial type who ten years before decided that this was not a way he was willing to endure—that, in fact, living like this was something he considered to be a fate worse than death?[18] This man now barely recognizes his family and is unable to read, though he still apparently enjoys sunshine and raspberry sherbet. In other words, what is the connection between the one and the other person: are they the same, separate, separable? Such considerations are basic to our understanding and acceptance of the whole concept of advance directives. If the present person has no real connection (other than a physical one) with the former, is the former entitled to decide for the latter? And, if not—since that person can't—who is?

We all know that our perception of what might be "a fate worse than death" changes—many teen-agers think that being fifty qualifies. We know from empirical evidence that our ability to judge the quality of life of another (or of ourselves before a contingency arises) is worth little. Not even those closest to a patient were, in one study, able to estimate how the person him/herself felt about their quality of life. It is a judgment that we cannot make for another as well as that other. If the professor in the classroom is another from the man in the nursing home, who is to decide?

We think that it must be possible to distinguish between at least two senses of personal identity. The first is the biological sense, which would have us live in the same body from birth to death; the second is the psychosocial sense, which would be predicated on our being aware of having a past, future and present within a community of others. Our biological personal identity is challenged by the fact that few of our cells (except for most of those of the nervous system) persist—there is an ongoing renewal process. In dealing with advance directives, however, it is primarily the psychosocial continuity that is in question. When we lose a limb or lose all of our limbs our being the same person (legally and morally) as we were before such a loss would not be questioned because intuitively we hold the psychosocial to be the essence of personhood. Losing a limb or two is quite a different matter from losing our memory of the past, our relationship to the present and our understanding of the future. In a very significant way the old man in the nursing home and the professor in the classroom are not the same person.[19]

As with all problems in ethics, we are not left with a clear direction or with a good and proper course of action. Ethical problems, by their very nature, do not offer "good" answers—what we generally forced to choose between are poor, bad and atrocious courses of action—i.e., courses of action which can be considered "good" only in relation to the fact that the others are worse. The choice here rests between allowing persons in the fullness of their mental and spiritual capacities to make reasoned choices. That is, it is to allow they, themselves, to look ahead to a time when their capacity to choose would be impaired or, on the other hand, to discount such a choice and to allow others to make it instead. The problem becomes more difficult the further the person in the bed before us is psychologically removed from the one executing the advance directive. In general, however, most of us would encourage Schubert to sketch a last movement for the "Unfinished Symphony" rather than to leave its composition either to a Schubert senile or entirely to another. We would be unhappy to see that great work marred by being finished with childish attempts at composing. Schubert's work of art would now no longer be Schubert's but rather that of a caricature of what once was. So in a sense, we come down to the same answer: if our man in the nursing home is the same as the professor in the classroom, then clearly the professor's choices have standing. If he has become but a caricature of himself then, perhaps even more, we should feel that the professor in the fullness of his capacity should be allowed to sketch his work of art. Allowing another—another who had no continuity either with the professor or with what the professor had become—to make such a choice is even more unacceptable. Allowing standing to advance directives is far from a perfect solution; but it is, among the solutions available, the least troubling.

Advance directives can, in general, be divided into two categories: "living will" documents and "enduring power of attorney for health care affairs" assignments. "Living will" documents speak to the question of "*what* shall we do?" "Enduring power of attorney" assignments speak more to the question of "*who shall decide* what should be done?"

"Living wills" have, in our view, many flaws:

1. They are easily set aside because they invariably stipulate that they shall be in effect when there is no hope left—if physicians think that there might be even the least possible chance, they may feel justified in ignoring such an instrument.

2. They presuppose that a particular situation can be foreseen with sufficient clarity to make a definitive choice—something we are rarely able to do.

3. They are frequently misinterpreted by physicians to mean that the patient wants no aggressive measures be taken—and this is simply not the case.

In general and for the most part living wills simply mean "don't be foolish" not "don't be vigorous." Thus, patients who might have been returned to previously acceptable function by their own definition may not be aggressively treated and may, therefore, die when this is not at all what they had in mind.

Enduring power of attorney for health care assignments (which appoint one or more persons as decision-makers should decisional capacity be lost) are much more specific instruments. An enduring power of attorney of this sort allows a person (or persons) whom the patient trusts and who knows and understands the patient's values, goals and world-view and is willing to act in accordance with such values, goals and world-view to make specific decisions in concrete and specific situations. The patient—within the body of the instrument—can provide general guidelines, but the person holding the assignment is the one who makes specific judgments in accordance with those guidelines.

The usefulness and ethical standing of either kind of document is greatly reduced if the process of obtaining such an instrument is flawed. Under a federal law, all patients admitted to a hospital must be asked whether or not they have executed an advance directive. [20] Superficially, such a law seems proper—unless health care institutions are aware of these instruments they cannot be expected to act in accordance with them. Unfortunately, some institutions (driven by the notion that the care of patients with AD's saves considerable money) have tried not only to inquire about the presence of such instruments, but have suggested to patients being admitted that such instruments should be executed at that time.[21] Setting aside the belief that persons with AD's cost less—a belief which needs more substantiation than is presently available—we are firmly of the belief that hospital admission is the very worst time to execute such instruments. The main merit of such instruments is the very fact that the process of executing them can lead to serious deliberation and dialogue about such issues. Instruments executed thoughtlessly without proper discussion and under considerable pressure are instruments whose value is, at the very least flawed. In fact, they may be worse than having no instrument at all.

In order to execute an ethically valid AD, just as in order to make a decision of any other kind, patients need to be fully informed. They need to understand what being on a ventilator, being resuscitated, being tube fed, and so forth means and implies. In our view the discussion has improperly focused on technical possibilities or means and has tended to ignore goals. It is, we believe, only the patient or the person speaking for that patient who is entitled to sketch the specific goals of the encounter; it is health care professionals who must judge the feasibility and determine the nature of the means needed to pursue these goals. For example: Stating that one would not wish to be on a ventilator is meaningless unless one clearly understands that being on a ventilator can mean a number of quite different things: (1) a temporary inconvenience; (2) a permanent inconvenience and (3) a comfort measure which alleviates air hunger.

Executing an AD is something that should be done with the help of health care professionals. It should begin while patients are far from the end of their lives and it should be revisited over time. Patients need to understand what they are doing, need to understand their own goals, their "work of art." Only then will they be able to understand such goals and the most appropriate means to their realization. One cannot properly say if one would or would not wish surgery, a ventilator or a feeding tube if one did not fully understand both what the situation entailed and what one's goals were. Such understandings are only attainable by an ongoing dialogue among all those concerned. Furthermore, AD should not be seen as something executed and finished, but as a process that is very apt to change over time, a process that needs occasional review and reaffirmation.

Advance directives may or may not play a decisive role in the usual end of life situations we are dealing with here. Many patients do not lose decisional capacity towards the end of their life. Unfortunately, it is not rare that a patient's mind remains clear while the capacity to act is radically reduced. In such situations health care providers frequently tend to turn from the patient to the patient's family when decisions have to be made—a process which justifies the patient's fear of losing control. We are not arguing that the family should be excluded—although in rare instances that is precisely what the patient may, in fact, wish. What we are arguing is that the patient, rather than being more and more peripheralized and objectified in the discussion of what should be done, should remain the central issue while, at the same time, being seen as a person enmeshed in their social nexus. Whether at the end of life or not, patients are neither freestanding asocial beings nor beings whose identity is subsumed into that of their family or social nexus. The relationship of individuals within their family or community is an organic one. That is, it is one in which family and community are necessary conditions for individual well-being.[22] Every effort in orchestrating the end of life must be made by all of the players concerned. This draws patients closer into the nexus of the family while emphatically allowing them to take the lead in determining their own destiny. When this is done well, patients will find themselves turning to the family for support, and families will be led to turning to patients for guidance.

When decision-making capacity is lost towards the end of life, advance directives can be most helpful. We maintain that the main virtue of these instruments is the process by which they are executed. If such instruments are blindly and unthinkingly followed in the hope that they will remove ethical responsibility for what is done by health care professionals (and, in that way, make health care professionals the mere instruments of another's will), they represent nothing more that a self-serving "Pontius Pilate act." That is, they allow physicians and others to wash their hands and do what they might, otherwise, consider harmful or wrong. When used in this way, such instruments form the quintessential ethical cop-out.[23]

In general, physicians and other health care professionals should follow the wishes of the patient stated on AD's. That, however, does not remove responsibility for their ultimate actions from them. Health-care professionals as we envision them today—and physicians more than others—are properly seen as having fiduciary responsibility for their patients, a responsibility which cannot simply be discharged automatically. Ultimately the responsibility for what is done is and must remain that of the person in charge—he or she who holds the pen is responsible for the consequences of what is or isn't ordered.

Physicians must make sure that the choices patients make are made by persons with proper decision making capacity and are made with sufficient knowledge and understanding to choose. They may not agree with the choices but if they are to help execute them they at least have to agree that they do not consider them to be morally repugnant choices. When surrogates choose (whether these are "legal surrogates" who chose by virtue of holding an EPA or close family and friends in a less formal setting) health care professionals transfer the responsibility for ascertaining the decisional capacity of the chooser from patient to surrogate. They must, in other words, be sure that surrogates are informed, understand, are able to articulate options and give a logical reason (commensurate with the patient's values) for the choices made. The problem when judging the holder of an EPA may even be a weightier one—health care professionals must gain the greatest degree of certainty possible that holders of the EPA are not acting maliciously and out of crass self-interest. It happens rarely but, in our experience, it has happened.

There has been a tendency in some states to legislate the process by which surrogates are picked. Such rules generally would prescribe a lock-step approach—the spouse, followed by parents, eldest children, other children and so forth. Using such rules as guidelines may serve as well—trying to apply such rules in a thoughtless fashion, on the other hand, may leave decisions in the hands of inappropriate decision-makers. Like most rules, they may be treated as having prima facie value—that is, they should be followed except when convincing evidence suggests otherwise. However, such rules often envision an "ideal" picture of the American family—a picture which, for better or worse, frequently does not exist today. Surely a wife separated from her husband for ten years is, *prima facie*, a less appropriate decision-maker than is a good friend with whom he has shared his thoughts and lived for eight years. Surely the eldest son with whom the mother has been at odds for a decade and who has paid little attention to her is not a good decision-maker. Even if such persons truly tried to act in good faith, their intimate knowledge of the patient's values, goals and world-views may well be impoverished. In such situations, health care professionals must attempt to seek out those closest to the patient and document why they might choose to follow their lead rather than that of the legally but not actually closer relative. The responsibility is and must remain that of the person who ultimately determines a certain course of action. Physicians cannot abrogate their responsibility for the patient to valid EPA-holders, surrogates or the law.

6.   THE QUESTIONS WE NEED TO ASK, THE METHOD WE MIGHT USE

In the last phase of life—which often but not invariably occurs in older age—patients may remain fully conscious and maintain complete decision

making capacity. Many do not maintain decision making capacity and some
(for example those who are young children or those with congenital severe
mental defects) may have never had it. Persons who have had a biography
that included the capacity for self-determination present a quite different
problem than do those who have never been able to choose for themselves.
Even in the latter group (those who never had decision making capacity),
one must differentiate between persons who had some ability to choose for
themselves (the eight year old, for example, who is struck with a fatal illness) and those who have never had such a capacity (the forty-year old who
has never been able to do more than make meaningless sounds and has never
recognized anyone).

When decisions need to be made about persons who lack decisional capacity we generally ask the question "what would they want done?" It is a
question that cannot be answered with complete confidence for patients in
any of these groups. However, it is a question that might be better answered
for the group having a history of decisional capacity. Patients who have
started their work of art and completed some of it have left suggestions of a
style that those who have never been able to do so have not done. We shall
come to this group a bit later.

We first want to consider the worst of these groups of patients: patients
who have never had any decisional capacity and who, therefore, have no
track record of values, likes or dislikes. Such patients are virtually opaque. In
such patients the question "what would they have wanted" or "what would
they want" is a question to which no reasonable answer can be given. Perforce our answer—should we attempt it—would come from our own set of
values and preconceptions. We cannot and can never know what (or even if)
such patients "want." Trying to approach the problem of treatment from that
angle is, therefore, bound to be fruitless. An approach that may yield more
asks the very opposite question: "what would such a patient not want?" The
answer to this negative question is easier for us to provide: there is a cluster
of common experiences which no creature at all aware of its environment
and at all capable of sensation would want. We can say with considerable
certainty that no one would want to have useless pain, to be cold, hungry,
dirty or socially abandoned. Even the most severely mentally handicapped
appear to react positively to some and negatively to other stimuli.

When patients have some capacity to decide—and most patients, even
the most severely affected do—one needs to consider their track record of
preferences. A patient may not have decisional capacity for medical matters
but may certainly be allowed to decide what to eat, how to dress, whether to
get up or stay in bed and so forth. The fact that we allow such choices means
that we acknowledge (even if in a narrow sphere) decisional capacity. Such
choices and preferences may give us a clue. The patient is less beyond our

reach and, in a sense, less opaque. We now can begin—gingerly, but begin nevertheless—to approach the positive question of what it is they might want.

The approach to specific problems that we will suggest in dealing with individual problems at the end of life or elsewhere in health care ethics is an approach similar to that used by a travel agent in planning a trip. In planning a trip three questions need be answered—the first question needs to be answered before the second can be addressed and in turn that must be answered before the last one can be considered. The first thing either a travel agent or an ethicist needs to know is the starting point of the journey. In medicine that starting point is the most probable diagnosis, how sure we can be about it and, in case of serious doubt, whether further data are needed to confirm or refute what we think we know. This information needs to be supplied to the ethicist and to the patient and family before one can proceed. When there is serious doubt, or when the patient or family simply does not believe their physician's diagnosis, consultation must be obtained. Good ethics, here as always, is dependent upon good and accurate facts.

The second question is the one that is ethically the richest: what is our destination? Here the "expert" (that is, the physician and the consultants) must offer a prognosis and provide a "best" and a "most probable" case scenario. It is then up to the patient or, when the patient lacks decisional capacity, the patient's surrogates to determine which alternative is most likely to realize their goals. Such goals depend upon the values and biography of the patient. Although physicians can and must determine whether such goals are or are not realistic ones, physicians and other health care professionals are not entitled to determine such goals. Patients and families usually have a number of goals that must be arranged in a hierarchy. Some of these goals may be mutually exclusive; others may support one another. This cluster of goals usually but not always has (at its center) the desire to minimize suffering.

The third question—how do we get from where we are to where we now know we want to go to—is a question of means. When answers to the first two questions are unclear trying to address this question is time consuming and generally pointless. Once we know where we are starting out from and where we are headed the possible means of getting to our destination become clearer and their choices more evident. Much of orchestration (the subject of the third chapter) deals with this question.

7.   JUDGING ACCORDING TO THE PATIENT'S INTERESTS AND SETTING OTHER INTERESTS ASIDE—IS THAT POSSIBLE?

Health-care ethics—like all other fields—has some taboos and fetishes. These, like most taboos and fetishes, are insufficiently examined and reflected upon and the very thought of questioning them tends to induce surprise if not anger. One of these fetishes is that those who decide for patients—i.e., surrogates—are persons who "must set their own interests aside and choose as the patient would have chosen." The other side of that coin is the taboo against making choices that are not entirely patient-centered. In many cases such attitudes are the result of s strong reaction against a long history of cultural and professional paternalism—a revulsion against letting others determine our fate or interfere with the completion of our work of art.

When patients have an enduring power of attorney for health care matters it is, one would hope, given to one who is close to the patient: someone close enough to understand the patient's values, attitudes and world-view. Likewise, when decisions have to be made for patients who lack decisional capacity and who have no AD's, we turn to members of the family and close friends for guidance. We do so because we have reason to believe that such persons where close enough to particular patients to understand their values, goals and world-views.

Dr. John Hardwig was one of the first (if not, indeed, the first) who began to emphasize the role of the family in ethical decision making. In so doing, he cast doubt upon the inevitable centrality of the patient's interests to the exclusion of all else.[24] In addition to the family, however, we also cannot totally discount communal interests. The interest of individuals, families and communities are perhaps conceptually separable but in reality are difficult to tease apart. When it comes to the interests of various people involved in making a judgment, we need to ask two questions. First of all: what does it mean to have an interest? Secondly: is it ever possible to set one's own interests aside?

For an individual to "have an interest" suggests that they (and their interest) are things which when examined and understood can stand alone, separate from their usual nexus. We are not here arguing that Joe's interest and Jim's interest cannot be differentiated. Instead what we are suggesting is that each of these interests is a complex thing which is difficult at best to define and impossible to describe without presupposing or invoking many others. True, we all have an interest in not having a burdensome life, in not having pain, in not being cold, hungry or dirty. But these are negative interests common to all feeling creatures. Such interests cannot describe Mary, Joe or Sam. What then is "a person's interest?" We would argue that our interests are composites of many other interests which overlap, interpenetrate, interreact and eventually create a mix definable as "one person's particular interest" but not anything that is easily delineable into its separate parts. Moreover, these interests do not simply coexist next to one another; they intermingle until this new entity, a particular interest, (unique in itself but containing a multitude of others) emerges. In another context, Stuart Hampshire has labeled such a process a compost heap—a "gemisch," whose initial components have since formed a new whole and are no longer separate or separable parts.[25] Among all others, one's own personal compost heap is unique—but it is a compost heap and not separable into component parts which can simply be removed or abstracted. As one of us (EHL) has argued: among others, "my interest" is made up of the interests of my wife, my students, my dog, my friends, my institution and many others. Should my wife decide for me, she could not very well abstract her own interest from mine without leaving my interest—as well as hers—damaged and bruised. The very reason surrogates are chosen, after all, is that they are closest to, and presumably intimate with, the patient. To expect surrogates (whether legal holders of the EPA or close family and friends) to abstract their own interests and try to represent the patient's true interest is asking of them not only the conceptually impossible. It is asking them to distort (often beyond recognition) the very interest they are supposed to be preserving.

Let us imagine a concrete (and in the United States an unfortunately not infrequent) case. Mr. Jones with severe Alzheimer's disease is in a nursing home. He is incontinent, is no longer seems to recognize anyone, is obviously beyond being able to make his own decisions, but does not appear to be suffering. His wife of many decades, who has been very close to him, is the acknowledged decision-maker. They live, as do many elderly Americans, on insufficient social security checks. With the help of what is left over from her husband's check, Mrs. Jones manages to live a bare but tolerable existence. She is, as it were, dependent on her husband's check that will, should he die, stop. If her husband's check were to stop, Mrs. Jones would not have enough to provide for a decent existence with only her own social security income: quite likely she would either be in the street, hungry or dependent upon charity. In making a decision about prolonging her husband's life, is it fair (or is it even possible) to ask her to ignore her own interest? Isn't her own interest an integral part of what was once her husband's interest? Would it be in his interest to have his wife homeless or hungry? These are questions with grave social and personal consequences and not questions that are soluble by some blind principle, abstraction or formula.

Not only is the interest of a person composed of a "compost heap" of other interests which are impossible to dissect apart but asking anyone to separate their own interest from any decision about to be made is impossible.

Consider, for example, what happens on the one hand when one is asked to decide for another of whom one has no knowledge (say, a person found unconscious on the street) and, on the other hand, when one is asked to decide for one with whom one has been intimately associated for a good part of one's life. Between these there are people about whom we do not know a great deal but know sufficiently to make them acquaintances rather than friends. The closer we come to intimately knowing another, the more difficult does separating interests become: the compost heap of the one deciding overlaps the compost heap of the one for whom a decision must be made. When, however, we know little or nothing about the person for whom a decision needs to be made, our compost heaps (and therefore our interests) are quite distinct from one another. But even in such situations when we must decide for another, who is a stranger, our interests matter. When we must choose for one we do not know there are, first of all, basic and neigh universal interests all sentient beings share—most persons would not wish to suffer useless pain, be cold, dirty, abandoned or treated in a callous or undignified manner. Having eliminated options that would conflict with such interests leaves other decisions to be made. And once again our own interests are not neatly separable. To have an interest means, among other things, to have certain values, beliefs, tastes and attitudes. A decision which would run counter to these values, beliefs, tastes and attitudes is one we are unlikely to make for another whose values, beliefs, tastes and attitudes are unknown to us. Since we have no more reason to assume that these values, beliefs, tastes and attitudes are radically different from our own or from those of the general community we share, and since we must, perforce, act on the basis of some values, beliefs, tastes and attitudes, we must "do the best we can." In short, we will act on the basis of our own values, beliefs, tastes and attitudes. Whether we must choose for those close to us or for those about whom we know nothing it is (and for different reasons) impossible to do so outside of the context of our own interests.

8.   ETHICS COMMITTEES AND ETHICS CONSULTANTS

In the last few decades ethics committees have been established in all hospitals in the United States and Canada.[26] It is, however, a peculiarity of the health care system as it exists today that hospices often lack ethics committees or ethics consultants. Ethics committees or consultants, it would seem, are particularly important components in managing the end of life well. Ethics committees are of three types:

1. IRB's or Institutional Review Boards which are constituted to scrutinize experiments with human subjects. (In Europe these are called "Ethikkommission", "Ethikkommittee" or "Comitee d'ethique").
2. Committees constituted to examine animal experimentation from an ethical perspective. The use of these committees is, unfortunately, not as widespread nor its standards as rigorous or its findings enforced as are those of IRB's.
3. Hospital ethics committees that serve to help with problems as they affect institutionalized (hospital or nursing home) patients.

The function of ethics committees is educational (first of all themselves but ultimately members of the hospital community and the public), review of institutional policy and help with individual cases. A well educated and functioning ethics committee can do much to help with end of life decisions not only as they affect individual patients but and perhaps most importantly as they affect policy. Compassionate, well thought out and flexibly applied policies can do much to prevent the occurrence of as well as deal with full-blown individual problems. Such policies, in turn, can profit in their development from the ongoing experience of practicing health care professionals who, consequent to utilizing such policies, discover problems with them or with their use.

Ethics consultants—optimally well trained ethicists who can be called upon as any other consultant to help with an individual problem—can be helpful. However—and this simply cannot be emphasized enough—neither ethics committees nor ethics consultants are decision-makers. The ultimate decision must be made by the persons most relevantly affected and the clinicians(s) in charge of the case. The responsibility for such a decision remains theirs. The role of ethics committees and consultants is to help clarify problems, ask questions, think through cases and help examine and determine the ethical standing of various options. In asking such questions, they need to remind health care professionals of the initial questions: who is entitled to make the decision in question and who is being treated. Ethics committees and consultants can serve an important function when patients have been ruled incompetent and a state guardian has been appointed. Often continuing active treatment in a terminal patient (or resuscitating such a patient) is clearly not in the best interest of the patient; at times it is. In such situations ethics committees and consultants can act as intermediaries between the guardianship commission and health care providers and institutions.

Ethics committees and well-trained consultants can (in individual cases as well as in the policy decisions they help to craft) help flesh out the concept of autonomy within an institutional setting. Ethics committees and consultants can, however, also be quite counterproductive, actually producing more harm than good. This can occur, specifically, whenever such entities

(a) See themselves as constituted to enforce a particular religious point of view

(b) Believe that they serve a police function

(c) Allow themselves to be co-opted by the institution in which they work, seeing themselves as but an arm of that institution

(d) Assume the role of decision-makers rather than consultants

Ethics committees and consultants are neither the patient's nor the institution's agent. Ideally, they are constituted to reason together, to raise questions, insist on definitions and help clarify problems. When they adhere to their functions of educating, scrutinizing policy and impartially helping with the analysis of individual problems, they can be true assets to both the institution and to the broader community they serve.

ENDNOTES AND REFERENCES

1. L. Fleck, *Genesis and Development of a Scientific Fact*, trans. by F. Bradley and D.J. Trenn, ed. by D.J. Trenn and R.K. Merton, (Chicago, IL: University of Chicago Press), 1979. Based on the preceding work, see also T. Kuhn, *The Structure of the Scientific Revolution* (Chicago, IL: Chicago University Press), 1970.

2. For a very brief account of ethical theory as it is used in health care ethics see E.H. Loewy, *Textbook of Health-Care Ethics* (NY: Plenum Publishers, 1996) p. 19-49.

3. One needs to appreciate the totality of Dewey's work to get a grasp on his view of what has come to be called "pragmatism" and what he himself preferred to label as "instrumentalism." See, among others, J. Dewey "Ethics" in *John Dewey: the Middle Works 1899-1924*, vol. 5, ed. by J. Boydston and P.F. Kolojeski, (Carbondale, IL: Southern University Press), 1978.

4. T. Kushner, "Having a Life versus Being Alive," *Journal of Medical Ethics*, 1984; 1:5-8.

5. E.J. Cassell, "Life as a Work of Art," *Hastings Center Report*, 1984; 14(5): 35-37.

6. EHL has discussed the concept of "rational compassion" and of "compassionate rationality" in a number of works. Among them see, E.H. Loewy, *Moral Strangers, Moral Acquaintance and Moral Friends: Connectedness and its Conditions* (NY: State University of New York Publishers), 1997 and E.H. Loewy "Finding an Appropriate Ethic in a World of Moral Strangers," *The Influence of Edmund D. Pellegrino's Philosophy of Medicine*, ed. by David C. Thomasma (Dordrecht, the Netherlands: Kluwer Academic Publishers), 1997.

7. I. Kant, *Foundations of the Metaphysics of Morals*, trans. by Lewis W. Beck (NY: Macmillan Publishing, 1990), p. XXXXX and I. Kant, *The Metaphysics of Morals*, ed. and trans. by M. Gregor (NY: Cambridge University Press, 1996) p. 165-166; 157-158).

8. For a discussion of the role of Christianity in the development of this notion see R.H. Tawney, *Religion and the Rise of Capitalism: A Historical Study*, (NY: American Library), 1954 and K. Kautsky, *Foundations of Christianity*, trans. by Henry Mims (NY: Russell and Russell), 1953.

9. E.H. Loewy, *Textbook of Health-Care Ethics*, (NY: Plenum Publishers, 1996), p. 64-68.

10. The libertarian point of view is exemplified by the works of Nozick in social philosophy and of Engelhardt in health care ethics. See: R. Nozick, *Anarchy, State and Utopia* (NY: Basic Books), 1974 and H.T. Engelhardt, *The Foundations of Bioethics*, 2nd ed., (NY:

Oxford Books), 1994 as well as H.T. Engelhardt, *Bioethics and Secular Humanism: the Search for a Common Morality* (Philadelphia, PA: Trinity Press International), 1991.

11. B. Freedman, "Offering Truth," *Archives of Internal Medicine*, 1993; 153: 572-576.

12. The idea of "sizing up" was one expressed by Eric Cassell in conversation with Hans Jonas and was quoted by the latter. See: H. Jonas, "Against the Stream," *Philosophical Essays: From Ancient Creed to Technological Man* (Engelwood Cliffs, NJ: Prentice Hall), 1974. Also see M.D. Good, "The Practice of Biomedicine and the Discourse on Hope," *Anthropological Medicine*, 1991; 7: 121-135.

13. A.L. Back, et al, "Physician-assisted Suicide in Washington State: Patient Requests and Physician Responses," *JAMA*, 1996; 275(12): 919-923.

14. E. Casell, "The Function of Medicine," *Hastings Center Report*, 1977; 7(6): 16-19.

15. P. Dalla-Vorgie, et al, "Attitudes of Mediterranean Populations to Truth Telling," *Journal Medical Ethics*, 1992; 18: 67-74 and D.R. Gordon, "Culture, Cancer and Community in Italy," *Anthropological Medicine*, 1981; 7: 137-156.

16. E.H. Loewy, *Textbook of Health-Care Ethics* (NY: Plenum Publishers, 1996), p. 68-70.

17. J. Moreno, "The Social Individual in Clinical Ethics," *Journal of Clinical Ethics*, 1992; 3(1): 53-55.

18. This concept of something being a "fate worse than death" is one we owe to our colleague Dr. Ben Rich.

19. This is not the place to discuss the question of personal identity at length. The following sources offer a more in-depth discussion of the question: A.E. Buchanan and D.W. Brock, *Deciding for Others: the Ethics of Surrogate Decision making* (NY: Cambridge University Press, 1990), esp. pp. 152-190; R. Dresser, "Life, Death and Incompetent Patients: Conceptual, Informative and Hidden Value in Law," *Arizona Law Review*, 1986; 28: 379-381; B. Rich, "Prospective Autonomy and Critical Interests: A Narrative Defense of Advance Directives," *Cambridge Quarterly of Healthcare Ethics*, 1997; 6(2): 138-147.

20. E.L. McCloskey, "Hopes for the PSDA," *Journal of Clinical Ethics*, 1991; 2: 172-173.

21. M.D. Gross, "What Do Patients Express as their Preferences in Advance Directives?" *Archives of Internal Medicine*, 1998; 158: 363-365.

22. We have previously suggested that the relationship between individuals and their communities (and a family is a small community) is not well described in terms of a competitive and necessarily adversarial dialectic. Rather that relationship is homeostatic in the sense that the various members balance one another in the pursuit of a common goal. This common goal is the survival and prospering of the community. Just as the prospering of the individual is a necessary condition for the prospering of the community the survival and prospering of the community is necessary to enable, underwrite and safeguard the particular goals of the individual. See: E.H. Loewy, *Freedom and Community: the Ethics of Interdependence* (Albany, NY: State University of New York Press), 1995; See also E.H. Loewy and R. Springer Loewy, "Lebensunwertes Leben and the Obligation to Die: Does the Obligation to Die Rest on a Misunderstanding of Community?" *Health Care Analysis*, 1999; 7: 23-36.

23. The danger that can be created by an unthinking endorsement of advance has been discussed in E.H. Loewy, "Advance Directives and Surrogate Laws: Ethical Instruments or Moral Cop-out?" *Archives of Internal Medicine*, 1992; 152: 1973-1976 and E.H. Loewy, "Ethical Considerations in Executing and Implementing Advance Directives," *Archives of Internal Medicine*, 1998; 158: 321-324.

24. J. Hardwig, "What About the Family?" *Hastings Center Report*, 1990; 19(2): 5-10.

25. S.T. Hampshire, *Innocence and Experience* (Cambridge, MA: Harvard University Press, 1989), p. 67-68.

26. There is a vast literature on the utility and function of ethics committees and ethics consultants. A few resources include: M.G. Kuczewski and R.L.B. Pinkus, *An Ethics Casebook for Hospitals: A Practical Approach to Everyday Cases* (Washington, DC: Georgetown University Press), 1999; F.E. Baylis, ed., *The Health Care Ethics Consultant* (Totowa, NJ: Humana Press), 1995; J.M. Gibson and T. Kushner, "Will the Conscience of an Institution Become Society's Servant?" *Hastings Center Report*, 1986; 16(2): 9-11; B. Lo, "Behind Closed Doors: Promises and Pitfalls of Ethics Committees." *New England Journal of Medicine*, 1987; 317(1): 46-50; E.H. Loewy, An Inquiry into Ethics Committees' Understanding: How Does One Educate the Educators?" *Cambridge Quarterly of Healthcare Ethics*, 1993; 2(4): 551-556; M. Siegler, "Ethics Committees: Decision by Bureaucracy," *Hastings Center Report*, 1986; 16(3): 22-24.

Chapter 4

The Concept of Orchestrating Death

1.   INTRODUCTION

When the end of life is approached, there are several considerations and issues that become important in orchestration. Thus, before addressing orchestration itself, some other topics must be briefly discussed. Central to these are the questions of resuscitation, the question of not initiating or of discontinuing therapy and the problem of limiting some but not abandoning all treatment. We shall also briefly address the problem of dying at home rather than in an institutional setting. For a fuller discussion the reader is referred to several standard textbooks on the subject as well as literature pertinent to these particular issues.[1]

Decisions not to resuscitate patients are, very obviously, decisions made when the end of life is near, though this is not universally the case. A younger patient who may well recover might ask that resuscitation not be attempted. This, however, as important a discussion as it is, is not germane to this particular work. What we are discussing here is the appropriateness of such orders in situations in which the patient is rapidly approaching the end of life.

The decision not to resuscitate a patient does not and must not denote either that other treatment and care should be stopped or even reduced. The decision not to initiate or to withdraw other treatment is quite a different matter and the simple notion of "being cared for," which is everyone's due, must never be reduced or stopped. Nor is the decision not to resuscitate one that necessarily denotes cessation of intensive care or the removal of such patients from Intensive Care Units. At times the kind of care provided in the intensive care setting (such as very frequent suctioning or other comfort measures) is appropriate to the patient's needs and must be continued.

Although throughout history there have been attempts to restore heartbeat and respiration the history of successful resuscitation is relatively recent. Initially used in cases of cardio-pulmonary arrest occurring in the course of acute cardiac events, cardio-pulmonary resuscitation rapidly spread (some would say metastasized!) to other conditions in which the heart stopped or/and respirations ceased. Whatever the cause, whenever a patient's heart stops or respirations falter, resuscitation, unless otherwise specified, is initiated. There is good reason for this. If resuscitation is not promptly initiated the patient is dead; if it is initiated it can, if warranted, be stopped. Therefore, do not resuscitate orders, along with "nothing by mouth" and similar orders are among the few negative orders which physicians write.

As resuscitation became fixed in medical practice and firmly embedded in lay persons' minds it took on a meaning and value far above the technical. People often look upon these resuscitative efforts today in much the same way as last rites used to be (and for some people still are) looked upon—as symbolic efforts. They are the symbols that we often feel are everyone's due, symbols that represent a proper death and symbols that comfort those left behind. Cardio-pulmonary resuscitation is, however, quite different from other symbols or rites of passage.

Religious rites are private in the sense that they are attended to by those of priestly function and by the patient. They are public only insofar as the family and those close to the dying person, while perhaps not present in a deeper sense, participate. And like any other rite of passage it guides people into a range of appropriate ways of behaving. Other cultural rites of passage are apt to be more broadly public with the dying person, the priest or shaman and members of the community all present and actively or passively participating. Cardio-pulmonary resuscitation is private in the sense that the patient is unconscious, the family excluded and those substituting for the priestly function are engaged not in easing the persons passage to the beyond but in preventing it. They differ further, insofar as the patient is the object of their purely technical efforts and not, as with other rites, the subject. Cardio-pulmonary resuscitation, contrary to other rites, tends to sever the dying person's contact with her community rather than fostering it. Nevertheless, in the eye of much of the public dying in a hospital today properly entails a last and often symbolic effort at resuscitation. Instead of anointing with oil, 400 joules of current are now passed across the chest. Perhaps this trend towards establishing cardio-pulmonary resuscitation as a rite or a symbol underscores the fact that in our modern, highly technicalized society humans still crave rites and symbols and perhaps it suggests the need to find more fitting ones.

We must, first of all, be quite clear what a "Do Not Resuscitate" (DNR) order implies. Its technical meaning differs slightly from institution to institution and health care professionals are well advised to familiarize themselves with the precise meaning in their particular institution. Strictly and traditionally speaking resuscitation implies cardiac massage, electrical defibrillation and ventilation. There are, however, circumstances in which the term need not apply to all three. Defibrillation but not external cardiac massage may, for example, be appropriate in a frail old lady whose ribs would shatter during routine attempts at massaging the heart. At times patients opt to permit chest compression and defibrillation but refuse ventilation or intubation. Often as not, Such refusal rests upon a lack of understanding that can be cleared up as soon as the terms are explained. Thus, ventilator support (often perceived as a terrible thing by laypersons) can be done for three, quite different, reasons: (1) to maintain patients over an acute event, giving them the chance to return to their previous state (as might be the case in a severe pneumonia or during resuscitative efforts; (2) to more or less permanently keep patients (as in amyotrophic lateral sclerosis) on ventilator support, allowing them to continue living; or (3) as a comfort measure (as in cases of pulmonary edema).

When resuscitation is discussed with patients and relatives, the language used is critical. Lay persons have no real idea of what transpires in the course of resuscitation. On the one hand they are given the message by the media that this is a highly successful and simple procedure. On the other hand (and often by the same media), they are told horror stories of pain and suffering. To make matters worse, attendings and residents are often inclined (whether consciously or not) to describe resuscitative efforts in flamboyant terms in order to get the answer they wish to get. Both authors have heard, time and again, attending physicians and residents describe chest compression as bone-breaking and painful (when in truth the patient is most often unconscious), defibrillation in terms of electrocution and ventilation in terms of "having a tube shoved down your throat." It is hardly surprising that a patient already ill, afraid and in pain will refuse to have anything at all to do with such procedures.

There are, at times, good reasons why a DNR order should be written. First of all, resuscitation, like any other medical intervention, is a procedure or treatment which patients capable of making decisions have a right to refuse. Beyond this there are two other reasons for writing a DNR order: the first is a technical, the other mainly an ethical one.

Regarding the first, technical reason, physicians are not obligated to offer or submit patients to fruitless treatments or procedures. Indeed, they are well advised not to do so. When the literature indicates that resuscitative attempts will be futile (if, in other words, the heart cannot be restarted without promptly stopping again) trying to resuscitate patients is useless and doing so, since it offers relatives unwarranted hope, may even be cruel. When resuscitation might be successful but has a high risk of returning the patient to a terminal and hopeless state—perhaps one associated with considerable pain or suffering—the decision is not one of inability (a technical judgment.) Rather, it is one that considers whether such a life might not be worth living. It is a judgment only patients or, when patients no longer have decisional capacity, their surrogates can make. Under some circumstance patients may well wish to prolong their lives even when doing so entails suffering. Such is the case when a patient still wants to witness some important event or to achieve some important goal. When the literature indicates that the heart could be restarted and might keep going for a given time but the patient would never again regain consciousness or leave the hospital alive the decision is made on the grounds that such a short and insentient life would not be worth living. Although most of us would agree with this, it is not the same thing as when resuscitation would simply not work. Ultimately it is a decision that ideally should have been discussed with the patient or family long before the event arrives.

The great enthusiasm that was felt for cardio-pulmonary resuscitation during the first years of its application has given rise to skepticism and distrust. Many resuscitative efforts end with a patient who, while technically alive, has severe brain damage secondary to a prolonged lack of oxygen and who now will live in an unconscious, vegetative or severely damaged state. While these results are sometimes due to efforts that, in retrospect, ought not to have been made, some are inevitable, and they are the price we pay for success. We tend to forget: permanently unconscious, vegetative or severely neurologically damaged patients are dependent upon artificial means to sustain their lives. Such means are not obligatory—they need not be implemented or when implemented may be withdrawn. Such "mistakes" can, in due time, be rectified; failing to attempt resuscitation cannot.

In the past, heated debates raged about a supposed difference between not starting treatments and discontinuing once a treatment is started. However, in the ethics literature, as in law, this issue has been fairly well settled. Under identical circumstances there is no ethical or legal difference between not initiating and withdrawing therapy.[2] In both cases there must be either a solid technical reason (the treatment has reasonably no chance of working) or an ethical reason (prolonging life would merely promote the act of dying or cause prolonged and useless suffering). In general, the technical reason is and remains a medical decision. While patients and families should be informed of such decisions, there is no obligation to seek their permission. Indeed, seeking permission to withhold something useless is logically inappropriate, distinctly misleading and is arguably unnecessarily cruel. The ethical reason, however, is different: it is one of individual values, goals and world-views. It is a decision that must be made by the patient—be it by a patient with decisional capacity deciding at the time or in advance or be it a decision made through surrogates.

This is not to say that for the health care team as well as for relatives and patients an emotive difference between failing to initiate and withdrawing does not exist. Not starting "feels different" than withdrawing. When we fail to start we can delude ourselves that we have simply not acted; when we withdraw we very evidently have. Not doing something seems more easily to let us off the moral hook. Nevertheless we must be clear about one thing: when the possibility of acting exists, failure to act is as surely an action as deliberate failure to choose is a choice. When we could do something and fail to do it we are invariably causally linked to the outcome. Had we acted to prevent something, it might not have happened. The emotive difference as well as the aesthetic difference is not trivial. The importance of the difference is that members of the health care team are just as much persons with feelings, interests and values as are patients and their families. While their feelings cannot be a deciding factor, they nevertheless need to be respected and dealt with. Here again frank dialogue among the health care givers is essential. We come back to one of our original questions which asked who, in fact, is being treated. The short answer, "the patient, of course," is disingenuous and unsatisfactory. The patient (at least as long as consciousness has not been permanently lost) properly is the centerpiece of our concern. But the patient is not the only concern that we can or should have. Family as well as members of the health care team must likewise be considered. This, for example, may mean that more time is spent in discussing withdrawing than is spent in not initiating treatment and that, at times, a middle road (such as continuing but not escalating treatment) might be chosen.

The question of limiting treatment is often a more difficult question than the more straight-forward question of refraining from or stopping cardio-pulmonary resuscitative efforts or some other kind of therapy. Stopping or not initiating treatment is generally a judgment more explicitly made than continuing some but not other forms of therapy. Many of the problems at the end of life and which legitimately enter into good orchestration are problems with limiting but not abandoning therapy. It may seem quite appropriate (and even necessary) to treat a patient's pneumonia in a nursing home but it may appear equally inappropriate to consider coronary bypass surgery—i.e., not because the patient is too frail to undergo surgery but because general mental conditions and signs of deterioration so counsel. The reason for such decisions is often not articulated. Often such decisions are not overtly made, as when a patient with sepsis is deliberately undertreated or one with severe coronary disease is not offered by-pass surgery.[3]

Such decisions are far easier when the patient either has decisional capacity or has an advance directive. In many cases—if not indeed in most—the patient is no longer capable of making decisions and surrogates will make such decisions. There are, we think, certain guidelines which we can offer and which will facilitate the making of such decisions. There is one word of caution: legal competence or incompetence does not denote that patients do or do not have decisional capacity and are capable of making their own decisions (see Chapter # 2). In deciding to treat or to forego treating, at least four considerations are appropriate:[4]

1.   The immediacy of the threat

When there is an imminent threat to life, the proper default judgment counsels treatment. This is done to "buy time" so that a proper decision can be made. Unless there is prior agreement that no treatment of intercurrent conditions will be attempted, health care professionals are well advised to treat. However, health care professionals are even more urgently advised to discuss such eventualities beforehand. Doing so will usually provide clear guidance in individual cases. Again: it is more important to discuss goals than means, values rather than technological possibilities. The situation is often not foreseen and not foreseeable—the goals and values, however, are far more stable.

2.   The relievability of the suffering caused by an illness

Conditions which cause a great deal of pain or suffering or which, in order to deal with the pain, require large doses of narcotics which distort the patient's ability to think and socialize, should be treated vigorously. This may include surgical intervention to set a bone or remove some other painful condition and it may include angioplasty to temporary relieve angina decubitus. Likewise, treating pulmonary edema in someone in whom a decision not to treat intercurrent illness has been made may be necessary so as to provide a more tolerable exit.

3.   The suffering entailed in the treatment.

Treatments that are severely or protractedly burdensome to the patient need to be evaluated with the patient or the surrogates.

4.   The patient's ability for sustained understanding of and cooperation with treatment.

Patients who are demented or otherwise severely mentally incapacitated are often incapable of understanding the goals of therapy or what therapy might entail. Patients in the intensive care unit after by-pass surgery or patients on dialysis will find the treatment burdensome but will realize that those to whom they have entrusted themselves are trying to help. Patients who are severely demented or otherwise severely mentally incapacitated cannot understand this: they have felt secure in a previously nurturing environment which now suddenly and inexplicably has "turned against them". Confidence is replaced by fear and the patient's remaining life is further burdened.

Physicians are not obligated to perform procedures or apply treatment that in their medial opinion is of no avail or might even be harmful. Thus if it is known with reasonable certainty that cardiopulmonary resuscitative efforts will fail (if the literature and the experience of the clinician indicate as much) then asking the family for permission to write a DNR order is inappropriate. That is, it is inappropriate to ask permission to refrain from "doing" something that simply cannot be done. The request unduly burdens families insofar as it suggests to patient and/or family a possibility of success that simply does not exist.[5] On the other hand, physicians and other health care professionals are not entitled to assume that a given life is "not worth living" and to make judgments that are the patient's or the family's to make. Assuredly, physicians and other health care professionals are not only entitled but also, we would argue, obliged to counsel patients and relatives. But they are not entitled to pressure, bully or mislead patients in the pursuit of their own values.

There are a larger number of patients in the United States who die at home than there have been in years past. Part of this phenomenon is due to hospice and the care it can offer and part of it is due to the patient's wishes and the capacity of the family to assist the patient. Undoubtedly, another part of this phenomenon is also due to a shifting attitude towards death in our culture. Death, which heretofore was often denied or hidden, has become a far more open theme of discussion. There are still, however, a number of hurdles. Whether a patient will or will not be able to die at home depends in large measure upon the ability and willingness of family members to assist with this. Taking care of frail, weak, often incontinent and frequently not altogether pleasant people requires an enormous amount of attention. It is a twenty-four hour job which many families are unable to attempt or, when attempted, fail to carry out. Families have other obligations than to the dying. The devotion offered to the dying person means that the same amount of time, energy and devotion cannot be given elsewhere (economists refer to this expenditure as "opportunity costs"). Family members have a multiplicity of other obligations—to their children, their spouses, their employer and, not the least, to themselves—that need be considered in such a decision.

Once the decision not to leave home but to die there is made, there are various practical conditions. When push comes to shove, many family members are simply not prepared to stand by and let patients die. It is something easier to contemplate in the abstract than to carry out in the concrete. Frequently what happens is that an emergency rescue team ("911") is called, responds and, of course, is generally obliged to do all to sustain life until patients can be brought to the hospital. At the hospital, active treatment is very likely to be started in the emergency room. Decisions to call "911" are motivated by a dread of not having done all possible for a patient as well as often by fear of such "neglect" being misunderstood by friends, neighbors and other members of the family. [6] Such problems can more easily be resolved (even if not solved!) by frank discussions among all concerned and by supplying relatives with a telephone number where help short of an emergency call to "911" can be obtained. For hospice patients, this is likely to be hospice; for other patients other arrangements can be made. Also some states recognize legal documents which release and/or prevent emergency rescue crews from initiating life-sustaining measures.

2.   CONCEPTUAL, LINGUISTIC AND EDUCATIONAL PROBLEMS

There are also some linguistic, conceptual and educational problems that stand in the way of managing the end of life well. All of us, when the chance of cure is gone and the chance of meaningful prolongation of life is remote, are likely to express the sentiment, "there is nothing left to do." When, however, there is "nothing left to do" trying to do that which cannot be done is, at the very least, foolish and arguably wasteful: our energies, we reasonably tell ourselves, might better be saved for a task which holds out hope of success. Such a way of phrasing and, thus, looking at things easily results in abandoning the patient. Physicians, nurses, family and friends will avoid a situation in which no chance of "doing anything" remains. This linguistic problem is transmuted into the concept that the care of the terminally ill is a largely passive activity in which enduring rather than doing is the issue.

Even when cure or prolongation of life is not possible, not meaningful or often not something to be desired, it is crucial to understand that much still remains to be done. Such "doing" is not a passive process to be endured but, if done right, is a very active process indeed. When we speak of doing something we have an end or goal in mind. Curing disease or prolonging life may be an unachievable goal. But that does not mean that no other legitimate and achievable goals remain. Orchestrating the end of life has two interrelated functions: to maximize the positive content of life, to make it enjoyable and worthwhile and to minimize the suffering so commonly experienced during that phase of life. The goal of orchestrating the end of life is to create a situation in which the patient's suffering is held to a minimum while the ability to enjoy what remains of life and to fulfill personal attainable goals is maximized. The goal of what we have called orchestrating the end of life may, in fact, include extending it, just as it may—as a last resort—include actively helping patients to die.

We need to realize that the task of medicine is not limited to effecting a cure, to saving or even to prolonging life. The task of medicine (as we noted in the first chapter) has progressively widened. As the ability of medicine to extend life and to extend relatively healthy and functional life has increased, so has ability to extend life that is no longer meaningful and has, in fact, become burdensome to the person living it. Between these two (extending relatively healthy life and extending life that is no longer meaningful but now burdensome to the person living it) lies one of the widening gray zones: one of medicine's achievements has been the creation of chronic disease. This is not said in criticism: extending the life of patients with diabetes, rheumatoid arthritis, birth defects, lupus or amyotrophic lateral sclerosis has often also managed to add years of relative function and happiness. But it has also meant that such success is paid for when extension proceeds beyond personal meaning. Medicine has to learn to make actual and ethically appropriate distinctions between prolonging what is merely biological existence (being alive) and prolonging biological existence as the necessary condition for desired experience. And it has to learn how to manage ("orchestrate") the end of life so that patients in their last few days, months or years continue to take satisfaction in being alive.

Not all patients who are at the end of life necessarily experience pain. Many do. Many more patients than those who experience pain experience suffering. In medicine we have a tendency to equate the two and to believe that to take care of the pain will also take care of the suffering. Although in the medical setting pain and suffering are often related, suffering is a phenomenon which is experientially and neuroanatomically quite different from pain.[7] To Freud, suffering comes to us from three sources: (1) the decay of our own body, (2) the natural forces "raging against us", and (3) (most grievously) our relations with other persons.[8] Frankl adds a critical point to the conversation: suffering becomes suffering when what we endure seems pointless to us. To help persons find meaning even as they approach their end is, perhaps, the main task before us. Analyzing what such a skill might look like is what this chapter is all about.

Ideally, orchestrating the end of life does not begin at the time when a diagnosis of a potentially fatal illness is made but should start long before. Just as the end of life is integrated into the totality of a life, so the care of that phase needs to be integrated into overall medical and social care. Physicians should seek to engage their patients in conversations that deal with the with the values, hopes, fears and ultimate wishes of those patients long before such a diagnosis is made. Part of medical practice—and a part we think equally important to the technical skills expected of physicians—is getting to know and understand the patient's "work of art." Creating this work of art is a work in progress and, therefore, the values, hopes, fears and ultimate wishes of patients may in fact change.

Unfortunately, in today's world it is not frequently the case that physicians have a long-standing relationship with their patients. Such a relationship, much as it may be desired, is often not possible. This makes record-keeping all the more important. Medical records should properly contain more than merely technical information dealing with symptoms, findings, lab data and diagnosis. A social history tersely noting the patient's medical status, habits and occupation does not exhaust what physicians need to know to provide good care. Medical records should also briefly sketch the patient's life, plans, hopes, fears and ultimate wishes. As these may and very likely will change over the years, it is important to understand not only a patient's "work of art" at a particular time but to be sensitive to and record appropriately its evolution with time and circumstance.

When we talk of dealing with persons at the end of their lives, we should not concentrate merely on the elderly or even only on adults. Although much more rarely than in past centuries or even at the beginning of this century, children do die. In societies other than our western industrialized world, this is often still the case. In addition, in the United States today many children who need not die do so because of diseases brought on by chronic poverty, malnutrition and lack of access to health care.

It is difficult to speak about "children" in any ethically coherent sense. In dealing with dying children (low birth weight or severely damaged neonates are beyond the scope of this book) chronology is not a reliable ethical—albeit legal—standard. But even in law, judges have progressively paid more attention to the expressed wishes of children than they did in former years. The problem is that the maturity of a child (which is what we are speaking of) is not only related to biological age: the cultural setting with its different expectations, the social circumstances and the personal history of the "child" are equally important when it comes to maturation. In former days (and in parts of the world today) many persons were married and had families long before they were eighteen. Furthermore, a child reared in adversity does not, if it is to survive, remain "immature" for long. Children who grow up in circumstances of chronic poverty, danger or illness mature much more rapidly than do, for example, children raised in a protected middle class environment.

In dealing with the realization of death, children go through various stages. There is a slow development from seeing death as a temporary separation (or as abandonment), to death as reversible and to a final grasping of the finitude of one's own and others' lives. The specifics of the developmental stages and the time when these may be expected to be presented is beyond the scope of this book.[10] It bears mentioning, however, that these stages are guide posts and there is (as with adults) a great deal of individual variation in a child's capacity to deal with concepts of death. An adult notion of death, like all else, develops slowly and incrementally and is associated with experience and context. In our society children today tend to be "protected" from encounters with death. They are often in their adult years before they are touched by the death of someone close to them.

It has been shown that most children who are gravely ill and whose life is drawing to a close are aware of their illness as well as of their impending end. There is also evidence that not dealing forthrightly and honestly with the child about this problem in order to "spare them fears and pain" can, in fact, produce exactly the opposite result. As with adults, enmeshing oneself and the patient in a web of untruths or lies makes communication difficult. The motives for not informing children (on their terms) are complex: the avowed reason of sparing the child is often combined with the desire to spare oneself the pain of this conversation as well as with the hope that the truth is, after all, not true. But dying children, like dying adults, apparently are generally quite aware of their approaching end and need, above all during such times, the comfort of truthful communication with their loved ones. Such conversations are admittedly terribly difficult and trying, especially for the parents. But such conversations are also difficult for health care providers whose humanity, likewise, needs to be recognized and respected. The help of psychiatrists, psychologists and psychiatric social workers who have special training in dealing with such children can be of crucial importance. While helping the child to deal with the situation is important, this cannot be done effectively without, and at the same time, helping the parents and siblings to do so. Children, like adults, should not be conceptually or actually separated from the social nexus within which they lead their lives.

With children, as with adults, orchestrating the end of life requires a multidisciplinary and integrated approach—something that is today, perhaps, far more effectively done with children than it is with adults. In general the effectiveness of dealing with dying children is due to extensive training of all who must deal with these situations as well as to the strict multidisciplinary team approach which is used in most centers. Those who deal predominantly with adult patients could learn much from the approach pediatricians take.

3. RELATIONSHIPS AND TALKING WITH PATIENTS

The living person maintaining some form of conscious awareness is inevitably involved in relationships. Relationships, according to the definition we will use, require mutuality: that is, to have a relationship requires an engaged and active interaction between two self-aware beings. We can speak of a relationship with anesthetized or unconscious persons only because of our prior relationship with them as self-aware beings and our expectation that their self-awareness will return. But during the time of anesthesia or unconsciousness that relationship is, so to speak, on hold. Most certainly we can have a relationship with our dog, our cat or our bird—they know us and respond to us in a manner that both partners can recognize. Having a relationship with a goldfish is, however, more problematic and a relationship with a houseplant is, essentially, a one-sided affair. We can claim to have a relationship with our house, with a bed-slipper that has been with us for many years or with a host of other objects. But such a "relationship" does not rest on mutuality and can be conceived as a relationship only in a symbolic sense. Our relationship with the dead too is, in part, symbolic but it is symbolic in a different sense: here what we feel to be an enduring relationship is based on prior and past mutuality. It, therefore, often allows the continuation of a now internalized "dialogue."

Symbols come into being as an epiphenomenon of the reality that they come to represent. They necessarily relate to something we believe exists or has existed. Often they outlast—and sometimes they substitute for and distort—the reality they represent. When we value the symbol more than the reality for which that symbol stands, we have changed sentiment to sentimentality.[11] Likewise we have to be cautious in dealing with patients who are permanently unconscious as though they were, in fact, conscious. As long as consciousness persists or can return (however impaired, however fleeting) the reality of the relationship persists. When consciousness is permanently lost, the relationship is frozen and exists only in our memory and in our past. At the end of life, relationships assume great importance—both to the person nearing their end and to those about them. It is only when the patient ultimately withdraws (as he/she often does) that such relationships begin to lose their prior rich mutuality.

The need for these social relationships and the need of bringing them to an authentic close is one of the reasons why, in days past, people feared sudden death. Sudden, unexpected death, especially in the fullness of life, obliterated the chance for meeting these social obligations. Persons felt that it was necessary to say the proper good-byes, to make the proper arrangements for and with those left behind and to partake in the religious ceremonials and symbols of approaching death. Today, people at the end of life often reclaim such feelings—we are not that different after all! They begin to feel the need to make their peace, they wish to assure others and be assured by them of their love and they wish to strengthen old and recapture lost relationships. Giving them that opportunity is part of what properly orchestrating the end of life is all about.

The relationship between physician and patient is often conceived in isolation, as though it—like all other relationships—did not partake of the entire context. Not only is the relationship of patient and physician embedded in a particular context, but both physician and patient have, in turn, other relationships, each with their own inevitable contexts. The relationship physicians have with patients are modulated by the relationships physicians have with other health care providers, with other patients, with their friends and, ultimately, with their community. There are some obvious examples of this: when health-professionals have had a "bad day," are sleep deprived, have had an argument with their spouse or have severe economic problems, all other relationships are affected. The importance of a well functioning health care team lies not only in each understanding their technical tasks and their boundaries well, but also in the often neglected fact that the relationship of each of the members with the patient is affected by their relationship with all others outside of as well as within the team. Furthermore: the team does not exist in a vacuum. It is a social construct and is enmeshed in an institution with its own internal and external dynamics and relationships. In turn, the institution is inevitably and inextricably connected with the narrower community and ultimately with the wider community in which it exists. These interconnections are a part of human life and ultimately connect us to all other humans—and we would claim, eventually to all sentient beings.[12]

Relationships, by their very nature, are complex and changing. No one can tell others the particulars of how they should relate to one another. Each of the authors has a different relationship with each of our students and they with us. If one of us were to claim that he or she had the same relationship with all students (no matter their personality and all that this entails) it would suggest having no true relationship with any of them. Furthermore: such a personal relationship today will be different from what it may be tomorrow, not only because one's tomorrow will entail different experiences than does one's today but also because one's relationship with a person today changes the relationship one has with that and other persons tomorrow.

Relationships are, in part, defined by responsibilities. It is difficult to define the concepts student, spouse, nurse, physician, teacher, policeman, friend and even enemy without pointing to the different obligations these relationships and their roles entail. The members of a health care team, likewise, are defined in part by the obligations they have to each other as well as to the patient. But once again, since these obligations do not occur in a vacuum they must be understood in the context of the larger community in which they occur.

Attempting to teach health care professionals how to relate to their patients and with each other can, of course, be done in general terms. Certainly one can tell health care professionals what not to do—it is not appropriate to convey the sense of being hurried, disinterested or uninformed. But, above all, it is important to teach people to allow themselves to be genuine: to be themselves and to interact with others in a way comfortable and suitable to them, the particular situation and within the context of a particular relationship. When students are taught to relate in a particular way, to say certain things or to smile in certain ways they are, in effect being instructed to relate in a superficial and inauthentic manner. The basis of relationships is mutuality and the basis of genuine relationships is mutual honesty and not a process of mutual posturing or game playing. Furthermore, the basis of relationships is a mutuality in which, in the process of a specific relationship, each learns from the other(s) how to relate. Relationships are dynamic, changing and evolving. To make of relationships stereotypic interactions, is to lose their sensitivity, their meaning and their value. Patients generally have little trouble sensing whether their health care providers are genuinely interested in them, whether they really care or whether they feign interest and pretend caring. At the end of life, patients have enough other problems without also being asked to play games.

Speaking with and above all listening to patients and their relatives (especially when informing them of bad news or exploring various treatment or care options) is of prime importance in compassionately caring for persons and their relatives. Often patients (or relatives) are not ready to hear or not willing to speak. Sometimes they may seem to listen and may even respond but soon thereafter will have "forgotten" (or totally misconstrued) much of what has been said. Such conversations are a process of feeling each other out, of exploring limits and of being sensitive to what is said, what is not said as well as to the body language accompanying the conversation. Patients (and relatives) can only be told what they are ready to hear. Again, such conversations have been well described in one paper as a "pas de deux" in which all must be sensitive to the particular needs and feelings of the others.[3]

Breaking bad news or speaking about diagnostic and therapeutic options is best done with the patient as well as patient selected family members. All must be given an ample opportunity to hear, to ask questions and to discuss. It is best not to insist upon an answer at the time diagnosis and options are presented but to permit patients to return home, discuss what has been said, formulate new questions and think things over. Rarely must decisions be made the same day. When health care professionals have to give "bad news" to their patients, especially when they have to discuss therapeutic options or end of life decisions, it is best to remember that patients and their relatives may not understand clearly what has been said or, at times, may not hear at all. Patients hear what they are prepared to hear and are apt to block that which they are not ready to handle. Beyond that, when several persons are told the same thing they are quite apt to go away with quite different impressions of what has been said. Hence, it is often a good idea to make a tape recording of these conversations, to allow the patient to take the recording home and to urge them and their family to listen to it on several occasions. When patients and families listen to the recording of what they as well as their care-givers have said questions which they neglected to ask and points which they fail to understand clearly will become more evident to them. As they continue the dialogue among themselves new questions will also present themselves. When such questions or points in need of clarification present themselves, patients and their relatives should be urged to write them down and bring what has been written down to the next visit. Likewise, and especially when some time has elapsed, health care providers will often benefit by listening to the tape again before the patient visits them. Not only is this a refresher in the particular human dimensions of the case, it enables health care professionals to detect critical information which may have been inadvertently omitted and to add it.

Listening to what patients have to say, speaking with rather than to them and listening to the interchange between patient, family and friends can be extremely informative for the physician and the entire team. One learns more about the inner dynamics of a family relationship—information that is critical to good orchestration and performing—by listening to patient and family talk with one another. The fact that a patient is totally dominated by his partner (or that he or she is the dominant voice) is, for example, a critical piece of information which can often be learned only by watching and listening. Personality traits and ways of behaving which were not evident before may become very evident now and relationships painted in a certain way may suddenly be seen in a quite different light.

Some ways of helping relationships flourish and communication succeed can be suggested. Such ways of helping relationships flourish are important throughout the encounter of health-professionals with their patients but become extremely important when orchestrating the end of life is the issue. The conductor and the other players need to have and to cultivate relationships with the patient. The ways we shall suggest to help communication so that relationships can flourish are, however, suggestions and guide-posts and not something which all health-professionals at all times and with all persons should mindlessly follow. Much depends upon the contingency of the situation, the personality of both patient and health care professional and the context within which the relationship occurs.

First of all, health- care professionals should not appear to be hurried. When pressed for time it is important that patients and families are told about time pressures in an honest way. Every effort to set a specific future time aside and communicate this to the patient should be made. To pretend to "always have time" is disingenuous; body language will generally convey the fact that we are hurried or pressed for time. When health care professionals are with their patients, they should attempt to devote their entire time and energy to that particular encounter. The term "quality time" has been overused but it is an extremely important concept. An hour spent distracted and obviously wishing to be somewhere else is as good as worthless when compared to ten minutes of real and evident attention.

Secondly, it is important to remember that sharing food and drink has a large symbolic significance in all cultures. In speaking to people it is, whenever possible, most helpful to do so over a shared cup of coffee or tea, to literally "break bread." This cannot be overemphasized especially when bad news has to be conveyed, difficult discussions have to take place or difficult arrangements must be made. Breaking bread, and sharing a glass of wine denotes a common humanity and signals that one is willing to share one's humanity as well as one's time.

Thirdly: it is helpful not to speak to patients who are bed or chair bound while looming over them in a standing position. Our physical position can now doubly intimidate the supine who already feel themselves powerless and dependent. Clearly, from Shaman to modern times, the garb of healers was culturally prescribed and met certain (and for healing not unimportant cultural) expectations. It symbolized a certain power and a certain commitment. But this can be overdone and instead of conveying re-assurance can convey power not just over events but patients themselves. Sitting down on or by a patient's bed rather than standing does a lot to put patients at ease. At the end of life the sense that physicians have at least some control over events (that they have the power to ameliorate pain and suffering) is important, but so is the sense of shared humanity which breaking bread and sitting together conveys.

Fourthly, all too often physicians as well as other health care professionals will turn to the family rather than primarily turning to the patient him or herself. Turning to someone other than the patient occurs especially often when patients are elderly, bed-bound or already (because of the nature of their illness) dependent. It is often done for the sake of convenience or from the false premise that to do so is to spare patients worry and grief. We are not arguing that the family should be neglected or excluded. We are saying that when a patient is self-aware and has decisional capacity he or she is properly the first and not the last to be turned to. Even when decisional capacity is tenuous, patients deserve our respectfully including them in our conversations. At times this may not be possible, but often it is.

Fifth, one must not forget the value of humor. There are few if any situations in life in which a shred of humor does not survive. An appeal to humor rather than deadpan, somber interactions can lighten the load and ease conversation and understanding. Humor used with compassion is a powerful tool. It also can convey a shared humanity and, when used appropriately and genuinely can convey a sense of compassion rather than—what is so often claimed—callousness.

Sixth, students are often advised to touch their patients, to put an arm around a shoulder or to take a hand. Such forms of interaction once again require mutuality: some adult patients or families will not wish such closeness and some health care professionals will find such closeness distasteful. It is not something that can be prescribed. Health-care professionals as well as patients and families can sense each other's limits readily and must respect them. Above all, one should be oneself and expect one's partner to act the same way. Relationships, if they truly rest on mutuality, must be genuine and authentic.

Communicating and relating to children at the end of their lives require some understanding of a child's world, of their way of thinking and relating, of their fears, hopes and imaginings. Children more so than adults will tend to relate in non-verbal ways, often through art and music. Often relationship is through an intermediate—a puppet, a stuffed animal or perhaps a pet. Sometimes children will speak about their own fears and pain as though such fears or pains were not their own but that of their pet or stuffed toy. On the other hand, children relate poorly to euphemisms. Circumventing the truth by using expressions like "going to sleep" or "going on a long trip" are more apt to bewilder or create fear than to help. Just as with adults, a straightforward, specific and literal but compassionate approach that gives the child permission to express grief, hopes and fears is of critical importance for all concerned.

4.   THE SCORE AND THE MUSIC

The "score" that the conductor uses in our setting is the patient. It is the patient that the conductors and musicians must know and understand. Thus, it is, first of all, necessary, to understand the particular patho-physiology which a patient's particular illness presents. Beyond this, however, all concerned must understand other medical conditions that coexist or precede the particular illness. Thus knowing that a patient has a small cell cancer of the lung and understanding what this implies is impossible without a thorough understanding of the totality of a patient's other medical circumstances. One must understand how the various medical conditions interact with one another as well as how the treatment of one may be affected or limited by the other. This is a complicated task. Relatively few patients at the end of their lives have but one illness. The illness a patient has, however, cannot be reduced to the sum of the diseases. Always it is a specific illness in the context of other pathological conditions and in a specific patient at a particular time and within a particular cultural setting. A patient has a history of which the medical history, as difficult as it is to know and understand, is generally not the most complex thing to know about a patient and often is not the most important thing to the patient. Knowing only the medical conditions and their interaction provides only a very few of the themes those involved with orchestrating the end of life must deal with and must seek to understand. Other themes—themes of cultural background, of personal history, of important relationships, of values, fears and hopes as well as the often most vexing issues of economic limitations—must be as understood as fully as possible if problems at the end of life are to be effectively dealt with. The score, then, is the patient in his or her totality and complexity. It is the patient who composes the music; it is the conductor and the players (the health care team) who, with the help of patient and family, must interpret that music.

In many symphonic performances, the composer is dead and can provide no personal guidance. In a sense, the dead composer's written score provides an "advance directive" which provides broad guidelines to those charged with performance. At the end of life, the composer of the score is still alive, able to interact and much of the time will have sufficient capacity to make (even if often not to implement) decisions (see chapter 2). The patient can and should actively participate in what is—so long as the patient is alive—a work in progress rather than a finished product. Patients in our analogy must, however, make their choices within the framework of possible options just as composers must write their symphonies within a framework created by the possibilities offered by the instruments available.

A symphony has several thematically interconnected movements that attempt to create a whole work of art whose conclusion is appropriate to its beginning and whose middle smoothly connects the beginning with the end. There are several—and not merely a stereotyped number—of movements. Likewise, the types and numbers of players vary according to what is being played and may, on some occasions include quite unusual instruments or vocalists appropriate to a particular setting.

Each performance is an act of creation as, in a sense, is what each listener does with that performance. Such creativity in end of life care—just as in some symphonic performances—may vary the score and at times may attempt to include instruments and settings other than the composer visualized. Thus a string quartet or a concerto may be orchestrated as a symphony or a symphony may be played as a quartet. In other words, the number of players or the role of a particular player in the performance may have to be changed to fit taste and circumstance depending on the contingencies of a particular case. One may, for example, not employ clergy when patients do not wish it or reduce the music to a solo performance—the latter, since individuals rarely have all requisite skills and unlimited time, will rarely be the case. However, one can conceive that a patient will not accept a particular skill as applicable to their case. Radiation or chemotherapy or even physiotherapy, may very well be something that would be medically indicated but may be something a particular patient, with decisional capacity and fully informed, still refuses. Thus the texture of a particular piece of music will have to be adjusted to the problem at hand.

Various movements may be compared to various stages which patients at the end of life encounter. The term "end of life" is, as we have said, at best vague and ill defined. Ideal end of life care (and with it orchestration) would begin much earlier in the planning than it does today. Most, but by no means all, people at the end of life are elderly and one could easily foresee an amalgam between geriatric care, end of life care and hospice. The first movement, ideally, is seen as the beginning of the process and might well start many years before the end. End of life care—like symphonies—may consist of various movements of various lengths. Each movement has different main themes, yet the common thread of the patient's values and particular philosophical perspective connects the themes of each movement. Thus aggressive and perhaps even curative therapy may well be part of the first movement, attempts to prolong even if not cure may be part of later movements and finally other movements, depending on the patient's capacity for autonomous mental as well as physical action, will follow.

Often in today's setting the last movement begins very late in the course of illness. Patients are treated as though their lives were eternal until they are actively confronted with a fatal illness that has proven to be beyond cure or meaningful prolongation. At that point patients, as often as not, are declared to be "beyond treatment" (see previous chapters) and efforts are at best limited to rigorous pain control—pain control which is often given at the price of mental and physical function. It is here that skillful orchestration (which must be an amalgam of specific medical knowledge and the hopes, values, fears and expectations of a specific patient at a specific time and in a specific setting) can play a major role.

Not all patients have a protracted course. Patients may die in a relatively short time, going from the hale and hearty to sick and miserable and finally to death in a matter of days or weeks. Here, too, appropriate orchestration can play an enormously important role. The piece of music chosen for such an occasion may not be symphonic. It may not have several movements; it may have only one main performer or it may be a rather short concert piece. The challenge in such cases is even greater for often the medical team and the physician does not know the patient, his or her life values or world-view and have little time to make appropriate judgments. No cookbook prescriptions here (or anywhere else in this work) can or will be given. However, it is always important to keep in mind that dealing truthfully and compassionately with patients, enhancing their understanding of their autonomy by offering them settings and methods which allow for the widest choices and being open to their individual needs are almost always in order. Enhancing patients' understanding of their autonomy is quite different from insisting that patients comply with our particular understanding of autonomous action. For particular patients, in particular cultural settings, autonomy is understood in quite a different way from that of much of western (and particularly American) society today. Good orchestration is sensitive to this fact and, thus, seeks to enhance not autonomous action in which people decide for a supposed isolated self but autonomous action in which patients are free to act in the embrace of their understanding of who and what they are.

5.   CONDUCTORS

Composers create the score that is turned into music by the conductor's interpretation. While composing is largely creating it is, nevertheless, creating from available materials. Conductors take a somewhat more restricted material (the composition) and from it create a unique performance. In the case of end of life management it is, until the very end, a work in progress. Musicians participate in this act of creation. The audience also—if it is to listen truly and not just passively attend—have a part in the act of creation: the music heard may be the same but the meaning that such music has to an individual listener may be quite different.

Part of planning end of life care (like composing) takes place away from the bedside (or concert hall). Composing or planning various options and designing various treatments for broad classes of diseases and patients is a theoretical occupation. From these theoretical constructs the good conductor fashions what, given the particular constraints of available musicians and instruments as well as the limitations of the concert hall, is appropriate in a particular patient setting. The knowledge gained from past as well as ongoing experience "feeds back" into the theoretical discussion, illuminating needs and enriching the theoretical discussion. The task is social in that, to provide a good performance (or to provide good end of life care) involves what may well be another illustration of Habermas' communicative action.[14] That is, the task is ongoing communication among the patient and all those concerned with end of life management.

Who conducts and what does it mean to be a conductor? Conductors are the ultimate point of reference for the orchestra and the ultimate coordinator of the progress of a given performance. In concert with players and with the potential or actual audience, conductors help select the music and guide its development. Conductors of orchestras must, first of all, assemble the different players of the orchestra. A common goal must be developed to which all can subscribe and follow. Conductors (at least if an optimal performance is to take place) should not be dictators. They will readily consult the composer, the players and ultimately the audience. Conductors, at their best, are persons who respect the composer, the composition and the general musical as well as the particular technical skills of each player. Good conductors (although they are ultimately responsible for the type and quality of the performance) not only direct but also seek counsel from the composer and from their musicians. Good conductors are not micro-managers who interfere with and control every player's action. While understanding the range of all instruments, they understand what they themselves would be incapable of doing. While firmly in charge of a particular performance the conductor nevertheless must be willing to hear and listen to the unique voices of the individual players. Having assembled the players and practiced with them, the conductor must direct the performance and, after it is done and in concert with all the players, must re-evaluate and learn from it. Here, once again, one can see the importance of cultivating relationships not only between health-professionals and their patients, but likewise among the members of the orchestra who must work together and, therefore, must seek to understand each other as human beings as well as professionals engaged in a common task.

Conductors must fully understand the score and know what instruments would be required for a successful performance. Beyond this, conductors must understand and utilize the acoustics of a particular concert hall in which the performance takes place and turn them to best advantage. In selecting the musicians conductors must be aware not only of the talents and shortcomings which each player may bring to the orchestra but also of that player's capacity to work together with others in the orchestra. Soloists often make poor team players. Particular players have to be selected and have to be fitted into their particular group of instruments. Players should not be picked merely because of their technical skill—technical skill is the necessary but quite insufficient condition. Players must also be selected with an eye to having their personality fit in with the rest of the orchestra. The conductor, thus, must not only pay attention to the technical skills of the players but likewise must be able to assess their skills as human beings undertaking a common task.

A good conductor is not only one who performs a technically good job and who adheres to the various queues provided by the composer. In part, a good conductor creates: he/she takes the raw material which is the composers creation and fashions it into a performance which is unique in itself and is rarely quite the same twice. In being human beings, conductors adjust their performance to situation, context, needs and past experience. A good and sensitive performance considers more than the technical capacities of each instrument and the technical facts of the concert hall: a good performance is one sensitive to the human dimension.

The conductor in our health care culture today is often, but not invariably, a physician. Other models are certainly thinkable. The conductor in orchestrating the performance at the end of life is the person who coordinates the players and the performance and who, ultimately, is responsible for its quality. Conducting takes more than merely technical skill. It implies a willingness to seek cooperation with and among all the players and it likewise implies a willingness to learn from the past for the present and from the present for future performances.

6.   PLAYERS

The players of the orchestra combine a number of critically important skills. Players need agree upon and jointly pursue a common goal. Most performances will employ a standard repertoire of players and skills: almost invariably an orchestra has strings, brass, woodwinds and timpani. Some music, however, requires additional instruments. Preferably these will not be ad hoc choices made on the spur of the moment but will be players used to playing with a particular orchestra. Patients' needs in the last few days, months or years of their lives may be vastly different. Persons ending their lives with advanced cardiac disease have needs quite different from the person riddled with metastatic cancer or dying in renal failure.

Who are the players who almost invariably will be a part of every performance? Obviously there are physicians, nurses and social workers. Each of these has an area of specific expertise. Part of the advantage of a team-approach is the opportunity to learn from one another, to see the problem from a different aspect and to consider each of these aspects in setting goals and making day to day decisions. Physicians may come from a variety of disciplines. It is critical, in our view, that physicians have and cultivate relationships not only with the patient and family, but likewise with the players. Optimally, such a physician will be a person who has known the patient and the family over the years or at least over the course of that particular illness. In today's world this is a goal which is often not realized. Societal as well as institutional forces mitigate against it: people move frequently, insurance coverage changes so that a particular physician may no longer be able to care for the patient and, therefore, fragmentation of care is more often the rule than the exception. Furthermore (see chapter on hospice) forces within the hospice setting as well as the funding of hospice often produce a state of affairs in which entering hospice means losing continuity with the physician who took care of the patient before.

Pain management is one of the critical issues in end of life care. There is the danger of reducing good end-of-life care to good pain control: a reduction which flies in the face of all collected data.[15] Having said that: pain control remains one of the essential (but certainly not the sufficient) conditions for good end of life care. Despite of the fact that the management of pain (at least in malignant disease) has greatly improved in the last few decades, there still remains a lot of room for improvement. It is often quite new to medical students and residents that one must inquire both into the degree and duration of pain relief and that degree and duration of pain call for different strategies. Insufficient relief of pain calls for an increase in dosage, insufficient duration of relief for a reduction in time interval. Likewise it has taken all too long to make clear to physicians the fact that analgesia must be prophylactically administered before pain returns. Here is not the place to discuss various strategies for supplying optimal analgesia to patients.[16] Suffice it to say that pharmacology is clearly not sufficient. We are all familiar with the fact that our psychological condition has a tremendous amount to do with how we perceive pain. The bored person will focus on, and the occupied person will be distracted from, pain. Likewise fear and anxiety is additive, whereas happiness, joy and satisfaction tends to diminish pain. We all know this from our own personal experience—yet it is all too often forgotten when managing patients. Moreover, the extent to which we understand our pain is culturally and socially different: pain is felt far more intensely and is more readily translated into suffering when the social situation is neglected than it is when the social situation is well understood and appropriately addressed. Physicians and other health care professionals who are involved with managing the end of life should be thoroughly familiar with strategies for optimal pain relief and should be ready to obtain regular consultation from specialists in the field of pain control. Indeed, since pain is so often (even if no means invariably) encountered at the end of life, specialists in pain control should be members of the team.

Often the clergy play an important part. It is surprising how rarely today physicians (be they resident physicians or attendings) know about their patient's spiritual beliefs. Students are trained to inquire into a whole array of physical, emotional and social facts but they are often most hesitant to ask about a patient's religion or other form of spirituality. And yet, if one is to manage the end of life well, such understanding can greatly enhance communication and ultimately, therefore, management. For patients who are members of a particular religious group, involving their clergyperson as a member of the team and not as an "outsider" can be most helpful. Chaplains who are especially trained in hospital work or work with sick patients can play an enormous role and be of great help—sometimes even with patients whose belief system is not based on any particular religious belief. When patients have had a long enduring relationship (be it with a physician or with a chaplain) every effort should be made to include these persons both formally and informally within the team caring for the patient.

Social workers have a critical role. The social situation in which one's life evolves inevitably shapes all that happens. The best conceived plan could be destroyed by a social situation into which such a plan cannot be accommodated or by one which distorts it. Social workers have the skills that can ferret out these situations, understand the social setting and its various configurations and ultimately provide concrete advice. Likewise, clinical psychologists or psychiatric social workers can provide insights, establish new ways of communicating or proceeding and very much help to clarify situations.

Many different types of therapists must be counted as among the regular players. Physical, occupational, nutritional and respiratory therapists—to name but a few—can be of immense help not only in the concrete tasks they perform but also in the particular insights that these skills entail. Rather than merely utilizing such persons and directing them to the performance of a particular task, we should listen to and seek to learn from them. There are many other types of therapy that may be critical today. Animal therapy at all ages has been found to be important and to bring a sense of inner peace to patients. Not only is it important that a patient's pet be included—also and not unimportantly for the sake of the pet—it is, oftentimes, critical. Consider a patient seen in ethics consultation on a ventilator and in the Intensive Care Unit. On her bedside stand was the picture of.a little dog and it was readily apparent that she very much wanted to see, touch and communicate with her friend. Bringing the dog to her—or in this particular case, arranging for her daily transport to an area where her respiratory support could be continued while she play with and pet her dog—was, arguably, of greater importance to managing her end of life care than any of the technical nuances on which so much time and effort had been expended. Pets should be considered as part of the team and not as another technical modality. They have desires, needs and ways of relating of their own. Allowing the interplay between patient and pet to continue and especially encouraging the patient to continue to care for and fulfill the needs of the pet and not only allowing the pet to fulfill the needs of the patient is critical. Most humans have a need to be socially useful. Caring for a pet is caring for another and may have an important function as the patient approaches the end of life.

In many persons and, apparently, especially in children, music and art therapy can play a crucial role.[17] In children, as well as in adults, the ability to express oneself in art and the opportunity to experience the sense of closure and transcendence that good music can sometimes provide, can convert a gray, dreary and discomfort filled period into one that can still be enjoyed and fulfilling. Furthermore, children will often express in art or music what they cannot or will not verbalize outright. Adults, too, may often seek metaphors or symbols as a form of conscious and subconscious expression. A skilled art therapist, one who is used to dealing with that sort of expression can be of immense help.

7. THE CONCERT HALL

The setting (the concert hall, as it were) in which the end of life takes place is critical to the success or lack of success of management. The concert hall in which the performance takes place has acoustics. These are the sounds sent back, distorted or rendered with fidelity which patients, conductors, players and family hear. These "sounds" are the explicit and, perhaps more importantly, tacit messages conveyed to patients by members of the team, by family, friends and associates. Such messages condition all else that the patient perceives and are an often-neglected aspect of caring for people.

In recent years architects have begun to plan, design and finally build institutional settings which accommodate not only to the physical needs of the users but which are, likewise, sensitive to the dimensions of patients' needs. Their work has concerned itself not only with such things as ramps or devices to help assist or lift weakened patients but likewise have come to concern themselves with creating a milieu in which such patients can be allowed to safely express as much autonomy as possible. The setting in which the last part of life takes place may be the home or an institution, and the requirements within these settings can range from low through intermediate to high intensity care. Each of these levels has different requirements. However, in each of these levels every attempt must be made to create a setting that allows patients to participate in the orchestration of the last phase of their life. Every effort must be made to help patients overcome their handicaps and safely express as much autonomy as possible. Patients who are very much weakened, patients who are confused or who have difficulties with express-ing themselves, can greatly benefit from the work of these architects.[18]

Hospice and the ethical problems associated with hospice will be dis-cussed in the next chapter. Dying, however, frequently takes place outside a hospice setting. For a variety of reasons some patients may not wish to resort to hospice care and, as is most often the case, spend only the last few days or weeks in the embrace of a hospice's care. The period that we understand as constituting the end of life begins generally long before a patient enters the internal or external hospice setting. Managing the pre-hospice part of the end of life, then, is of the greatest importance to end of life care and in many im-portant ways conditions the way that hospice care is accepted.

The loss of self-determination, the inability to decide and carry these de-cisions into action, is what most patients fear most. Above all, those con-cerned with helping patients along this path must conscientiously try to nur-ture and avoid suppressing this autonomy. It is so easy to try to help the in-creasingly enfeebled patient more than one should. It is often so much more convenient and it often seems to be so much more humane to "wait on" such patients rather than to allow them to act for themselves. Dependence, just like independence, can become a habit, crushing the willing and acting of progressively more helpless patients as all too easy and all too readily done from the best of motives and out of the greatest love. It is often no favor to the patient. Inactivity (whether of the mind or the body) creates a deadening passivity that leads to more helplessness, more dependence and ultimately more depression.

Hopefully patients who enter the last stage of life have discussed the way they see their life completed with loved ones and health care providers. Many will have executed a formal advance directive, an instrument hope-fully fully discussed between the patient, those close to them and the health care professionals involved. In addition to such instruments, the dialogue about such matters should remain open and discussions should continue. Pa-tients' perceptions of illness changes as they move from merely contem-plating the illness and the experiences the illness entails to actually experi-encing it. Decisions made a year prior to an event and at a time when a pa-tient was still in the fullness of health and feeling well may be quite different from the actual arrival of the anticipated and feared experience. Reality may be better, worse or (rarely) just as expected and, thus, wishes and directives may change. When formal directives have not been executed (and some pa-tients for a variety of reasons are loathe to execute such a directive), infor-mal discussion among health care givers and relatives should continue in an ongoing manner.

Health-care professionals, while ready to give advice to patients, should attempt to refrain from stamping their own values and ways of living on their

patients. The power of health care professionals is immense and power necessarily tends to corrupt not only politicians but all of us. We "know what is
good" or "what is right" and we (explicitly or tacitly) try to lead patients to
"see it our way." Often the attempt of health care professionals to enforce
their view of what a desirable end of life might be is not done explicitly and
with force but quite tacitly—not rarely, for example, by inspiring guilt in the
patient. Patients do not wish to offend or damage the very people they depend upon to provide them with help during their last few months and, thus,
are can easily manipulated so as to comply to a given health care provider's
world-view. As often as not this is well intentioned, but well intentioned or
not, it robs patients of self-determination and of the last vestiges of a dignity
that most patients crave.

Even when it is familiar from past experiences—and often it is not—the
medical setting is both threatening and reassuring. It is threatening in that it
is surrounded with an aura of mystery not unlike that of religious institutions: it has its own rites, its ways of behaving and its peculiar and clandes-
tine activities. It is reassuring insofar as patients have traditionally seen the
medical milieu as supportive, nurturing and worthy of trust. Birth and death,
illness and health are, and remain, among the universal phenomena for
which explanations are sought and for which often mystical explanations
have been and continue to be given. Physicians and nurses are seen as high
priestesses and priests who by their presence and actions have the power to
influence events in ways and by methods but poorly understood. Patients—
even physicians, when they become patients—are or feel themselves dependent upon health care professionals. The relationship is complicated—trust,
fear, apprehension and resentment at the power others have over them and
over the course of events are all intermingled. Throughout the course of their
last few months or even years patients must be encouraged to maintain their
self-determination as well as to have trust in their care-givers. Trust, like all
relationships, is a two-way street: one in which patient and health care professional must actively participate and which, at its best, is not a passive
"giving up" but a mutual and dynamic "participation with."

One of the things persons fear most is to become useless—that while
their own needs are fulfilled they cannot serve to fill the needs of others. To
feel socially responsible is to maintain a necessary contact with the world
and to feel fulfilled. It is a crass mistake to attempt to shield patients from
the day to day worries of the family. Patients will, when and if they enter the
stage of withdrawal, readily make their lack of involvement evident. To feel
socially useful means to have responsibilities, to participate in decisions and
to be, in some sense, not only a "patient" (one who is acted upon) but also an
agent who has responsibilities and control. Rather than be shielded during
this stage, patients should be actively encouraged not only to participate but

also, when appropriate, to lead in decision making for themselves and their family. It is not rare that patients at this stage of life will make their will, but making one's will should not be seen as the end of control and responsibility. It is simply one more thing to do.

Here again, pets are an immense help. Patients should continue the care of their pets—walk or feed the dog, groom the cat, clean the birdcage. Such activities are part of communication and being responsible for such activities is important in maintaining a person's hold on life. Beyond this, a patient's pet is someone who will (in greatest likelihood) survive the patient and (sometimes more than the relatives!) grieve the patient's death. The tacit messages (the acoustics) sent back by the pet when they interact with the patient are as important as are any others.

8.   CONFLICTS

There will, at times, be conflicts among all concerned. Players may disagree with one another, the patient or the family. The conductor here must play an active role in facilitating understanding and those concerned must learn the art of communicating and truly listening to one another. Much of this communication and the resolution of disagreements depend upon mutual trust, a state of affairs which is unlikely to come about when the various actors rarely speak unless it is to resolve such disagreements. A well functioning team develops a life of its own—an illustration of what Rousseau calls the *volonté general* or general will.[19] Such a will does not come about unless people intimately interact and dialogue with one another. It is essential to the whole enterprise.

Disagreements can have a variety of sources. The disagreement may be about means or end. That is, there may be different opinions about what the legitimate goals are as well as different opinions as to what the best means to reaching such a goal might be. Not that ends and means are totally separate. Often a given goal serves as the interim means towards a further goal. Thus the interim goal of successfully eradicating an intercurrent infection is but a means towards the larger goal of prolonging a person's life. The larger, overall goal of therapy needs to be clearly negotiated and one needs to stand ready to change that goal as the case develops. But never should the interim goals be allowed to over-shadow or compromise the overall goal of the therapy that has been negotiated.

When there is disagreement about diagnosis or about the various options available, further consultation with appropriate specialists must be sought. Sometimes in today's world patients may wish to resort to what has come to be called "alternative methods of treatment." Such alternative methods may be herbal or other "traditional" forms of medicine or they may consist of faith healing, shamanism and other officially unrecognized approaches to a particular treatment. One must differentiate between a patient who comes out of a particular cultural background and wishes to utilize treatment appropriate to such a setting and a patient who is suddenly desperate to avail themselves of means they would otherwise ignore or which is not commonly used in their culture.

When patients from a given culture wish to employ healers of their particular cultural group, it is often wise to include such persons among the players right at the outset. It is common experience that such healers not only can bring peace to the patient but also may prove to be important allies to the entire team. They must be treated for what they are, colleagues who, even when the means they utilize may seem strange, share the same broad set of goals with the rest of the team.

When patients inquire about or wish to utilize medications not generally used in western medicine, one must differentiate between those medications which may have no beneficial (but are unlikely to have a harmful) effect and those which clearly can prove harmful. Many herbal medications, for example, are generally harmless and may (who knows?) even be beneficial; others, however, may create rather toxic complications and will have to be avoided. When patients who have used western medicine their entire lives suddenly wish to try other means of treatment, it is often a signal that they are desperate and that something in the orchestration of their end of life is missing or has gone awry. Re-assessing the situation, reasonably allowing the harmless and trying to steer away from the potentially harmful medications and treatments is much more effective if one understands the reason for the patient's (or the family's) sudden desire.

Not all conflicts can be resolved. Those that cannot despite the best effort of all concerned may require a change of team members and/or conductors. Such a state of affairs should happen rarely and constitutes a failure that should become a topic of retrospective discussion and analysis by the health care team.

9.   PUTTING IT ALL TOGETHER

Orchestrating the end of life, we have said, has two interrelated functions: to maximize the positive content of life so as to make it enjoyable and worthwhile and to minimize the suffering so commonly experienced during that phase of life. Orchestrating the end of life, conducting the performance, engineering the concert hall and its acoustics, playing and being the audience is not something which can be reduced to the particular actors concerned.

Nor is it something any person, however skilled or devoted, can do single-handedly. Orchestrating the end of life well depends upon a team approach in which all share a common purpose and pursue a common, agreed upon and frequently re-examined end. Such a team consists not only of the primary clinician and the members of the health care team but includes patients, friends and family.

In many cases such orchestration might fruitfully start long before the end is near. End of life is not, except arbitrarily and retrospectively, a definable period of time in a person's life. End of life planning, like planning for retirement, should start well before one realizes that one's days are drawing to an end. Obviously, the course of events depends upon the particular illness: a myocardial infarction (sudden, unanticipated, devastating) is something quite different from a cerebro-vascular accident with moderate or severe sequellae and this, in turn, is quite different from the slow declines that often characterize either metastatic disease or progressive emphysema. The problems are different, the time course is different and the type of orchestration must be tailored to fit the disease as well as the patient.

Eventually one has to "put it all together." The score, the conductor, the players and those who construct the concert hall have to reach decisions which, translated into the clinical world, will determine what, when and how it is done. One might perhaps best start with the patient whose life (and whose work of art) it is. A course needs to be steered between paternalistically making decisions for the patient and having the patient make all the decisions for the conductor and the team. Ultimately decisions must be made, but neither by health care professionals for patients nor patients alone. Properly, decisions are the product of ongoing, interactive dialogue between patient, family, health care professionals and the other players concerned with the patient. Such a way of proceeding—another illustration of Habermas' model of communicative action—is something that must start early and, as the disease process develops, be frequently revisited.

It is best to ask the patient to bring key members of his family and friends into such a conversation and to have not only the conductor but also key members among the players participate. Decisions made should be subject to frequent revisions as the burden of illness may change some of the attitudes and values which patients may have. It is not unusual that a given state of affairs which a patient has not experienced and which he, in anterospect, felt intolerable is found to be tolerable or, at least, to be preferable to the alternative of non-existence. On the other hand, a state of affairs that before the fact appeared to be one a patient might wish to tolerate may prove, once experienced, to be unexpectedly burdensome.

In engaging in this kind of dialogue between patients, family, players and conductors much can be learned that will not only be of benefit to the particular clinical problem at hand but which will likewise be helpful in developing more successful approaches in the future. In addition, engaging in such dialogue creates understanding between the members of the team; it allows them to examine and illuminate their own values and assumptions and, ultimately, creates a more cohesive team. There is a certain camaraderie that benefits not only a particular patient but patients the team will deal with in the future.

The task is not finished once the patient has died. In orchestrating the end of life, the affected person must, of course, be the center of concern. However, the patient does not stand alone. He or she is surrounded by a group of caring persons attached by bonds of love, obligation and mutual caring. Once the patient has died, these people are very much alive and very much in need of ongoing concern. It is not enough to send relatives and friends to "support groups." Some may indeed profit from participation in such groups. Others, however, will find that such a form of group interaction does not suit them. They will find that they see what some look upon as sharing of grief as parading their grief and concern in front of complete strangers. Already the language used by such different people is significant: "sharing" to some, "parading" to others. It is important to tailor the type of support to the needs of the person, to adapt it to their particular work of art. In the process of interaction during the last few weeks or months of life, the needs of such persons should have become clear. The way such persons are treated during their grief process will go a long way in helping them to cope with the rest of their life and eventually with their own end. Next of kin (especially widowers and, to a lesser extent, widows) have a high mortality during the first few months and years after the loss. It is important to gently suggest further medical follow up for those who have been especially close to the patient.

In orchestrating the end of life it is important that the humanity and pain of the conductor and player be recognized and acknowledged just as is the pain of patients and relatives. As people work with one another they necessarily bond—patients and health care providers become friends. The pain and sense of loss experienced by health care providers can be profound. Since the smooth functioning of the team depends to a great extend on the psychological health of the care givers, attention must be paid to the members of the orchestra and its conductor just as it must be paid to the patient and family. Debriefing sessions should be made available to professionals to encourage them to express and deal with their feelings. Skilled psychological support is just as important for helping health care professionals deal with their personal sense of loss and grief as it is for encouraging good work and maintaining good work relations.

ENDNOTES AND REFERENCES

1. Among others, see T.L. Beauchamp and J.F. Childress *Principles of Biomedical Ethics* 4th ed. (NY: Oxford University Press), 1994 and E.H. Loewy, *Textbook of Health Care Ethics* (NY: Plenum Publishers), 1997.

2. A. Meisel, "Legal Myths about Terminating Life Support," *Archives of Internal Medicine* 1991; 151: 1497-1501.

3. S. Hilfiker, "Allowing the Debilitated to Die: Facing our Ethical Choices," *New England Journal of Medicine*, 1983; 308: 716-719.

4. E.H. Loewy, "Treatment Decisions in the Mentally Impaired: Limiting but not Abandoning Treatment," *New England Journal of Medicine*, 1987; 317: 1465-1469 and the discussion in E.H. Loewy, *Textbook of Health-Care Ethics* (NY: Plenum Publishers), 1997.

5. L.J. Blackhall, "Must we always use CPR?" *New England Journal of Medicine*, 1987; 20: 1281-1284.

6. G.H. Stollerman, "Decisions to Leave Home," *Journal of the American Geriatric Society* 1988; 36: 1497-1501 and E.H. Loewy, "Decisions not to Leave Home: What will the Neighbors Say?" *Journal of the American Geriatric Society*; 1988; 36: 1143-1146.

7. There is an extensive literature on pain, a much smaller one on the concept of suffering. See: E.J. Cassell, "The Nature of Suffering and the Goals of Medicine," *New England Journal of Medicine*, 1982; 306(11): 639-645; E.J. Cassell, "Recognizing Suffering," *Hastings Center Report*, 1991; 21(3): 24-31; E.H. Loewy, *Suffering and the Beneficent Community: Beyond Libertarianism* (Albany, NY: State University of New York Press), 1991.

8. S. Freud, *Civilization and Its Discontents*, trans. by J. Strachey, (NY: W.W. Norton, 1961), p. 24.

9. V. Frankl, *Man's Search for Meaning* (NY: Simon and Schuster), 1963

10. There is an excellent body of literature concerned with dying children, their ability to come to terms with their own (and with others) death and the way in which children (as well as parents and siblings) can be helped to cope with this tragedy. See K.W. Faulkner, "Talking about Death with a Dying Child," *American Journal of Nursing*, 1997; 97(6): 64-69 and *Hospice Care for Children*, edited by A. Armstrong-Dailey and S.Z. Goltzer (NY: Oxford University Press), 1993.

11. J. Feinberg, "The Mistreatment of Dead Bodies," *Hastings Center Report*, 1985; 15(1): 31-37.

12. The interrelationship between individuals and between various associations is discussed in E.H. Loewy, *Freedom and Community: the Ethics of Interdependence* (Albany, NY: State University of New York Publishers), 1995.

13. B. Freedman, "Offering Truth," *Archives of Internal Medicine*, 1993; 153: 572-576.

14. Habermas, in his *Theory of Communicative Action*, suggests that rules of justice can only be evolved in the context of an interactive social dialogue. What EHL suggests here is that this notion is applicable to a variety of other activities such as are found in orchestrating the end of life. In essence, it is a living example of democratic interaction aimed at dealing with a problem recognized as common to all participants. See J. Habermas, *The Theory of Communicative Action* (NY: Beacon Press), 1985

15. Pain control is not what patients fear most when they ask physicians to actively help them die. See A.L. Back, *et al*, "Physician-assisted Suicide in Washington State: Patient Requests and Physician Responses." *Journal of the American Medical Association*, 1996; 275(12): 919-923.

16. See, for example, *The Oxford Textbook of Palliative Medicine*, edited by D. Doyle, *et al.*, (NY: Oxford University Press. For an excellent brief review article of that subject, see M. Levy, "Pharmacological Treatment of Cancer Pain," *New England Journal of Medicine*, 1996; 335: 1124-1132.

17. There have been some excellent studies about the effect of art as well as music in children at the end of life. The pictures they paint or draw often gives us insight into their fears, hopes and understanding and the process of creating such pictures can be an important release mechanism. See, for example, J. Bertoia, *Drawings from a Dying Child* (London: Routledge), 1993 and K. Keipenheuer, "Spontaneous Drawings of a Leukemic Child: An Aid for a more Comprehensive Care of Fatally Ill Children and their Families," *Psychosomatische Medizin*, 1980; 9: 21-32.

18. There has been a fair amount of literature about this subject. See, for example, M. Calkins, *Design for Dementia: Planning Environments for the Elderly and the Confused.* (Baltimore, MD: National Health Publishing), 1988 and S. Heeg, *Bauen für verwundbare Menschen*, (Bauwelt), 1993; 29(10): 420-426.

19. Rousseau's general will is often misunderstood. It is what develops when persons working well together in grappling with a given problem interact and it cannot be reduced to the sum of its parts. See J.J. Rousseau, "The Social Contract or Principles of Political Right," trans. and ed. by G.D.H. Cole *J.J. Rousseau: The Social Contract and the Discourses* (NY: Everyman's Library), 1993.

Chapter 5

Sudden Death and the End of Life

1.   INTRODUCTION

While in former days sudden death was something that was feared, today it is something that many of us would far prefer to a protracted downhill course. There are many reasons for this, some social and some due to the fact that the down-hill course can today be almost interminable and is often associated with protracted suffering (see chapter one). Patients who die unexpectedly are often victims of accidents, myocardial infarctions or some other pathophysiological disasters or, as is not infrequently the case today, victims of murder or suicide. While such deaths can occur at all ages, they are especially pronounced in the younger age group. When patients die suddenly the ethical problems confronting health care professionals are quite different: they are problems of dealing with the family, problems of organ donation or of autopsy. Very often—far more often than in those whose decline occurs over months or years—such persons have given little thought to their possible death and have, therefore, made few preparations. In cases of sudden death, the question, "who is being treated," must be answered in terms of those close to the patient and of those associated with the patient's care. Once a patient dies some obligations to support and care for the living remains. This obligation is not only to the family and loved ones but also to others. It is an obligation grounded on the physician's duty to alleviate suffering and strengthened by the relationship with the bereaved—a relationship almost inevitably associated with the treatment of the actual patient.

Between those who die suddenly and those who linger in a slow downhill course are patients who are struck by a sudden, unforeseen but nevertheless devastating illness and who then go rapidly downhill and die. Examples of such illnesses include severe sepsis, extensive acute myocardial infarction, stroke or trauma with death not at once but in a few days. Frequently such patients have not anticipated severe illness or death and, even more frequently than others, have given little thought to death. Often they have executed no advance directives. The ethical problems in such cases involve, first of all, finding proper surrogates (see also chapter two). As long as hope for meaningful (on the patient's terms) survival exists care must, of course, be patient-centered; when hope dwindles and is finally snuffed out attention needs to be turned to problems of futility as well as to the problems of family, organ donation and autopsy mentioned above. We shall, throughout this chapter, discuss the role of the health care team in taking care of families.

2.   ORCHESTRATION IN SITUATIONS OF SUDDEN OR RAPID DEATH

Orchestrating the end of life for patients who die suddenly is quite a different issue. Nevertheless, even here the team that orchestrates the end of life may very well serve to help the bereaved deal with the problem in a more than perfunctory manner. Often the family is in great need of medical, social, psychological and spiritual support, the type of coordinated support that a well functioning team should be skilled in providing. When patients die suddenly the team is often without adequate information and must act on what it can gather from previous caretakers. Often the team will end up being informed by its own instincts—in a practiced team those instincts can be quite good and can serve well.

When patients die suddenly or soon after the onset of a devastating illness, it has become the custom to attend to the immediate need of the family and perhaps to give them a follow-up call in a week or two. Such a stereotypic approach—while it may serve public relations purposes and deal with some of the health care providers' problems—is not generally helpful. People, their cultural backgrounds, their family constellations, their basic beliefs and their social situations are quite different from one another. Some people prefer to grieve alone and perceive outside help as an annoying intrusion. Such persons will feel their perceived obligation to socially engage with others to be a further burden rather than a relief. Other persons will be most grateful for a good deal of outside help. Some people are religious and would welcome interaction with a clergyperson, others are not and would not. A call in two weeks is far too far away for some and for others may rip open new wounds or be perceived as annoying. Sensitivity towards the individual needs of families and close friends—often an instinctive matter but sometimes something which can be gently inquired into—is essential if one is to support grieving persons well. It is often useful to have the help of a team, which is precisely what the team skilled in orchestrating the end of life is so well suited to do. Reminding those left behind of their other obligations can be most helpful: inquiring after the well being of a pet or showing concern about the relatives job may help direct attention back to the world of the living and to their needs. Seeking to show people that, sad as it may be, the person who has died no longer needs them but others do, can help them over the hump. But above all sincerity and a sense of humor may be most helpful in dealing with a tragic situation. Pretended grief is worse than callousness. Health-care providers as well as patients are persons in their own right. As such they have unique ways—appropriate to themselves—of showing their emotions. Insincerity is not only ethically unacceptable—it is generally rather quickly found out.

Attention should also be paid to the possible medical needs of relatives and friends. Although at times hypnotics or tranquilizers may be indicated, simply pulling out a prescription blank and prescribing such medications may complicate rather than alleviate the grieving process. It certainly does not substitute—even though in some cases it may complement—the support that those left behind need. Relatives and friends are under terrible stress, stress, which not only is a bad thing in itself, but which can seriously exacerbate pre-existing illnesses. Relatives who have heart disease, diabetes or other chronic conditions are especially vulnerable during such times. Long term effects should not be neglected: the incidence of death from a number of diseases is significantly increased by bereavement. Inquiring after the medical situation of relatives and doing what one can to direct them to proper treatment and at times and, with their permission, contacting their health care providers is part of such orchestration.

When patients are struck by a sudden devastating illness that causes their death in a few days or weeks, orchestrating their end of life is still terribly important. What has been said before on the subject holds here, but in a far more rapid, more truncated and more urgent way. Every attempt to allow patients to express themselves, to interact with family, loved ones and pets, every effort to minimize pain and suffering and every effort to minimize disturbing interventions must be made. When hope for meaningful recovery exists all measures to achieve such recovery, provided that they are not refused by the patient or by surrogates, are in order. But once reasonable hope has vanished the goal properly becomes consultation, orchestration, palliation and making what remains of life as peaceful and meaningful as possible.

While the patient is critically ill, close communication with the family is essential. One of the problems with patient-physician relationships (and one which can be a factor in legal action) is the (generally subconscious) attempt by health care providers to appear optimistic, knowing, fully competent, beyond mistake—in short, fully in control. It is extremely important to speak to relatives several times a day, to share with them not only hopes but also doubts, uncertainty and fallibility. Sharing fallibility is not something that comes easily to most physicians and yet, like all humans, physicians too make mistakes. Most lay persons are fully aware that physicians are fallible: sharing fallibility with them, saying outright that the risk—especially in critical situations—of error is ever present, will enhance rather than diminish respect, communication and understanding; and it will, in fact, reduce the risk of malpractice suits. Furthermore, physicians (like all human beings) are apt to delude themselves, to believe that no error has been made or, if it has, that it made no difference to the outcome. Such a course of self-delusion is ethically problematic—especially insofar as it can and does stand in the way of significant improvement and learning. Unfortunately, health care professionals, like all humans, make mistakes.

While health care providers should share the agony of the family, the health care team likewise is well advised to share their own agony with the family. Losing a patient is not and must not become an easy thing. Physicians and nurses as well as other members of the team are human and normal humans suffer when confronted with another's pain: especially when they find themselves unable to accomplish the goal they desire, for which they have been trained and for which, in good measure, they feel responsible. To share such feelings with the family is to share humanity and may help put everyone's grief and frustration into the larger context of the human condition.

In those final days questions which will become acute after a patient's death can be suggested to the family—questions about organ donation or autopsy, but also questions about future planning for those who have been dependent upon the patient. A well functioning, multi-disciplinary team approach can be most helpful in preparing relatives for some of the questions they will soon have to deal with.

3.   SURROGATES

When patients have lost decisional capacity and have not executed advance directives surrogates are traditionally consulted about important patient care decisions. Surrogates are not only those persons who know a patient and a patient's work of art so well that they understand their values, hopes and wishes, but are those willing to help finish that work of art not in their own but in the patient's style (see also chapter two). That is a daunting task and one that can never be perfect. Physicians and other members of the health care team have the most difficult task of trying to discern who is best able to speak for a given patient. Such a task is not a legalistic one and, even though some states suggest a hierarchical list of surrogates, cannot be discharged in a stereotypic manner. It is, for example, not the case that the spouse is always the proper surrogate: persons may be legally married to one another but estranged for years; the oldest child may have been at odds with the parents and the youngest closest to them. Such nuances of family relationships are difficult enough to know when one has known a patient for years; they are most difficult to discern when patients have been struck by a sudden illness and are being taken care of by strangers.

Physicians and others concerned with making decisions in those cases where patients have lost the capacity to make their own decisions are still (at least in the way ethics is understood in our western world) ethically compelled to attempt to follow (or at least to give serious attention to) the presumed wishes of the patient. In selecting surrogates, therefore, they must be attentive to selecting those surrogates that can help clarify what the presumed wishes of the patient might have been. When—as is the case in some states—surrogates are specified in hierarchical order, physicians are still obligated to make certain that such surrogates can, in fact, best express the patients will. An alienated spouse or oldest child is not a proper surrogate and can for a compelling reason and with proper documentation in the chart be set aside in favor of a consensus of others. Let us look at a case:

> Mrs. Pushkin, who has been widowed for twelve years, has been brought to the hospital after a massive stroke that has left her paralyzed and semiconscious. Neurologists say that there is no hope for meaningful recovery (viz., for her regaining sufficient sentience to make decisions). Her family consists of three children and among the surrogates deemed appropriate is also her best friend with whom she has lived for six years. She has had close contact with two of her children but only sporadic contact with her oldest son who lives across the continent, who speaks to his mother at Christmastime and who has not seen her for at least five years. The two children with whom she has had close contact as well as her friend say that Mrs. Pushkin has often stated that a life in which she is severely dependent and/or incapable of thinking clearly is not a life she would wish to have prolonged. They are agreed that, sad as it may seem, no further efforts to maintain her life or to treat intercurrent illnesses should be made. Her oldest son who is contacted by telephone adamantly insists that "everything should be done."

When there are no previous caregivers who know the patient and their social situation well, the difficulty is compounded. There are no pat answers in such situations. Physicians can, however, learn a great deal by having a family conference instead of meeting singly with diverse members of the family. They should carefully listen as the members of the family and friends speak with one another. Often relationships which seemed obscure before will become quite clear; sometimes intentions and motives will become apparent; and listening to such conversations, to stories about the patient and about their wishes and ways of going about things will always be helpful in guiding the next step to be taken. An initially almost opaque situation may become far clearer.

In a case like this one (and the eldest son could just as well have been an estranged husband), physicians are well advised to record these conversations in the patient's chart carefully. It is obvious that in this case the patients friend and her other two children know the patient and understand her artwork best. Health care providers would be well advised, ethically speaking, to follow the counsel of those who know the patient best and to set the wishes of the eldest son aside. Health care providers need (in physician progress as well as nursing notes) to document carefully why the person who under normal circumstances would be expected to be closest to the patient and, therefore, best able to speak for him or her should in this instance not be allowed to do so. In such documentation (which can be quite terse and brief and nevertheless quite complete), the names of the people involved in reaching this conclusion should be included.

It is often difficult—especially in situations in which the patient and the family have previously been strangers to the physician—to determine who is and who is not a proper surrogate. In such cases physicians are well advised to contact previous health care providers and to obtain from them all the available social information. Often communication with previous caregivers is not seriously attempted or, when it is, only the technical medical data are discussed. This is a mistake. Physicians who have taken care of patients for a long time often have a wealth of social information about patients. Such information can be most useful in guiding future decisions and in choosing proper surrogates. When patients do not have a long-time primary care physician who knows them and their social (as distinct from only their medical) situation well, the intensity of the situation may allow the health care team to understand the patient, the family and the complex interrelationships well enough so as to allow a reasonable decision as to the proper spokesperson.

In talking with surrogates, physicians need to be careful about the language they use. First of all, physicians must be clear as to what goal they are pursuing. When a patient hopelessly unconscious develops pneumonia there is every prospect for healing the pneumonia but none for benefiting the patient in any other sense. This distinction must be kept in mind and pointed out when speaking with relatives. Secondly, when a case is truly beyond hope physicians are apt to tell relatives that "there is little (or virtually no) hope." This often leaves relatives the impression that, although there is little (or virtually no) hope for recovery there is, in fact, some. When there is no reasonable chance for recovery, physicians need to state this fact clearly and forcefully: the language of "little or virtually no hope" introduces a slim, unwarranted and, thus, unrealistic hope and it is, for this reason, unnecessarily cruel. It also greatly complicates decision making because relatives are now apt to feel that if they decline further treatment, they will have had an active part in the patient's demise. As a result, they will often feel a sense of unwarranted guilt. They often feel that they have participated in (and often feel they have made) a decision to stop possibly (even if only remotely possibly) effective treatment when, in reality, it was a situation in which no effective treatment was possible. Thirdly: when appropriate, one must gently point out to relatives and friends the difference between prolonging life and prolonging the act of dying.

4. FUTILITY

Whether we are dealing with patients who are, after a lingering illness, at the end of their life or who are suddenly struck down by unanticipated illness or accident, we reach a point where we must ask ourselves whether what we are doing is futile. With the ever-increasing capacity of medicine to stabilize physiological conditions and to prolong biological existence (as well as with the increasing costs attendant on this), the problem of futility has become one of the more critical contemporary issues. On the one hand, patients are afraid of being kept "alive"—whether in a permanently insentient condition or in a condition in which they are in pain, suffering and incapable of meaningful communication. On the other hand, health care institutions are loath to take on the tremendous costs of maintaining patients when further treatment is considered to be "futile." And ultimately society (which has severe problems in meeting health care costs) has an interest in having resources (material as well as time, effort, love and devotion) used to meet societal goals.

Futility, as defined by the Oxford Dictionary, is an action "incapable of producing results," "failing utterly of the desired end," "useless," "ineffective" or "in vain." In speaking of a means being futile, some goal must be in view. Goals can be undesirable, but goals themselves cannot be futile. When speaking of futility we must be clear about what our goals are—giving artificial fluid and nutrition to a permanently vegetative patient is not futile if the goal is to prolong bare biological existence. It is futile if the goal is to prolong a life meaningful to the patient him- or herself.[1]

In a narrow definition, the Hastings Center defines futility as "treatment which would fail to reverse a physiological disturbance." Such a definition would make altering a physiological disturbance (say giving dopamine to a permanently comatose patient in shock without altering the final outcome) the goal of treatment. The narrowness of this definition forces the definition to become almost inapplicable. In practical terms, very little of what most think of as "futile" would be so considered.[2]

Leaders among those who have written about futility are Drs. Jecker and Schneiderman. According to them futility in the medical context exists when "a treatment has not worked in the last 100 cases" (futility in the quantitative sense) or when treatment "merely preserves permanent unconsciousness or cannot end dependence on ongoing intensive medical care" (futility in the qualitative sense). Jecker and Schneiderman also distinguish between a treatment effect which merely alters some part of the patient's body and a treatment benefit that can be appreciated by the patient and enables the patient to escape total dependence on intensive medical care. They consider treatment that merely alters some part of the body (or its function) without being appreciated by the patient to be futile.[3]

There are some difficulties with this view of futility. The difference between a qualitative and a quantitative sense of futility seems to be arbitrary. For example, treatment that "has not worked" demands a definition of "working" and "not working." Has treatment that keeps persons alive so that their families can finish grieving or see them a last time "worked?" Has treatment "worked" if it cures pneumonia but does nothing about severe dementia? Has treatment "worked" if the patient did not want it and still doesn't? Has treatment "worked" if the patient was forced to have it and now is glad he did?[4]

The fact that "treatment hasn't worked in the last 100 cases" and, therefore it is useless carries implication that it won't in the 101st case. This may, in fact, be a simplistic way of looking at statistics. But, again, it also evades the question of what "worked" means. The quantitative definition, therefore, has a lot of qualitative elements. Beyond this, unless open to the possibility of progress and willing to try new treatments one will tend to create a self-fulfilling prophecy: just because "x" is an untreatable and (until today) universally fatal illness does not mean that it, therefore, must continue to be. In such cases, trying to treat such a condition is not futile—it is experimental.[5]

We cannot expect absolute certainty in everything we undertake to do and, therefore, if something has not been successful for a given number of times it can be called futile. We might quibble about the numbers and these numbers would, we think, have to be adjusted to the particular problem under consideration; but the principle that somewhere a line needs be drawn is legitimate. But in a recent paper, Schneiderman goes beyond this: if something has worked one, two or three times out of a hundred, he would be inclined to put this into the same rubric and call it "futile." Now, if one has cancer and the chance that an intervention may cure or prolong life is, say, 2% and even if, furthermore, that intervention entails a good deal of suffering it is not futile: a patient may or may not wish to take that risk and endure the suffering. Physicians whose values differ from those of their patient are ill equipped to make such a decision—and such decisions ought not then to be hidden under the rubric of futility.

The qualitative definitions have even more serious problems. They take for granted that a permanently unconscious life or life totally dependent on intensive care is not worth preserving. This is a value judgment—and while we ultimately do have to make value judgments and while it is a value judgment we may personally agree with—we must be clear about the fact that what we are doing is, in fact, making a value judgment. In addition, Schneiderman argues that "if it is empirically likely that physicians will inflict pain and suffering on one hundred patients in pursuit of the chance that perhaps one will survive" this might well be considered to fall under the rubric of futility. Such a state of affairs does not denote "futility." It simply means that, all things considered, the burden of pain outweighs the benefit of a highly unlikely result. Whether to pursue treatment under such circumstances, we would suggest, is not a decision for the physician but for the patient to make. We are not dealing with something that is truly impossible to achieve by the means at hand but are dealing with something that we are unlikely to achieve and that, furthermore, is very burdensome—or something which we ourselves (but perhaps not our patients) consider to be undesirable. Only patients advised by their physicians—not physicians alone—are entitled to make such a decision. After all, the burden will be born (and the unlikely benefit enjoyed) by the patient, not the doctor. We believe that, above all, we need be honest about what we are about. Some patients may decide that, despite the suffering an intervention might cause, they wish to take that slim chance. It is a value judgment and not one that ought to be assigned without discussion to the rubric of "futility."

We agree with Schneiderman that to call something futile because it is extremely expensive or because using it would seriously deplete our resources is a misuse of the term: such a thing is not "futile" but is simply too expensive. Here the goal may be appropriate, the goal may be within the limits of what we understand legitimate goals to be, and the means contemplated may be appropriate to reaching the goal: but doing it is simply too expensive. Society, which ultimately must bear the burden of the costs, may decide (we think legitimately) that a given intervention is too expensive. That is well and good: but call it too expensive; do not call it futile. Such decisions are decisions of rationing of resources—a legitimate thing for a community to do, but a topic beyond the scope of this work. The broader the definition of futility, the greater is the danger that it will define futility for the ends of persons other than the patient. If a treatment is too expensive, we ought to say so: but we shouldn't call it "futile" merely to put on a veneer of probity!

When we say that something is futile and cannot accomplish our goals, we need grapple with the question of the legitimate goals of medicine. Is it one of the acknowledged goals of medicine to keep permanently unconscious persons alive? Is it one of our goals to intervene when our chance of success is very low? What are our goals? Once we have enunciated the goals we can then more readily grapple with our obligations. These, as we know, have shifted over the years. Only lately has sustaining life become one of medicine's goals and, therefore, one of its perceived obligations.[6] Prior to asking what these goals should be, we should asking who is entitled to set these goals.

We have argued in the past and shall argue here that the goals of medicine are social goals: goals that cannot be set by the profession itself, but goals that professionals certainly must play their part in setting. The practice of medicine is a social task. It is a practice rooted in, enabled by and done for the benefit of the community and its members. The values of the community inform and guide medical practice and values, just as the values and technical possibilities of medicine seep down and guide the community's understanding of it. The definition of futility is one made within the context of a particular culture, within a particular time frame and within the embrace of technical possibilities. Goals are determined within this same framework. The ends of medicine are not immutable: they are changeable and living, adapting, as they must, to situation and context. The goals of the profession, in part a product of the work that people involved in the health care professions do, cannot be independently set by workers in the field. Medicine can no more evolve its goals independent of the community in which it functions, than the community can evolve such goals without the advice (and ultimately consent) of those who must perform the tasks. Essentially, setting those goals involves a dialogue between various health care professionals as technical experts (who know the limits of possibility) and the community. Speaking about medical futility presupposes a clear understanding of societal values as well as of technical possibilities. Such a dialogue is, in fact, possible. It has been held in an ongoing fashion in the both the so-called Danish ethics counsels and in various attempts throughout some of the member states of the United States.

Society must make some hard choices and these choices, while they cannot be driven by economic considerations, cannot help but be affected by them. If keeping a permanently vegetative patient alive by artificial means constitutes one of the goals society considers legitimate, then society must be willing to pay for it and forego something else. We are not suggesting a particular choice society should make, but we are suggesting that choices must be responsibly made. If keeping vegetative patients alive is decided not to be a goal of medicine then, and only then, can doing so be considered futile—and then only for that particular society and for that particular time. As matters now stand, keeping patients in a permanent vegetative state alive is frequently a matter of personal choice. Most patients and families will feel that doing so does not meet their or their relatives' goals. If, on the one hand, patients and families feel that keeping a permanently vegetative patient alive does not meet their goals and is, therefore, not a benefit, trying to do so now becomes "futile." On the other hand, some patients and their families may feel that keeping such patients alive is (for a variety of religious or philosophical reasons) very much one of their goals. In such a case doing everything one can to keep them alive may be one of any number of things, but it is not, in fact, futile. Until society speaks, until a consensus (which does not denote uniformity but does not denote a slim majority either) is formed by ongoing and intelligent discussion, the status of supporting such patients is moot—-viz., it may be futile in one sense and not futile in another.

5.   AUTOPSY

In the last few years far fewer post-mortem examinations than in the past have been conducted. Since autopsies play a significant role in the development of medical understanding and progress this decline, at least in our view, is a shame. It is often argued that with modern diagnostic technologies the cause of death is generally known and, therefore, an autopsy is superfluous. This, first of all, is not necessarily true. If we assume that our technology invariably yields correct results and prove our results by appealing to that technology we have created a self-fulfilling prophecy to make our point. Secondly, it is extremely shortsighted: finding out what a patient died *of* is often not as important as finding out what that patient died *with*, i.e., what illnesses went undiscovered, what complaints which had been ignored or not diagnosed were missed, etc.

Physician enthusiasm (or lack of enthusiasm) for having autopsy examinations performed on their patients easily translates into the relatives agreeing or not agreeing to giving permission. A hesitant, embarrassed or half-hearted approach is more than likely to meet with a refusal. Psychologically, the time just after a patient has died is a very bad time to mention autopsy for the first time. It is a most negative time for family and friends. The idea of an autopsy is something patients and family have often not thought about. They may have preconceptions about it that are associated with words like "mutilation" or they may feel that "patients have suffered enough." When done in a gentle and compassionate manner (and especially when done by physicians who themselves truly believe in the importance of these examinations), a careful explanation of the intent and purpose of autopsies, combined with a gentle reminder that the suffering of their loved one is over can often encourage the family to give their consent.

We have personally known a physician who more often than not brought a discussion of autopsy into the routine conversation with patients and relatives long before there was any thought of their dying. This was done simply by explaining diagnostic or therapeutic options in terms of "what we had learned from autopsies." Such conversations frequently led to a discussion of autopsy and to a greater understanding of both patient and family of the reasons for requesting them. It also made evident to patient and family that the physician was likely to request such an examination. The same physician would, at times, mention autopsies in the course of speaking with relatives whose patients were in the intensive care unit. When request for examinations were made that could not yield positive results for the particular patient, part of the explanation for the request was that "what we could find out would be highly interesting but of no value for this patient at this time. While we should seek to know the answer to the question, one does not perform autopsies on the living—much as one needs to perform them on the dead." And lastly, this particular physician almost always himself attended the autopsies. He let the family know that he would and that he would share the findings with them. It should come as no surprise that this physician had an autopsy rate of over 90%.

It is, of course, essential to stress that autopsies are not only useful to science and to future patients but also that they can serve to give relatives a greater ultimate peace of mind. Relatives could now rest secure in the knowledge that nothing important had been missed—or, if it was, that they would be informed. Often relatives feel considerable guilt when active treatment is withdrawn or no resuscitation is attempted. When it can be confirmed by the autopsy (and it usually is) that further efforts would have been futile, such knowledge can help families cope with their feelings. It is, therefore, important to communicate with relatives and to let them know when the autopsy is done and what the findings were. Sometimes it is advisable to send a brief note outlining the findings to the relatives.

6.   ORGAN DONATION

When patients die suddenly or after severe and unanticipated illness they often are ideal organ donors. Often they are young and otherwise healthy. Some patients have executed valid donor cards, while others have not. When such patients die the situation is severely emotionally charged. Patients who are considered to be potential organ donors today are persons who are judged brain dead. This is not the place to discuss either the problem of brain death or the problem of organ donation in detail. However, the ethical dimension of end of life issues demands at least a short discussion of it.

Brain death means that the entire brain (from brain stem to neocortex) has permanently ceased to function. The rest of the body can be kept alive only by the use of a ventilator and other artificial support. If the ventilator were to be withdrawn, the patient's other vital functions would soon cease. In most western nations today, brain death is the legal equivalent of death and all treatment may be stopped. The introduction of this concept, unfortunately, came about as a result of the need for organs and is, therefore, a definition of convenience rather than of logical reasoning. If permanent insentience is the reason for declaring someone dead, then permanent coma or the permanent vegetative state do not appear to be different. If reliance on artificial means without which other organs would soon cease to function were the issue, then artificial pacemakers and other means of permanent support would likewise be so definable. The Danes are unique in refusing to accept this definition: after considerable debate in the Danish ethics counsels it was decided not to equate brain death with death of the whole organism. Rather, and with proper instruments of donation executed in advance by the patient or at the time by relatives, organ removal and donation is permitted. As Hans Jonas said long ago, it is time that, rather than manipulating the definition of death to suite our convenience, we "squarely faced the issue of the rightness of continuing to support solely by our artifice what may still be called life."[7]

Nevertheless, brain death in the United States and most of the western world, is an accepted legal concept. Once patients are declared brain dead they may (legally and with the proper instruments of donation) serve as organ donors. Their doing so can save many lives and help others to lead more productive and less circumscribed lives. In many states the relatives of patients suitable as organ donors must (by law) be asked if they might wish to donate. In most states of the United States a system of "presumed refusal" is the rule—that is, patients or relatives, must expressly permit the removal of organs. In some states and in some other western countries "presumed consent" is the rule. In "presumed consent" patients (by prior directive) or relatives are asked not whether they would consent but whether they would object to having organs used in this manner.

After a tragic and unanticipated death has occurred is a poor time to ask a grieving family for "a favor"—staggered by their grief, withdrawn into their inner shell, it is likely that they will refuse. If donation is the rule rather than the exception it is more likely that they might not refuse. It is important to remember and to point out gently that donating organs will save other lives and will help return function. Sad as the death of the patient is, the death of another who might have been saved had organs been donated is equally sad for others—and perhaps quite unnecessary. Relatives may thus be led to discover that from this disaster some positive value can be wrested, that perhaps the best that can be obtained from the death of one is the gift of life for another. Many families have found solace in such thoughts.

In virtually all states patients are asked to express their desire to donate organs by filling out a portion of their driver's license and having it witnessed. Such a properly executed and witnessed card serves as a legal instrument. Unfortunately, despite a legally valid donor card, no hospital today will remove suitable organs if any of the family members refuse.

Ethically and legally it is appropriate that the team salvaging organs and the team treating the donor patient are clearly separated. Unless such a separation exists, in fact, a clear conflict of interest—i.e., the preservation of organs versus the preservation of patients—could occur. The treating team, however, is not precluded from speaking to relatives of patients whose prognosis is grim about the fact that once brain dead a request would be made. Introducing this topic early—just like introducing the notion of autopsy in a timely fashion—can help prepare the family and prevent a deluge of requests from following the final (and often shattering) news.

7.   CLOSING REMARKS

When patients die relatively quickly much of the team's attention is legitimately turned to the family. While the patient is dying he or she remains central to our considerations but even then, every effort needs to be made to include the family and its considerations within the embrace of the team. Patients are not freestanding asocial individuals. Rather, so long as they are alive, they are enmeshed in a real way in a social nexus. Subsequently, they, in a symbolic way and as far as those who have known them are concerned, continue to be enmeshed in a social nexus that, in many respects, includes members of the health care team. This is true when patients die after a long illness, but is also true when their illness has not been long standing. The support the team can give to patient and family will, in many ways, be repaid by the support the family, in turn, can provide the health care team. Taking care of patients in the last phase of their life can be enriching and deeply satisfying experience for all concerned.

ENDNOTES AND REFERENCES

1. Oxford English Dictionary.
2. *Guidelines on the Termination of Therapy and the Care of the Dying* (Briarcliff Manor, NY: The Hastings Center), 1987.
3. L.J. Schneidermann, *et al*, "Medical Futility: Its Meaning and Ethical Implications," *Annals of Internal Medicine*, 1990; 1112: 949-954; N.S. Jecker," Knowing When to Stop: the Limits of Medicine," *Hastings Center Report*, 1991; 19(2): 5-10; L.J. Schneidermann, et al, "Futility in Practice," *Archives of Internal Medicine*, 1993; 153: 429-431.
4. For a fuller exposition please see: E.H. Loewy, *et al*, "Futility and its Wider Implications: A Concept in Need of Further Examination," *Archives of Internal Medicine*, 1993; and E.H. Loewy, "Futility and the Goals of Medicine: Concepts in Need of Social Definition," *European Philosophy of Medicine and Health-Care*, 1993; 1(2): 15-29.
5. This section is adapted from a discussion between Dr. Schneiderman and myself. See, L.J. Schneiderman, "Medical Futility," *Wiener Klinische Wochenschrift*, 1998; 22: 775-778; and E.H. Loewy, "The Social Dimensions of Futility: a Response to Schneiderman," *Wiener Klinische Wochenschrift*, 1998; 22: 804-806.
6. D.W. Amundsen, "The Physician's Obligation to Prolong Life: a Medical Duty Without Classical Roots," *Hastings Center Report*, 1978; 8(4): 23-31.

Chapter 6

Suicide, Assisted Suicide and Euthanasia

1. INTRODUCTION

Patients with decisional capacity whose only options are either to live and suffer longer or to die and (from their perspective) suffer less may request physician assistance in dying. This request can present in various ways: (1) as an inquiry into available methods for ending life and how to employ them; (2) as a request for a prescription (easily at hand to use or not) which might end life painlessly and peacefully; or (3) as a plea that the physician directly administer medications to end life. At times, it may be a combination between the latter two requests. For example, a patient may ask a physician to be ready to supplement the drug she has taken should it prove not to be efficient.[1] Two things are common to such requests: (a) they are made by patients with decisional capacity; and (b) they are made under conditions in which options have been narrowed to living longer and suffering more or living shorter and suffering less.

Each of these three requests is often seen as ethically quite different. In the first (sharing of information), physicians or nurses see themselves as much less implicated than they do in the other two. In the second (prescribing an agent that, if taken in sufficient quantity would cause death), physicians and nurses often still feel that, since the final action which causes the death was done by the patient, they still are not causal agents. In the third (directly administering an agent that will cause death), physicians and nurses are liable to feel that, because they are directly part of the causal chain, they are also directly responsible. Here, perhaps, is a nice illustration of the difference that personal morality and emotion make in the approach to a problem. First of all, personal morality (often derived from religion or tradition) may proscribe something for an individual which broader ethical considerations leave open. Secondly, the process of advising "feels" different from the act of writing a prescription and yet unlike administering an injection causing death. These are not trivial differences and they may lead to quite different courses of action. But, ethically speaking, physicians or nurses who advise, prescribe or inject are all necessary links in the causal chain leading to a person's death. Without their advice, prescription or injection the patient will not have died when he or she had. Now, it may be argued that if a physician or nurse refused to advise, the patient could more or less easily get the same advice elsewhere. Furthermore, one could argue, but with much less force, that a prescription is not necessary. That is, a patient might choose another method or obtain drugs or a prescription elsewhere. However, when a patient is helpless and unable to swallow (be it because of weakness, nausea or whatever reason for the inability) and is then reduced to asking for an injection to end his or her life, there is little question of some other option. Thus, one of the differences between these various ways of active help is the relative power patients have to select other options and carry them into practice.

The emotional impact on the health care team of these various courses of action are not trivial. Health care professionals—just like patients—are moral agents committed to their own moral points of view. It is one thing to claim that patients have a right to decide the time of their own death; it is another to argue that health care professionals are ethically obligated to help them carry out their wishes. This difference is quite evident when it comes to advising or prescribing: other courses of action are (at least in theory) open to the patient. The difference becomes tenuous when patients (because of profound weakness, nausea or inability to swallow) have become the virtual captives of the health care establishment. Such difficulties can be avoided or at the very least greatly reduced by timely discussions with patients and families. Patients who discover that there are unbridgeable incompatibilities between their own and their health care givers moral views should be strongly urged to select other health care providers.

In this chapter we will focus on what we hope will remain an unusual event: active participation by health care professionals in bringing about the deaths of patients who wish to have their suffering ended, who are mentally clear and who have no further options than to live a longer and suffer or to end their suffering and, thereby, their life. It is the thesis of this entire work that orchestrating the end of life well will do much to diminish the desire to commit suicide and, therefore, the requests for help with committing suicide (see the chapter entitled, "Orchestrating the End of Life"). Nevertheless, the problem—while we think it can be greatly reduced—will not disappear.

The discussion about suicide as well as about euthanasia is by no means a new one.[2] It dates back at least to the ancient Greeks and most probably goes back far longer than that. Most, but by no means all, ancient philosophers—among them Plato, Socrates and the Stoics—found euthanasia ethically acceptable; others, notably Aristotle (if one can infer this from his attitude towards suicide) and the Pythagoreans did not. Hippocratic ethics, which was significantly influenced by the Pythagoreans who presaged Christianity, opposed euthanasia; but it is important to realize that only a minority of Greek physicians belonged to the Hippocratic School. Early Christians opposed all killing. Indeed, killing, whether in the form of self-defense, war or capital punishment was, to the early Christians, morally unacceptable.[3] Euthanasia, therefore, was opposed by the church. In medieval times many, if not most, physicians were priests and medicine was quite thoroughly under church control. Despite these circumstances, Sir Thomas Moore (1478-1535), a pious Catholic, favored a society in which, among other rather progressive ideas, euthanasia would be available.[4] The idea of euthanasia has become ever more popular thanks largely to two forces: (1) increasing individualism and with it an increased emphasis on an individual's right to self-determination and (2) advances in medical science which have made the often nearly indefinite prolongation of life a practical reality.

2.   DEFINITION

Physician assisted suicide differs from euthanasia. In physician assisted suicide physicians prescribe—whereas in euthanasia physicians administer—a potentially lethal agent. Though euthanasia can be non-voluntary, what we are speaking about here is only voluntary euthanasia: viz., bringing about of a patient's death by advising on method, prescribing or actually administering an agent that causes death. For the sake of this discussion, it is considered only after the direct request of the person being killed. If we will not grant a person's ethical right to ask for their own death at the time they want to die, we surely could not accede to such a wish made in advance or allow another to speak for them. For the sake of this discussion, we want to go beyond the traditional translation of euthanasia as being a "good death." Rather, we wish to consider the ethics of euthanasia under the following definition:

> Voluntary euthanasia is the deliberate participation in the killing of consenting persons with the intent of sparing them an inevitable, slow and agonizing death.

Thus, for our purposes, any instance of euthanasia must share at least the following conditions: (1) it must be deliberate; (2) it must be stopping a life filled with relentless suffering and which, without such an action, would continue on; (3) it must be under circumstances in which the death of the individual is reasonably felt to be inevitable and shortly at hand; and (4) it must be only by the request or wholehearted consent of the person who is to die.

During the Nazi era, euthanasia took on a new and far more menacing meaning, a meaning that unfortunately has continued to infect discussions about euthanasia. Thus we want to differentiate clearly between what the Nazis (and some before them) termed "euthanasia" (but which, in fact, was simply murder) and what has been and currently is understood by that term. The term euthanasia as generally used, means the bringing about of another's death solely with the good of the person being killed in mind: a benefit (supposed or real) to family, state or institution is not a consideration. Even in non-voluntary euthanasia (sometimes termed "mercy killing"), it is the benefit of the person being killed and nothing else that (rightly or wrongly) motivates such an action. What we may consider to be a benefit to another may, in fact, not be a benefit: but at any rate and however wrongly conceived, it is the benefit of the person killed and no one else's benefit which motivates the action. Euthanasia as used by the Nazis was a different matter: the "benefit" to the person killed was never at issue. What mattered was that killing such a person allegedly benefited the state or society. Documents make this amply clear.[5] The euphemism "euthanasia," as used by the Nazis was simply a thin veneer of "double speak" for what they knew all civilized beings would simply call "murder."

Allowable (ethically or legally) killing—in whatever context—raises the legitimate fear that what could arguably be ethically allowable killing would open the door to what clearly could not be ethically accepted. Such a "slippery slope" argument, in some ways a distant cousin of the Nazi argument, which says that once we permit a foot of this sort in the door, a deluge of misuse is likely to follow, is not without substance. Allowing killing, for any reason, is undoubtedly a dangerous move. It is, however, a move which we do not seem to hesitate to make when it comes to the killing of our enemies in war (personally unknown and often indiscrete as when we bomb cities), executing criminals or killing in self-defense. In these instances we feel that we can isolate and distinguish such specific acts of killing sufficiently so that the social impact in promoting other forms of killing will be small. Such acts of killing, however, differ from euthanasia. Killing in war, executing criminals or killing in self-defense is done not to benefit the dying person who wishes to die—the hallmark of euthanasia in the sense we use the term here. Rather, it is done to benefit an individual or corporate other. Recently, the concept used by the Nazis to describe the chronically ill or otherwise "defective" individual slated to be killed by the Nazi state, i.e., *Lebensunwertes Leben*, ("life not worthy of life"), has subtly begun to re-enter our thinking. We will discuss this development in greater detail later.

In and of itself the slippery slope argument is tenuous. Many, if not most of our activities can constitute "slippery slopes." As examples, having a glass of wine may lead to drunkenness and eating a good dinner can be the first step on the road to gluttony. Slippery slopes are unavoidable. Rather than to disallow certain considerations or actions, the presence of the slippery slope merely counsels caution in making choices.[6] Discretion, which makes actions safer, if not safe and less bad, if not good, proceeds in a social context in which choices must be made. After all, one of the features that "greases" the slippery slope to begin with is the irresponsible drive to view all of the options we ultimately choose or decide as "the good" or "the right" rather than "the least bad" or "the least wrong" of a range of less than good or right alternatives.

3. SUICIDE AND LETTING DIE

Voluntary euthanasia has many similarities to suicide. In suicide rational persons, for whatever reason, decide voluntarily to end their lives; in voluntary euthanasia another person in some way assists in carrying out the wish. Common to both is that the decision to end life is made by the person who ends up dead. In suicide, the method chosen is direct: persons end their own lives by their own means or at least by their own hands. In voluntary euthanasia, an agent is interposed between persons wishing to end their lives and the means used. Even when one becomes the instrument of another person's desire, reason would still incline one to regard the patient's wish as suicidal. Agents who willingly serve as middlemen must now grapple with their own consciences: inevitably they become part of a causal chain that culminates in someone's death. If we consider suicide to be ethically wrong under all circumstances we could not find an ethical justification for the practice of euthanasia. Those who have traditionally opposed suicide have done so for reasons that either directly or indirectly appeal to religious values. Even when Kant attempts to argue against suicide on what to him seem to be perfectly rational grounds (viz., that in committing suicide one is treating oneself merely as a means and fails to treat oneself also an end in itself[7]), a religious motivation appears to peak through.

Personal choice, individualism and autonomy are much emphasized in our culture, too much so, some of us (including the authors) think. Nevertheless we also think that all of us would agree that personal choice and freedom to make one's own decisions deserves high standing in a hierarchy of social values. If, then, we consider respect for a person's autonomy to be at least a conditional ethical obligation (i.e., if we believe that in most instances persons have a right to self-determination as long as this self-determination does not in a significant way harm others), it is difficult to see how one would argue against at least a conditional right to commit suicide. Certainly, there are many occasions when suicide might be felt to be ethically problematic. Arguably, persons who have an important obligation that they can reasonably fulfill towards others (say persons who are their family's main material or psychological support or people who have a critical task to fulfill) have an obligation not to destroy themselves and, in that process, seriously harm or even destroy others. But in this discussion we are speaking of patients in the final stages of a painful and debilitating illness. Patients in the final stages of such an illness certainly continue to have obligations but, in most instances, such obligations are negative: to act ethically. For example, they cannot deliberately harm others, lie, steal or kill and they are expected to minimize the burden they impose on others. The capacity to act in a more positive manner (the ability to support one's children, to teach one's students or to treat one's patients) is, at the very least, attenuated if not indeed already lost. In a country in which individual rights not only are respected but also have, in many ways, become a national fetish, objections (especially legal objections) to suicide really ought to strike the vast majority of us as peculiarly illogical and inappropriate.

The argument that persons who commit suicide leave their families and friends with considerable mental anguish is an argument which has often been made and which, undoubtedly, is sometimes valid. Such a judgment would, we think, depend not only on the circumstances that surrounded the act itself but also, in many ways, on the way the act was carried out. (Certainly, this is something that could, one would think, be empirically determined.) In many instances when patients are terminally ill, the decision to commit suicide (or, in fact, in the Netherlands to undergo euthanasia) is one made in the embrace of loved ones. When suicide becomes illegal or is viewed as somehow shameful or ethically illicit, the ability of the patient to discuss such an alternative with family, friends or caregivers becomes severely constrained. As a result, the possibilities that those left behind would suffer mental anguish would, comparatively speaking, tend to be enhanced rather than diminished.

Few today would argue that suicide, under any and all circumstances, is ethically wrong. Even if we objected to suicide on personal secular or personal religious grounds, most of us would grant such a right at least conditionally to others in similar circumstances. And even most of those who think that suicide as well as voluntary euthanasia are morally illicit, find little wrong with not prolonging the life of a moribund or severely suffering patient. It is psychologically quite fascinating that an apparent majority of us who object to active interference, hold that passively "allowing someone to die" is somehow less morally culpable than actively bringing about the same result.

Patients who are suffering intensely and who have no further realistic hope of amelioration or cure (patients, in other words, who are confronted with a choice between living a bit longer with protracted and unrelievable suffering or having their suffering shortened by a self-chosen earlier death) do not, for the most part, wish to die. They merely wish not to continue living in the way that circumstances now inevitably force them to live. Such a difference is critical and underwrites the importance of properly orchestrating the end of life so that life is, all things considered, again viewed positively.

There are at least two different senses of "allowing" someone to die: (1) we may—when we easily could—refrain from interfering in a train of events which will, without such interference, inevitably lead to death (e.g., by not treating sepsis or pneumonia with antimicrobials) or (2) we may become a bit more active and discontinue a therapy upon which a patient's life depends (e.g., by removing the ventilator in a permanently ventilator dependent patient). In either case we may claim that we did not cause the death but that the patient's underlying disease caused the death. However, while such a statement most certainly has some truth in it (if it were not for the underlying condition my acting or failing to act would not have caused death), it is morally disingenuous. We cannot evade the fact that our failure to act (e.g., refraining from using antimicrobials) when we easily could have acted or our action (e.g., removing the ventilator) when we easily could have refrained from acting, inevitably makes us part of the causal chain leading to a person's death. Like it or not, either way—acting by acting or acting by omitting—inevitably makes us an integral and essential link in a causal chain. Had we not wished death to occur (or had we not at least been reconciled to the fact that, all things considered, death here was the lesser of possible evils), we would not have acted or failed to act as we did: we would have done otherwise.[8]

4.   TERMINAL SEDATION AND SELF-STARVATION

In the recent literature means of euthanasia have received some considerable attention: one is terminal sedation and another is to suggest to patients that they can stop eating (and perhaps drinking) and thus hasten their death.[9]

Terminal sedation essentially places a patient under anesthesia during the dying process. Supportive care is stopped and patients are placed under sufficient drugs to render them unconscious. The expression "terminal sedation" is, we find, peculiar. It is done with the full knowledge that no further active treatment will be done and that patients, as rapidly as possible, will now die as a result of their underlying disease process. Most patients are, in fact, sedated and given analgesics at the end of life. Thus the term "terminal sedation" is, at the very least, misleading and euphemistic. Terminal sedation, we would claim, differs from some form of voluntary active euthanasia mainly insofar as it has not been and is unlikely to be legally challenged. Terminal sedation may well shorten (and most certainly does not prolong!) life. Terminal sedation aims to keep patients asleep or unconscious until they die. The death of the patient is one of the goals of this process. It is *not* a by-product that is neither anticipated nor desired. When patients ask for—and appear to require—sedation sufficient to render them unconscious at the end of life there is little ethical objection in selected cases. Patients—whether injected with overdoses of a drug with the intention of causing their deaths or kept unconscious with the intent of keeping them unconscious until death ensues—are both, in the end, very much dead. To say in the former case (the injecting of a drug to directly cause death), that death was the intended consequence but to deny in the latter case is, at the very least, contrived and disingenuous. Presumably, the difference is maintained for two reasons: (1) to escape legal difficulties and/or (2) to maintain a form of self-delusion aimed at giving comfort to the physician and the medical team. There is basically nothing wrong either in accommodating to the law (when doing so does not conflict with ethical values) or in trying to minimize the anguish of the medical team. But making a virtue of self-delusion—because of its tendency to produce and perpetuate a form of *naïve* dishonesty—is not something to be encouraged.[10]

The other macabre option of recent literature is that patients who ask for physician assisted suicide be advised simply to stop taking fluids and nutrition and, thus, hasten their death. This method of approach—i.e., suggesting to patients that they starve themselves—leaves health care professionals free to claim that they were not directly involved and are, therefore, neither legally nor ethically culpable. Note: believe it or not, this has been suggested not just for patients who do not wish to eat or drink, but for patients who are still quite willing to do so. Such a suggestion, in our opinion, is not one aimed as much at easing the patient's plight as it is letting the health care professionals off the hook—especially the legal hook!

Eating and drinking have a significance far beyond the nutrition or fluids they supply: eating and drinking is a human activity that continues to connect us to our fellows. Sharing food and drink has deep atavistic significance and deep individual meaning. To stop eating and drinking is something social beings are certainly entitled to do. But to suggest it to persons who still are willing or even want to engage in the social ritual of eating and drinking is, to our way of thinking, inordinately insensitive and cruel because it could so easily suggest that, by analogy, they sever themselves from the social community as well. Such a suggestion is, in our view, not an ethically legitimate, or even minimally acceptable, option.

5. HARMING PATIENTS

Physicians are, above all else, traditionally enjoined to "do no harm." In general "doing no harm" is interpreted, at least, as causing only the minimal amount of avoidable or unintentional harm necessary to achieve a mutually (by patient and physician) desired goal. Expecting physicians "not to do any harm" whatsoever, would condemn the modern physician (and probably would have condemned his ancient counterpart) to virtual inaction. The injunction against significantly harming is what has caused health care professionals serious and perhaps quite appropriate misgivings when limiting treatment in dying patients (so as to allow an earlier death to occur). It has caused many physicians to look at any form of active killing (be it for "beneficent" euthanasia or in the service of the state) with horror. A revulsion against killing is seen as a proper professionally and socially conditioned reflex, a reflex that largely safeguards both individual patient and society.

"Harming," as used in the ethics literature, is not always a very clear concept. We tend to equate killing with harming. To be killed is, we think, equivalent to being harmed; to have one's life saved is to be benefited. In most, but not in all, circumstances this intuitive belief will be found correct because being alive (the biological and objective fact) is the necessary condition for having a life (the subjective and biographical fact). And being able to experience our daily lives and pursue our plans is, under normal circumstances, something we all want to do[11] Most persons associate the notion of harm with that of being injured or damaged: being caused unnecessary pain or having one's plans thwarted, when having one's plans thwarted could be avoided, are things we associate with the concept of harm. And most certainly physicians ought not to thwart their patients' plans unnecessarily or to seek to cause them unnecessary pain. The notion of harming and benefiting in the medical context is, however, a far richer one than can be encompassed by merely curing illness, prolonging life or alleviating suffering. When all is said and done, only the persons acted upon can ultimately decide whether something harmed or benefited them. What is considered a benefit by one patient may very well be considered a harm by another. That is, there are circumstances when patients view prolonging life (which is coming to an end and which they now consider a grave burden) as being done a harm. Likewise, patients who are too weak and physically dependent to kill themselves and who plead for the help of health care providers might look upon a refusal of help as a form of being harmed, abandoned or, at the very least, of not being helped or benefited. The language of "harm," then, does not get us very far.

The way the question of euthanasia is framed is critical to our discussion. If we frame euthanasia as "killing" or as "murder" the answer we give is apt to be quite different than if we were to frame this question as one of "preventing suffering" or of assisting the freedom of the will in those who lack freedom of action. The function of medicine is not only to sustain biological life but, and at least with equal force, to relieve suffering. Which of these sometimes conflicting obligations takes precedence depends upon the context, the situation and the actual possibilities. When sustaining life can be done only briefly and then only at the expense of intense suffering, refraining from sustaining that life is said to be morally permissible. On the other hand, when relieving suffering can only be done at the expense of terminating a biological existence no longer desirable to the patient, terminating this existence, while not necessarily morally worse than failing to sustain it, is proscribed. Whether we fail to sustain the patient and allow him or her to die or actively and gently terminate that life, the patient is imminently going to be dead.[12] In the former instance, however, the dying may be prolonged and agonizing; in the second, more rapid and gentler. That killing is, under all circumstances, more reprehensible than letting die is, at least in clinical medicine, neither intuitively nor reasonably obvious. The notion of what it is to "do harm," likewise, fails to provide us with any pat answers.

6.   SEPARATE QUESTIONS IN THE EUTHANASIA DEBATE

In considering euthanasia three distinct questions must be kept separate. First, the ethical question: Is killing a human being ever a defensible act and if so, under what circumstances? Second, the professional question: Is there some reason why persons in the role of health care professionals should not participate in the killing of a patient? Third, the social-political-cultural question: All things considered, is legalizing euthanasia a wise thing to do? These are separate questions. Discussions about euthanasia or physician assisted suicide have all too often foundered on the attempt to discuss all these issues all at once.

Is it ever morally permissible to kill another human? Most of us would concede that, at the very least, self-defense is morally permissible provided the most minimal force to safeguard oneself adequately is employed. That does not make killing another in self-defense a "good" thing: but it makes it permissible because, all things considered, it is a lesser evil than allowing an innocent person to be killed. But we tacitly condone other killing: when we set speed limits higher instead of lower or when we decide to mine coal or build high rise buildings we know that a certain number of deaths which would not otherwise have occurred are more apt to occur. We go to war and many of us count the killing of our enemies by our friends as acts of heroism; and in America we (unfortunately in our view) execute criminals—or those we believe to be criminals. Further, and perhaps most tellingly: we continue to structure our society so that many are hungry, poor, homeless and without medical care while some live in opulent luxury. And deaths due to hunger, poverty, homelessness and lack of medical care could, at least in our society, largely be prevented. To say that we always hold the killing of other humans to be unallowable is simply not true.

What then are the minimal conditions that might make killing of humans, while not good, at least the better alternative? There are social reasons: building high-rise buildings, mining coal or driving cars at the legal limit are examples. But in these examples those who will die have engaged in the activity causing their death with open eyes. Construction workers, coal miners and drivers all know that they run a risk and they are presumably free to take it or not.[13] Killing in a defensive war (an extension of self-defense) or killing in a war to safeguard innocent others may likewise be ethically defensible. Other social reasons for condoning death are hardly voluntary: the poor, homeless, the hungry or those without medical care only rarely knowingly and willingly embrace their fate. Given these facts of life in our society it is difficult to argue that helping a person to die who has decisional capacity, no further range of options and who pleads for help in ending their suffering is ethically necessarily and in all circumstances wrong.

Communities can make a reasonable argument that condoning killing will encourage others to kill. There is a not unreasonable fear that the practice could brutalize society as well as the profession. Brutality and callousness in society and on our streets has certainly risen. Often we fail to help persons in distress: persons being robbed or even raped while others look on without interfering is not a rare event. Above all, we read of the hunger of children and the homelessness of families, and, often, shrug our shoulders. It is a callousness towards suffering which is, in many ways, society's ill. If precept is an important factor in molding attitudes, communities will arguably be encouraged to be more callous, rather than less, when we over-value being alive and under-value the importance of having a life and of suffering.

We would argue that the killing of people, for their own benefit and at their own request when these are the only two options, may not be a moral good, but given the choices, it is arguably a far smaller evil than the alternative. But just because euthanasia may, under these narrow circumstances, not be ethically impermissible does not mean that anyone is obligated to help patients achieve their end. Nor does it mean that there may not be something in the social concept "health care professional" that might make participation by a member of this group problematic.

Killing others who are terminally ill at their own request, when they are incapacitated and unable to implement their own wishes (if, for example, they are too weak, have intractable vomiting or an obstructed esophagus) is a form of assisted suicide in circumstances when non-assisted suicide is no longer possible. If we do not acknowledge an individual's right, at any time, to take his or her own life, then assisting in suicide is clearly wrong. If, however, we are to grant others, at least at certain times, the right to commit suicide, then it is difficult to see why those who aid such persons can, necessarily, be faulted. Personal morality (or the particular morality of our particular moral enclave) may or may not prevent some of us from participating, just as personal morality (or the morality of our moral enclave) may or may not prevent some of us from committing suicide or from assisting with abortion. But such personal morality is personal and difficult to generalize to an entire professional group.

This brings us to the second question outlined earlier: the professional question of whether the peculiar ethical precepts of health professionals would preclude their participating in any active form of killing. Even if active euthanasia were to be considered a morally acceptable option and even if its legality for non-professionals were to be established, a severe moral concern for physicians remains. The issue "touches medicine at its moral center." The feeling that "if physicians become killers or are even merely licensed to kill the profession will never again be worthy of trust and respect as healer and comforter and protector of life in all its frailty" is a powerful one.[14] Physicians and other health-professionals are dedicated to life and to its preservation. Even if one were to acknowledge that the tradition to prolong life lacks ancient roots[15] it has, nevertheless, become a powerful motivating force for today's practicing physician. Society in its social contract with healers assumes this dedication as the tacit underpinning of the contract.

Put another way, is the "moral enclave of medicine" (the basic worldview which health care professionals share) incompatible with the notion of helping a patient to die? Professions, as well as other forms of association, share particular ideas of permissible behavior by the members. In a way, adherence to these socially established norms is a tacit, and sometimes explicit, condition of membership. Such a world-view is not static but evolves with time, circumstance and social changes. Its acceptance depends upon a wide consensus among the members of the group that condones or condemns a particular form of behavior. Health-care professionals are today sharply divided on the issue of physician-assisted suicide and euthanasia. No consensus can be said to exist.

The tradition of medicine has encompassed many changes. It has developed from meticulously avoiding the care of the dying to finding such caring to be a compelling obligation. Unquestioned paternalism, in which the "good" is interpreted by the healer, has been largely replaced by a more collegial model in which the "good" is jointly sought and pursued. The tradition has evolved and grown. And the tradition is, in many ways, what we, as individuals and as a profession, interpret it to be. To bring about a "good act of healing in the face of the fact of illness,"[16] which is undoubtedly what the profession is about, can be interpreted in many ways. Alleviating suffering, as well curing disease and not causing death, are important and simultaneous obligations. Professionals, in establishing hierarchies of values, bring to that activity all the preconceived and communally derived beliefs and viewpoints they brought to their particular understanding of the medical ethos. When obligations clash—when, for example, hopeless suffering can be alleviated only by causing the death of the patient—the individual's prior understanding becomes central to the issue. Determining which of these compelling obligations takes precedence, is a personal decision that must be made personally by each healer. Inevitably it will be made in the context of that particular person's background and beliefs. Such a decision will say more about the particular character of the actor than it will about the issue itself.[17]

Occasionally the suggestion has been made that, if euthanasia were ever to be accepted, it should not be health care professionals but others specifically trained to perform the act. Health care professionals would then, so the argument goes, be able to escape the evident conflict which euthanasia poses for them. In our view, such a suggestion, superficially attractive though it may be, has severe practical drawbacks. When laypersons enter medical school, they are embarrassed or disgusted by many of the things they must see and do; as time goes on, they become used to such activities: examining naked persons of the opposite sex or dealing with excreta has become a matter of routine. Creating a professional group who would kill daily instead of rarely (even if such killing were done in the service of decreasing suffering) runs the danger of creating a group of people no longer bothered by the gravity and finality of their actions. Socially, that does not seem to be desirable. Further, the person who relieves suffering by killing a patient, should know and understand the patient (and preferably the family and friends) well. It is not something to be routinely done in the normal course of a day's

work. Being *causally* involved in the death of another—whether by forego-
ing or withdrawing treatment or by a more direct act—should not be *casual*;
it should hurt. Such an act is never "good" in itself. At best, it is better than
the alternate available choices. To revert to the orchestration analogy: why
should the conductor be replaced just before the final movement? Lastly,
there are technical problems. Ending a life with as little suffering as possible
may not be as easy as it sounds. In the first place, it requires an understanding of and experience with pharmacology, physiology, psychology and other
disciplines that one cannot expect a lay person or a technician (who also
must act under a physician's direction) to have. Besides, if they were to ac-
quire this knowledge, understanding and experience they would be physicians! In the second place, it requires an understanding of and experience
with the peculiarities of the particular patient being cared for.

Finally, we come to the third, the socio-political-cultural question. Even
if one were to find active euthanasia an ethically acceptable option under
some circumstances and even if one were to affirm the probity of having at
least some physicians voluntarily participate, the advisability of legalizing
euthanasia would still be far from clear. On the whole, the issue—not as
much ethical as it is political—can be briefly stated: is it safer to outlaw a
practice which will inevitably continue to go on uncontrolled or is it safer to
permit it surrounded with many controls and safeguards?

There can be no doubt that the practice is far more widespread than most
health care professionals will (publicly) admit. What happens currently in
those jurisdictions where assisting patients to die is illegal is that decisions
are made idiosyncratically and are beyond professional (albeit not beyond
criminal) control. Clearly, where there are no guidelines, it is evident that
those who participate are informed by personal standards and do so at enormous risk. Yet, physicians who have actively shortened patient's lives have,
despite overwhelming evidence of their "guilt," often been adjudged "not
guilty" or given a slap on the wrist. This leaves physicians without guidance,
patients confused, powerless and insecure, and ultimately leaves justice be-
trayed: a wink and a nod is no way to deal with such critically important issues.

On the other hand, officially permitting such a practice also has distinct
drawbacks. The United States is not Holland, where the practice of active
euthanasia has (if we are to give credence to most albeit by no means to all
reports) worked fairly well. Even in the Dutch setting troubling problems
remain: recently proxy consent given for children and requests by non-
terminally ill psychiatric patients have been honored. American culture tends
to do two things: (1) it tends to readily allow finances and personal or corporate profit to drive decision-making and (2) it tends to abuse many liberties

by failing to take equally seriously the inevitable responsibilities that accompany such liberties.

On the positive side is the Oregon experience. However, this experience has, at this writing, been studied little more than one year.[18] Not only can such experience not be universalized to other cultures (any more than can the Dutch experience), it is far too early to attempt to draw any conclusions from it. The Oregon law is, so far, unique in the United States. It is clearly written and, in the first year that it has been in effect, it has been carefully and thoroughly analyzed. For these reasons, and because it may well serve as a model for similar laws in other states, a brief description is indicated. The so-called "Death with Dignity Act" delineates the circumstances in which physicians may prescribe a lethal dose of medications for their patients. The law forbids active euthanasia. That is, it forbids physicians to administer a medication to patients with the intention of directly producing death. It is questionable if the difference between giving a prescription and administering a drug can be legally sustained. It may (as some have argued) be contrary to the fourteenth amendment, which guarantees equal protection of the law for all persons within the jurisdiction of the United States. It is also questionable whether there is a compelling difference between a patient able to swallow and one who, because of esophageal obstruction or severe nausea and vomiting, is incapable of doing so. Paradoxically, the former would (under this law) have the right to end his life; the latter would not. At this point the question needs to be legally decided—ethically and logically speaking the difference appears trivial.

According to the Oregon law certain criteria must be fulfilled before a physician may prescribe lethal medication with the intent of causing death to a patient. The patient must be (a) at least eighteen years of age; (b) a resident of Oregon; (c) adjudged to have decisional capacity; and (d) suffering from a fatal illness that, in all probability, will cause death within six months. In addition:

1. The attending physician must receive from the patient two oral requests to prescribe a lethal medication. These requests must occur at least fifteen days apart.
2. The attending physician must also receive a written request from the patient.
3. A second physician must see the patient in consultation and must agree with the diagnosis as well as agree that the patient has decisional capacity. In case of the least doubt as to the patient's decisional capacity psychiatric consultation must be obtained.
4. Should the patient appear to suffer from severe depression psychological counseling must be sought.

5. The physician must advise the patient as to alternative courses of action such as palliative measures, hospice, etc.

6. The physician must ask the patient to inform and consult with the family but cannot insist that this be done.

In the last year, twenty-three patients were prescribed a medication for the purpose of committing suicide. Fifteen of these actually killed themselves, six died of their basic illness and two did not use the medication at the date of this report. Prescriptions consisted of 9.0 gm of either Secobarbital or Pentobarbital occasionally with an anti-emetic. The median time from ingestion to unconsciousness was five minutes, to death twenty-six minutes. No adverse effects were reported. In eight cases the physician was at the bedside when the patient ingested the medication and in six cases the physician was present at the time of death.

The legal status of euthanasia in the United States today is well known. Suicide has been decriminalized in most (but not all) states and, de facto, where laws against suicide exist they are not enforced. Physician assisted suicide is illegal in many states and neither directly forbidden nor permitted in many others. It is an anomaly that in some states where suicide is *not* held to be illegal, assisting someone with suicide (what is, after all, a legal act) *is* held to be illegal. In several states there have been attempts, generally through voter initiatives, to legalize both physician assisted suicide and euthanasia. Such laws, along with laws expressly forbidding physician assisted suicide or euthanasia, have been argued through several levels of federal courts. A narrowly crafted supreme court decision in 1998 essentially stated that the constitution was moot on this issue and that states were free to make their own laws regarding the legality of physician assisted suicide. Thereupon, Oregon again passed a voter initiative that made physician assisted suicide (but not active voluntary euthanasia) legal. At this writing the House of Representatives has passed a law that would forbid physicians to prescribe controlled substances for the purpose of causing a patient's death. Such a law if passed by the Senate and signed by the President (both of which are questionable) would effectively cancel the Oregon law.[19] There is no doubt that such a law would be challenged in court. Those of us who (at least in theory) are not totally opposed to the legalization of physician assisted dying have had, in addition to some positive, also some very troubling negative information to contend with. There have, for example, been interesting suggestions in the literature to the effect that we may, in fact, have an obligation to die.[20]

An obligation or duty to die seems a peculiar obligation to have. Having an obligation to do or to refrain from doing something implies a relationship between the person or persons having this obligation and the person or persons who are owed these obligations or duties. Such relationships occur in a community. The community shapes these relationships and shapes the consequent duties and obligations. While one might argue that one has an obligation to take certain risks or undergo certain discomforts for the benefit of or in the defense of family or community, it would be difficult to argue that we have a duty not only to risk death but to die or bring about our certain death. People who do this (by throwing themselves on hand-grenades, for example) are said to have acted in a supererogatory manner and are judged to be heroes. Their action has been "beyond the call of duty." If we have a duty to die, does our family (or community) have a justified claim to insist (and enforce) that we do? Intuitively we feel that no one can be required to go to certain death for the sake of another.[21]

In the debate over physician assisted dying, the fear of creating social conditions in which persons will, under certain circumstances, feel an obligation to die has figured as one of the arguments against legalizing such a procedure. Disabled persons are concerned that they would become even more threatened than they already are. Given the experience of recent history in both Europe and the United States—and coupling this with the American penchant for treating benefits and burdens primarily in terms of economic considerations—such a fear is an understandable and perhaps justified one. Those of us who have felt that under some very restricted circumstances physician assisted dying (be it by physician assisted suicide or be it by active voluntary euthanasia) is ethically acceptable, have right along hesitated to grant legal standing to such a process. Still, some of us feel that legalization under strictest control might be preferable to the current state of affairs where physician assisted dying is completely uncontrolled and is often left to the personal caprice of an individual physician.[22]

Attitudes that suggest we may have an obligation to die have once again made explicit the danger lurking in legalization. It is one thing to argue that family considerations do matter and that the attempt to isolate a patient's autonomy in situations in which the family as a community is involved is not only unrealistic but, in fact, philosophically untenable.[23] That is, it is one thing to feel that families should have some input into patients' decisions to end their lives—an input, by the way, that most of us have felt would be one which would tend to discourage suicide, to counsel patience or, and as a last resort, to lend support to a tragic choice. It is quite another thing to suggest that a patient who becomes "a burden" has an obligation to stop active treatment or might even have an obligation to seek or bring about his or her own death. And it is also quite another to change the counsel of families from one which might dissuade or might, with sadness, support such a tragic choice into one in which families are given license not only to let their own self-interests predominate but to insist (if dying, indeed, is a duty) that their self-interests *should* predominate and that they have a justified claim against their relative's life!

Human beings have, as do all other biological beings, an inbuilt drive to survive. The decision to end one's life is not one made (except perhaps in severely pathological psychiatric states) because people "want to die" but because they see dying as the only way to avoid "living this way." In other words, the only way that they can rid themselves of "having" an intolerable life—given the alternatives to them—is to stop "being" alive.[24] It is this desire to shape the end of life in a manner tolerable to patients so as to decrease the request for physician assisted dying that has prompted the effort to orchestrate the end of life. But orchestrating the end of life well is, in itself, something that presupposes a community willing to provide the social conditions that make such orchestration humane and effective.

Creating an "obligation to die" is an ethical violation of some rather core human values: these are core human values because they are part and parcel of common human experience and capacity. They are deeply rooted in our biological existence as animals, an existence that is the necessary basis for all else we may want, know or do. Beyond this, creating an expectation that at some point we have an obligation to seek our own death violates the sense of community that underwrites a viable and successful solidarity. Such solidarity comes about because individually we feel ourselves integrally enmeshed with others in our community and because we know that all of us will feel a mutual obligation to come to each other's aid. Communities are an association of individuals who are joined together for a particular, or a set of particular, goals. But communities transcend the summing of individual goals and interests. They are united by what Rousseau calls a "*lien sociale*," or social bond. Without this *lien sociale* a community is but an aggregation of individual interests. Individuals, however, are not merely the particular building stones of a community. Individuals and their communities are so interrelated that defining one is impossible without invoking the other. Neither has "primacy" over the other; the interests of neither can be accomplished outside of a decent respect for the interests of the other. But it does not end there: communities (whether these are families or larger communities) are corporate individuals which are, again, a part of the larger community within which they find themselves. Ultimately we, individually or corporately, are members of the world community and inextricably linked with its fate and destiny. To examine any one of these components outside the context in which they occur may be analytically useful, but cannot complete the task of examination. Seeing only individuals—be they actual individual selves or corporate entities—without seeing them as integral, interrelated and interdependent with the whole is, in the final analysis, myopic.

Insofar as a family shares burdens and benefits in pursuit of a common goal, it is the prototype of a community. Knowing that our families will be ready to stand by us—knowing not only that our families will be eager to share in our good times and it's benefits, but also that they are ready to support us when times are bad—is what creates solidarity. Without a sense of solidarity, a family is little more than a group which happens to share beer and hot-dogs together. Such a group has no true social bond of commitment. Just as some individuals have been termed "good-time Charleys," such families would deserve the same name. They have only a sense of personal gain and no sense of shared commitment.

The family community is integrated into the larger community of which it is a part. Just as individuals within a family must be ready to share burdens and benefits, individual families within a larger community must share their burdens and benefits with the larger community. This means, among other things, that families should not see themselves as isolated individuals (that they should not subscribe to a "myth of the asocial family") any more than should the individuals who compose it. Communities share rightfully in the bounty of individuals and families which compose them—the well off, in a just society, are expected to carry a heavier burden (of taxation, for example) than do those who are less well off. Individuals (individual families as corporate individuals or actual individuals), in return, rightfully expect support in time of need; it is what shared commitment is all about.

To argue that one has an obligation to seek death when staying alive would cause others untold suffering is one thing. To argue that one has an obligation to seek death so as to spare others the "agony" of paying more taxes or decreasing an already bloated income somewhat, is quite another. Arguing that one has an obligation to die so as to spare one's family an intolerable burden that is unrelievable in any other way is quite different from arguing that it is easier to encourage people to kill themselves than to encourage communities to play their supportive roles by relieving the family's suffering through appropriate communal support. Such a "duty to seek death" can easily be expanded to become a "duty" when you no longer are able to actively contribute: only the actively productive would, in such a point of view, be worthy of living. Those who are unproductive would not: a group of people who would then be classifiable as *"lebensunwertes Leben"* ("life unworthy of life"). If that thought does not (in light of recent history) have a chilling ring, it should!

There is, in this whole discussion, a very dangerous materialistic overtone: it is evident that the poor or persons from poor families, persons from small families or the poorly insured would, by this argument, have a greater and, presumably, an earlier obligation to die. Communities which look upon individuals as expendable units whose usefulness (or at least whose ability not to be a drain on communal resources) determines their standing are communities quite ready to dispense with their weak, poor and ill. In Nazi Germany, it started with the T-4 program and rapidly moved on to the wholesale extermination of persons deemed undesirable.[25]

The tacit message seems to be that when communities—through practices that underwrite their social institutions—systematically fail in their responsibility to any certain subset of its members, individuals ought to develop the ultimate heroic virtue of self-sacrifice. Certainly, an activism that reconstructs the responsibilities of community by curbing its mundane collective wants must be a more ethically relevant and promising choice than reconstructing the responsibilities of a set of individuals to include a heroic "duty to die."

An obligation to die when we are no longer productive members of our family and community is a step in the direction of the T-4 program and an affirmation of societal neglect. Creating a situation in which the community affirms an obligation to die does two things. First, it affirms that we are prepared to deal with the problems of the poor, the weak, the old, the disabled and the sick in a lethal manner—namely by "allowing" them heroically to "choose" death—rather than make what would be a relatively small shared effort to provide adequate communal (and not simply economic) support. Second, it negates the notions of mutuality, reciprocity and shared commitment inextricably linked with the belief in a just and caring community. As a result, solidarity—and with it the community—are weakened.

7. HOLOCAUSTS, GENOCIDES AND WHAT CAN BE LEARNED

The Nazi experience has been alluded to several times. It is so often mentioned in the context of the debate about physician assisted suicide that a few words specifically directed to it is in order. What in the literature has been called "playing the Nazi card" (using the alleged fact that "the Nazis did it" as an argument which trumps others) is often used as a pseudo-argument against physician assisted dying. Just as there are some analogies there are, likewise, profound differences.

The first lesson that we can learn from the Nazi tragedy (as well as from the events in Rwanda and elsewhere throughout history) is that the medical profession is no more immune to evil doing than is any other. Indeed, physicians, nurses and even some clergy were key players in Germany. They were involved in preparing the soil that made this tragedy possible. They were involved in implementing it; and they derived personal (or institutional) benefit from it.[26] The anti-Semitism of both Protestant and Catholic churches played a key role in preparing people's minds just as did the emphasis on racial hygiene by physicians.

The second lesson is that very ordinary individuals can be socially manipulated, seduced or coerced to participate in the most outrageous and atrocious evil. In all of us there lurks a member of the SS, just as in all of us there resides a great potential for good. It is the social setting that we create and endorse by our daily acceptance of it that determines which of these shall predominate.

The third lesson is the danger of euphemisms. It is the danger of changing our language so that what we are, in fact, doing is called by a far more palatable name. Speaking of the "final solution," of "special treatment," of "resettlement" tries to make of murder, abandonment and alienation something other than what they, in fact, are. This has its parallel in today's medical milieu. We cite here only two common examples. Quality control is often merely a euphemism for cost control. "Repatriation" (when very sick patients who have been brought to one hospital are forced to be transferred—sometimes at considerable risk and often against their will—to another institution) is merely a euphemism for what would, analogically, be considered extradition.

The fourth lesson is that, as important as economic factors are, they cannot be permitted to become the drivers of social policy. In making the destruction of the disabled or the socially undesirable palatable the Nazis appealed to economic factors. School children were asked to calculate how much money not having to care for disabled or hopelessly ill people would save and how much, thereby their father's salary might increase.[27] A famous placard showed a German worker. Across his shoulders lies a heavy stick weighted down on one side by a physically disabled person and on the other side by a mentally disabled one. The caption reads: "Du trägst mit" (you are carrying them along). The correct answer to that—"of course and why shouldn't I? I am lucky to be who I am"—was not what was implied. The appeal to crassly selfish and largely pecuniary motives was obvious. Here in the United States, we carp about the cost of providing "illegal aliens" with education and emergency medical care, as if they contributed nothing of positive value and came unbidden from some hostile and dangerous world.

Of course, costs have to be contained, some form of rationing is inevitable. It is one thing when cost control and rationing is done for the sake of saving communal resources so that better care can be given to more people. It is quite another matter when it is done in order to maximize profit for stockholders and pay enormous salaries to chief executive officers. When we begin to speak about an obligation to die because we may be burdening others, we begin to enter a morass in which the Nazi analogy becomes all too evident.[28]

There is another lesson well worth remembering, a lesson that has some application to the practice of medicine and to the end of life. The weak and disadvantaged among us can be treated in two ways. We can see them as part of our community or we can see them as different from us (a "they" and not a part of the greater "us). In the first instance, our relative strength and their relative weakness confers a special obligation on us. In the second instance, their weakness—their "otherness"—gives us, from our position of strength, the right to deal with them as we see fit. In short, we can see the weak and the dependent as truly a part of "us" or we can look at them as different beings—as "they."

The holocaust did not start with mass killings. It started by preparing the soil by, among other things, the constant disparagement of one group by a powerful institution within society (viz., the church). That prepared the soil and kept "them" from becoming a part of "us." From such purely social marginalization of a weaker population group, it then moved on to extermination. The progression from (1) you shall not live as one of us (social ostracism) to (2) you shall not live among us (ghettoization) to (3) you shall not live (extermination) is something that should give all of us pause. The weak, the sick, the elderly and those dying are not others who can be socially written off by such maneuvers as, for example, advising them to stop food and drink (an excellent means of social ostracism). They are not people who should be—when it can be helped—physically isolated and they should never be abandoned; above all else, they are not people who should be socially manipulated to collude in their own extinction.

But the Nazi card can be overplayed. What the Nazis did in the T-4 institutions, in the children's euthanasia program and in Auschwitz does not speak against euthanasia merely because the Nazis expropriated that language. We need to examine more carefully what the Nazis did, analyze and learn from it.

8.   RESOLUTION

Euthanasia is, in many ways, a distasteful topic. No one likes to envision the killing of others, the killing of patients by health care professionals or a society that condones killing. And yet, euthanasia, like illness and death of which it is a part, needs to be faced squarely. It will not do to obfuscate the issue or claim that what we are, in fact, clearly doing is not being done. Furthermore, euthanasia and its practice all too easily become the property of what many of us would consider to be, at best, questionable practitioners and perhaps charlatans. Instead of furthering the discussion, as some have claimed that it does, such grandstanding has done much to detract from it.

The better our care of terminal patients, the less will be the need for euthanasia. This is analogous, in many respects, to the abortion issue: the better our birth control program, the fewer will be the instances when abortion becomes an alternative. Orchestrating death by giving content and meaning to the last, as to every other, stage of life rather than focusing on dying can do much to reduce the need for euthanasia. Nevertheless, while the need for both euthanasia and abortion will be diminished, it will not vanish.

When all is said and done, we think that the following truths must be faced:

1. No society can claim that it condemns or disallows all killing; in many cases, if not indeed in most, physicians (whether they like to admit it or not) are causally implicated in the death of their patients.
2. Somewhere along the line the decision that "enough is enough" is and will continue to be made; persons who have no further options except either to die later with more protracted suffering or to die earlier but with shorter suffering may often choose to die earlier.
3. Physicians, because of the power they hold in the medical setting and because of their role in intimate, trusting physician-patient relationships, will inevitably be asked to help patients who choose euthanasia.
4. Euthanasia may be an unavoidable part of good "orchestration."
5. Laws that entirely forbid the practice invariably threaten to sweep the activity under the carpet and remove it from social and public control.

As a society and as a profession we must grapple with these issues and, in a democratic way, come up with decisions with which we can live, from which we can learn and through which we can adapt and improve. It may be the case that society, while rigorously setting its limits and controlling its practice will carefully choose to allow it in cases when patients who are terminally ill and who have no options other than living longer and suffering more or living shorter and suffering less repeatedly ask that such be done. Health-care professionals who wish to participate would be controlled but not stigmatized; those whose moral scruples would not permit them to participate would be free without penalty or stigma not to participate. Eventually, having learned from such a practice, it may well be that changes in either direction will be made. It may be found that the practice has served us well and that, perhaps, euthanasia requested by advance directive or asked for by appropriate surrogates could be tolerated. On the other hand, experience may teach us that the practice has not served us well and that it should be eliminated. A thoughtful analysis and dialogue—instead of the strident rhetoric that appeals to mercy on the one hand and tradition or religion on the other—would serve us well.

The current interest—not only among physicians and ethicists but above all in the general population—in physician assisted suicide and euthanasia indicates that there is grave dissatisfaction with the way in which the end of life has heretofore been managed. Since the end of life is not something most people gladly embrace, there will always be dissatisfaction—but it should be sorrow that life is ending and not fear that interminable suffering need accompany the last stage. It is one of our main theses that requests for medical assistance in dying will greatly decrease when the end of life is orchestrated well, just as requests for abortion decrease drastically as good birth control methods are readily available and utilized. Requests for such assistance in dying will not disappear—not all suffering can be reduced sufficiently for this to be a realistic expectation. However, requests for physician assisted dying should be seen and studied as failures of orchestration. Such a failure may, on further analysis, not have been avoidable but such information is also useful in guiding further developments in this field.

The debate about physician assisted dying and the insistence that all should be entitled to palliative care at the end of life and to a death with dignity may accomplish three desirable goals:

1. It may make the skill of orchestration a legitimate field of study.
2. It may induce us to teach these skills to all health care professionals within a multidisciplinary and disciplined setting using a rigorous approach
3. It may lead us to establish an equitable health care system whereby all care (including, but *not* starting with, palliative care) is available to all and the opportunity for a death with dignity is conceived of as a logical conclusion to a life with dignity.

ENDNOTES AND REFERENCES

1. The problem is beautifully described in a short story by Richard Selzer who offers an insight into the emotional problem health care professionals encounter in such situations. The story does not offer a solution—indeed it neither sets out to do so nor can. But as a description of a terrible moral (even if not ethical) problem is has no peer. See R. Selzer, *Down from Troy: A Doctor comes of Age* (NY: Chivers, North America), 1992.
2. P. Carrick, *Medical Ethics in Antiquity* (Boston: D. Reidel Publishers), 1985.
3. In the first century, early Christianity forbade all killing whether as capital punishment, in war or even in self-defense. This posed a great problem for the Roman Empire. On the one hand, they could not ignore an ever-growing segment of their population. On the other hand, they could not condone capital punishment or give citizenship to persons who refused to serve in the army. The first church-state accord resulted. The church

permitted killing those who were fighting an unjust war and those who had broken a just law. The definition of what was "just" and what "unjust" was left up to the state. Curiously enough, killing in self-defense remained proscribed until about the time of St. Augustine. An excellent description of this "doctrine of innocence" can be found in J. Rachels, *The End of Life*. (NY: Oxford University Press, 1986), pp. 11-13.

4. See Sir Thomas More, *Utopia*, trans. and ed. by R.M. Adams (NY: Norton), 1975. One of the best and earliest discussions of this book can be found in K. Kautsky, *Thomas More and His Utopia*, trans. by R. Ames (NY: Russell & Russell), 1959. Another excellent source is G.M. Logan, *The Meaning of More's Utopia* (Princeton, NJ: Princeton University Press), 1983.

5. Euthanasia as conceived by the Nazis was neither a "good death" nor a death brought about so as to benefit (or to prevent harm to) the person killed. While this program was carried on in semi-secrecy, the propaganda made for abandoning persons termed "nutzlose Fresser" ("useless eaters") was clearly visible to all. The extermination of the Jews was not termed "euthanasia:" the euphemism "euthanasia" was too evidently a euphemism to allow its use even at that late date. It is frightening to realize that the tentative lists of persons believed to be "genetically unfit" and proper subjects at least for sterilization, was later used when it came to the Nazi "euthanasia" program. For example, "the feeble-minded, the pauper class, the criminal class, the epileptics, the insane, the constitutionally weak, or the asthenic class, those predisposed to specific diseases or the diathetic class, the deformed, those having defective sense organs, as the blind and the deaf") was a list first suggested by an American, Bleeker Van Wagenen, at a conference in at the University of London in 1912 in his "Preliminary Report of the Committee of the Eugenics Section of the American Breeders' Association to Study and to Report on the Best Practical Means for Cutting off the Defective Germ Plasm in the Human Population," *Problems in Eugenics*, Ed. by W.C. Adelphi (NY: The Eugenics Education Society), 1912. The most definitive work on this subject is E. Klee, *Euthanasie im NS-Staat* (Frankfurt a/M, Deutschland: Fischer Tachenbuch Verlag), 1991. As background, the following also can be recommended: L. Alexander, "Medical Science under Dictatorship," *New England Journal of Medicine*, 1949; 241: 39-47; R.J. Lifton: *The Nazi Doctors*. (NY: Basic Books), 1986 and K. Moe, "Should the Nazi Research Data Be Cited?" *Hastings Center Report*, 1984; 14(6): 5-7.

6. E.H. Loewy, "Drunks, Livers and Values: Should Social Value Judgments Enter into Transplant Decisions?" *Journal of Clinical Gastroenterology*, 1987; 9: 436-441.

7. I. Kant, *Foundations of the Metaphysics of Morals*, trans. by Lewis White Beck (Indianapolis, IN: Macmillan Publishing, 1986), p. 47.

8. The point that patient's in hospitals today rarely die when nothing to prolong their life can be done, is a point evident to all who have worked as nurses, physicians or ethics consultants in a hospital. The point is made in two papers: E.H. Loewy, "Futility and its Wider Implications," *Archives of Internal Medicine*, 1993; 153: 429-431 and E.H. Loewy, "Futility and the Goals of Medicine," *European Philosophy of Medicine and Health Care*, 1993; 1(2) 15-27.

9. T.E. Quill, "Palliative Options of Last Resort: A Comparison of Voluntarily Stopping Eating and Drinking, Terminal Sedation, Physician assisted Suicide and Voluntary Active Euthanasia," *Journal of the American Medical Association*, 1997; 278(23): 2099-2104.

10. There is a fairly substantial literature on the problem of self-delusion. See: M.W. Martin, *Self-Deception and Morality*, (Lawrence, Kansas: University Press of Kansas), 1986.

11. E.H. Loewy: *Moral Strangers, Moral Acquaintances and Moral Friends: Interconnectedness and its Conditions* (Albany, NY: State University of New York Press), 1997.

12. J. Rachels, *The End of Life* (NY: Oxford University Press), 1986.

13. Of course, one can, with some justification, argue that the "free consent" of persons whose livelihood depends on such a risky activity is rather less than free. In a capitalist society and given the economic conditions of the times many will doubt the actual freedom of workers in such industries.

14. W. Gaylin, *et al.*, "Doctors Must Not Kill," *Journal of the American Medical Association*, 1988; 259: 2139-2140.

15. D.W. Amundsen, "The Physician's Obligation to Prolong Life: A Medical Duty Without Classical Roots. *Hastings Center Report*, 1978; 8(4): 23-31.

16. E.D. Pellegrino, "Toward a Reconstruction of Medical Morality: The Primacy of the Act of Profession and the Fact of Illness," *Journal of Medicine & Philosophy*, 1979; 4(1): 32-56.

17. L.R. Churchill, "Bioethical Reductionism and Our Sense of the Human," *Man & Medicine*, 1980; 5: 229-247.

18. See A.E. Chin, *et al.*, "Legalized Physician-assisted Suicide in Oregon—the First Year's Experience," *New England Journal of Medicine*, 1999; 340(7): 577 – 57; the details can be found on the Internet under http://www.ohd.or.state.or.us/cdpe/chs/pas/ar-index.htm (1998).

19. R. Pear, "House Backs Ban on Using Medicine to Aid in Suicide," *New York Times*, 28. October 1999, Vol. CXLIX (51,689); p.1, 29.

20. J. Hardwig, "Is there a Duty to Die?" *Hastings Center Report*, 1997; 27(2): 34- 42.

21. There are a number of papers that speak to this issue. Among others, see D. Ozar, "AIDS, Risk and the Obligation of Health Professionals," *Biomedical Ethics Review*, ed. by J. Humber and R. Almeder (NY: Humana Press) 1989 and E.H. Loewy, "AIDS and the Human Community," *Social Science and Medicine*, 1988; 27(4): 297-304.

22. E.H. Loewy, "Healing and Killing, Harming and not Harming: Physician Participation in Euthanasia and Capital Punishment," *Journal of Clinical Ethics*, 1992; 3(1): 29-34.

23. J. Hardwig, "What about the Family?" *Hastings Center Report*, 1990; 19(2): 5- 10.

24. T. Kushner, "Having a Life versus Being Alive," *Journal of Medical Ethics*, 1984; 1: 5-8.

25. The T-4 program, if a reminder is needed, was the destruction of life deemed "unworthy of life" ("lebensunwertes Leben")—precisely life which had become a burden to the community. It actively pursued the destruction of the mentally defective, the crippled, the severely tuberculous, the epileptics and persons deemed to be "asocial." Propaganda posters at that time graphically portrayed how much the community could save by not having to support such persons; mathematics examples in schools often asked students to calculate by how much not having to support "x" numbers of such "defectives" would increase the wages of "y" numbers of people. Shall we try to introduce such fine examples into our classrooms?

26. There is a vast literature dealing with this point. For a general review, which includes discussion about the implication of the churches in both preparing the soil for and failing to resist the Nazi atrocities see, for example, J. Weiss, *Ideology of Death: Why the Holocaust Happened in Germany* (Chicago: Ivan R. Dee, Publishers), 1996 and R. Hilberg, *The Destruction of the European Jews* (NY: Holmer and Meier Publishers), 1985. For the role of physicians in the holocaust, see A. Mitscherlich and F. Mielke, *Medizin ohne Menschlichkeit: Dokumente des Nürnbergers Arzteprozesses* (Frankfurt a/M: Fischer Tachenbuch), 1986 and H. Friedländer, *The Origins of Nazi Genocide: From*

Euthanasia to the Final Solution (Chapel Hill, NC: University of North Carolina Press), 1997.

27. M. Burleigh, *Death and Deliverance: "Euthanasia" in Germany, 1900-1945* (NY: Cambridge University Press), 1994.

28. E.H. Loewy and R.S. Loewy, "Lebensunwertes Leben and the Obligation to Die: Does the Obligation to Die Rest on a Misunderstanding of Community?" *Health Care Analysis*, 1999; 7: 23-36.

Chapter 7

Hospice and the End of Life

1.   INTRODUCTION

In this chapter, we will provide an introduction both to the philosophy of hospice and to the particular conditions under which it is actually practiced here in the United States today. Though brief, it should be sufficient to enable us to identify and discuss the persistent re-emergence of a particularly paternalistic attitude and approach in patient/clinician encounters that we consider ethically problematic. In short, we will argue that the most recent incarnation of the ideal of hospice, given the way it has been structured and funded in the U.S., not only fails to remedy today's growing disparity in expectations between laypersons and clinicians about the nature of the patient/clinician relationship. We will argue that it can work—even if unwittingly—to exacerbate it. In addition to examining the reasons for this failure, we suggest a more radical and fundamental remedy is required than is presently available.

The rise of the hospice movement here in the United States has been viewed by many as a refreshing and long overdue corrective to a medical establishment that has become increasingly preoccupied with a single aspect of medical therapy, viz., cure. Such a preoccupation, it has been argued, has encouraged clinicians (the term used in this chapter to refer collectively to professionals involved in co-ordinating the provision of health care for patients) to adopt a much narrower understanding of the nature of health care and the health care professions. As a result, it has caused clinicians to miss much of what has, until recently, traditionally been central to the medical encounter: *not* the treatment of illness, disease or disability, but the treatment of *patients* as subjects who have lives that will eventually come to an end. In other words, patients are not merely passive objects within the landscape to be maneuvered along the never-ending road to eradicating disease and re-pairing malfunctioning body parts.

The breath-taking advances that have been made in biotechnology—wel-come as they may be—threaten to replace instead of complement that older and much more broadly humanistic experience of medicine. And, they threaten to do so whether that experience takes the foreground as an intimate personal encounter or lies in the background as that impersonal relationship we all have with medicine in its public aspect as a social institution. Unfor-tunately, as we have discovered, the fact that biotechnology is often neces-sary for the preservation of bare biological existence says nothing about its effects on the quality of that existence or on the lives of all of those partici-pating in and most relevantly affected by the clinician/patient relationship. In other words, like bare biological existence, technology has potential but no actual content or meaning—it is, as it were, value neutral—until the context in which it occurs is factored into the equation.

This mixture between the broad, traditional goals and values generally associated with medicine one the one hand and the unique relationships and tacit expectations between individual clinicians and their patients on the other is what establishes the special obligations of health care professionals. These obligations extend to their patients, to themselves, to their profession, and to the community who not only solicits, but recognizes and subsidizes their expertise. While their expression may differ, depending on each indi-vidual case and its particular context, these special obligations have tradi-tionally included (listed here in no particular order of importance):

1. Promoting health via education
2. Relieving pain, symptoms and/or suffering (when possible)
3. Avoiding gratuitous harm or unnecessary risk to patients
4. Curing (as opposed to merely prolonging biological life)
5. Maintaining and improving function
6. Minimizing dysfunction
7. Bearing witness and/or representing patients, especially when any or all of the above are no longer possible

But, again, these obligations remain, just like bare biological existence and biotechnology, empty placeholders. While they point towards certain possibilities, they have no actual content or meaning—i.e., they are value neutral—until the bio/psycho/social context in each particular case can be specified. This requires a careful examination of the unique antecedent con-ditions that structure each and every particular situation. These antecedent conditions make it possible for the benefits and burdens of the goals and in-terests in each particular case to be identified and discussed by all whose lives will be relevantly affected by the effects of intervention. Without such examination, interventions are doomed to remain at the level of blind impulse or force of habit, rather than rising to the level of prospective, critical reflection, the sine qua non of intelligent practice. Parenthetically, this is the case whether the subject matter in question is labeled "art," "science" or "ethics."

In addition to underscoring the importance of context in providing meaning to the content of obligation, we seek to draw attention to another equally important point: obligations do not cease to be obligations when they conflict. That is, simply because the collaborative efforts of all of those relevantly affected have identified (provided content to) a particular hierarchical ranking of the clinicians' specific obligations in any given situation does not mean that those obligations that happen to fall lower on the list will simply cease to be obligations. The special obligations of clinicians arise from—and, thus, represent—a diverse set of goods, values, goals and interests some of which will, inevitably, conflict. This is simply an empirical fact of human existence.

But unmet obligations, whether real or perceived, can be costly—and not simply in material or socio-economic terms, but in non-material social terms as well. Whenever obligations are ignored or set aside—for whatever reasons—the bonds that tacitly hold society together are placed under stress and an "opportunity cost" of some sort is incurred. Some of these opportunity costs may be difficult to measure—e.g., alienation, loss of trust—but they are as real—and costly—as those more easily measured in concrete terms. Thus, one of the central purposes—whether tacit or explicit—behind clinical expertise has always been to meet one's professional obligations, and to do so in such a way as to preserve as many goods, values, goals and interests as possible and to avoid having to choose one rather than (i.e., to the exclusion of) others! In other words, an essential element in deciding how to rank goods, values, goals and interests is to assess the degree to which each has the potential to preserve, if not enhance, the rest.

The failure of clinicians to recognize and fully appreciate the conflicting obligations this diversity of goods, values, goals and interests can create helps to explain why the narrow preoccupation with cure in recent years has contributed to a growing disparity within the healing relationship. It resides in the tacit—and sometimes unrealistic—assumptions and expectations of laypersons on the one side and clinicians on the other. The current popularity and support of the phenomenon of hospice is due, in no small part, to the fact that patients—and all of us are potential patients—want a remedy to that disparity. Thus, we see, in the more closely co-ordinated and context-specific orchestration of care that an interdisciplinary hospice team typically provides, a movement in the right direction.

2.   HOSPICE: PHILOSOPHICAL IDEALS AND PRACTICAL REALITIES

The word "hospice" actually shares the same ancient roots linguistically with the words "hospital" and "hospitality" and has long been connected throughout Western civilization with the idea of a safe haven for sick and weary travelers. Since the late 1960's, however, the term "hospice" has been used to refer specifically to a special kind of care instituted to better meet the needs of terminally ill patients. This "modern" hospice movement began under the direction of Dame Cicely Saunders, a physician who established St. Christopher's Hospice in London in 1967. It was shortly thereafter that Kübler-Ross' now classic text, *On Death and Dying*, rapidly became a public phenomenon and spurred a renewed interest in discussing death and the way dying occurs in modern life.[1] Patterned after the inpatient hospices created by Dr. Saunders, the first hospice in this country was opened in Connecticut in 1974. By the late 1980's, there were nearly 1700 hospice programs spread across every state. Today, in only ten years' time, there are over 3000 programs located in the 50 United States, the District of Columbia, Puerto Rico and Guam.[2] However, more than 90% of all hospice care hours are provided as outpatient services within patients' homes (this includes nursing "homes").[3] So, what exactly is "hospice" here in the United States...how does it differ from Saunders' original concept and why?

Dorland's Illustrated Medical Dictionary defines hospice as "a facility that provides palliative and supportive care for terminally ill patients and their families, either directly or on a consulting basis."[4] This is a rather straightforward description and is, presumably, a rather fair representation of how most clinicians who are not hospice practitioners and laypersons think of hospice. Indeed, the National Hospice Organization (NHO), which describes itself as "the largest independent national non-profit membership organization devoted exclusively to the promotion of hospice care in the United States,"[3] offers this view of the philosophy of hospice:

> "[H]ospice" refers to a steadily growing concept of humane and compassionate care which can be implemented in a variety of settings—in patients' homes, hospitals, nursing homes or free-standing inpatient facilities.[5]

However, we are troubled by at least two caveats that bear mentioning here—both of which, interestingly, can be traced to arbitrary economic constraints over which hospices and their clients have increasingly little, if any, direct influence. First, while it is true in principle that such care can indeed "be implemented in a variety of settings," hospices are, in fact, under the gun financially to minimize the time their patients spend at any type of inpatient facility. As mentioned earlier, over 90% of all hospice care hours are provided in an outpatient setting. Beginning in 1995, Medicare and Medicaid paid for over 73% of all hospice services here in the United States.[3] These are capitated programs which, during the same time, provided home care (again, this includes nursing "homes") per diem re-imbursement rates of approximately $94.00 and general inpatient care per diem re-imbursement rates of approximately $419.00.[3] Extremely few patients have the resources to pay for diagnosis-related inpatient services not covered by the terms stipulated by these government plans. And patients and their families have no way of knowing, in advance and with any certainty, just how much expense this might entail.

Second, while NHO's membership includes over 2100 hospice programs and 47 state hospice organizations,[3] the cost of NHO membership (as of 1999, six dollars per admission per year) represents a hardship for many hospices. The Sacramento hospice facility affiliated with University of California, Davis, for example, is not a member of NHO for precisely this reason. Thus, it is important to bear in mind that a number of otherwise quite excellent programs—and their statistics—are not, in fact, represented by this organization, and that what information is available from NHO represents, predominantly, the views and statistics of its member hospices.

Our research indicates that there is, as yet, neither systematic collection, standardization and research of hospice data nor any recognized clearinghouse for the isolated, disparate and, undoubtedly, overlapping sets of data that are out there. Hence, as has been noted in several recent national and international journal publications, it is quite difficult to assess the representative validity of, much less to draw firm conclusions from, the information that is readily available here in the United States.[6] That being said, it is still the case that the NHO represents a majority of hospices in this country and is considered, by an overwhelming majority of hospice personnel, to be the most appropriate spokesperson for the philosophy of hospice care. Thus, for the purpose of discussion and analysis we, too, shall consider the NHO's position to be the closest thing we have to a corporate representative of hospice clinicians and organizations here in the United States.

The NHO has identified and published prominently five characteristics of hospice, which they claim differentiate it from other types of health care. We quote them here:

1. Hospice offers palliative, *rather than* curative treatment
2. Hospice treats the patient, *not* the disease
3. Hospice emphasizes quality, *rather than* length of life
4. Hospice considers the entire family, not just the patient, the "unit of care"

5. Hospice offers help and support to the patient and family on a 24-
    hour-a-day, seven-days-a-week basis [italics ours][5]

Most hospice clinicians have, either tacitly or explicitly, incorporated
these claims into their philosophies of practice, and most hospice teaching
centers utilize the literature from NHO in their information packets and
many in the classes they teach as well. Frankly, we find each of these claims
more or less problematic, and will deal with them one by one, albeit briefly.

As reflected in the first claim listed above, hospice care has come to be
equated—certainly in the minds of most hospice clinicians, but in the minds
of many other clinicians and laypersons as well—with "palliative" care and,
yet, the two are not, in fact, the same. In common as well as in general medical parlance, the term "palliative" still retains a much broader meaning. According to *The Compact Edition of the Oxford English Dictionary*, "to palliate" is derived from the Latin, "palliatus," to cloak or to hide, and its various
meanings include the following: to invest, to mitigate, to disguise, to excuse,
to appease and to cure superficially or temporarily.[7] According to Dorland's,
"to palliate" means simply "to reduce the severity of; to relieve."[4] In fact,
there is nothing in standard lay or medical dictionaries to suggest that palliative care is appropriate uniquely, or even only predominantly, to the care of
the terminally ill.

While palliation is a central feature of the type of care provided by clinicians in a hospice setting—and, certainly, in many terminal cases, it is the
central feature—the idea of palliative care has never entailed (i.e., required)
that the patient being given such care be terminally ill. We have argued in
numerous places elsewhere that, historically, part of the tacit understanding
in any patient/clinician relationship—irrespective of prognosis—is that palliation is one of the primary goods in any health care relationship between
patient and clinician. Palliation is one of the core issues that must always be
taken seriously in the course of helping patients (a) to understand the nature
of their situation, (b) to identify their own particular goals and (c) to weigh
the benefits and burdens of the alternative plans of care suggested by the
health care team.[8] Unless such core issues are squarely addressed, it is very
difficult for clinicians to develop and sustain the kind of trust necessary for
the health care relationship to succeed.

Thus, while hospice care is often considered synonymous with palliative
care—to the point that many working in or writing about the field use the
terms interchangeably—there are important theoretical and practical differences. These differences merit careful consideration (especially when one
considers the unique way in which both are practiced here in the United
States). For example, clinicians working within palliative care units or "pain
clinics" tend to place greater emphasis on comfort and the preservation of
function than they do on cure and/or prolongation of biological life. Clini-

cians working in hospice care generally tend to emphasize comfort and the preservation of function—and here, we borrow the language of NHO—*rather than* cure and/or prolongation of biological life, a subtle but important distinction nevertheless.

On the one hand, the type of palliative care currently offered by traditional medicine in the United States tends to focus rather narrowly on physiological pain (as opposed to the broader, bio/psycho/social phenomenon of suffering) and ranges from acute interventions to long-term chronic treatments. Such therapy does not ordinarily occur as part of a more comprehensive and integrated effort by a multidisciplinary team of clinicians. For example, while every patient seen by palliative care units or pain clinics is supposed to have a primary care physician, there is often little, if any, ongoing communication between the palliative care clinicians and the primary care physician. Such communication, we would argue, is foundational for providing an over-all long-term integration and co-ordination of their respective plans of care. But, even when the effort is made, palliation too often remains a narrow, biotechnical concern with little consideration as to how—or whether—it complements or is at odds with the larger, more global and long-term goals of the patient.

On the other hand, the type of hospice care available here in this country has been successful in providing a co-ordinated multi-disciplinary team approach that is (a) dedicated to treating the patient as a "complex whole," composed not only of the person dying, but his or her family and significant others as well and (b) structured specifically to address some of the broader bio/psycho/social elements of each patient's particular situation. Such an approach makes possible the inclusion of such things, for example, as bereavement counseling both before and for up to one year after the patient's death occurs. Unfortunately, it is also the case that hospice care is presently (c) restricted to terminally ill patients who are actively dying from their illness and have (to the best estimates of their clinicians) six months or less to live and (d) committed (increasingly, for economic reasons) to a stringent co-ordination of home care to avoid hospitalization or keep it to an absolute minimum. But, simply because palliation is a particularly appropriate tool for hospice does not mean that it is any less appropriate for any other type of medical care! No clinical specialty can escape issues of non-terminal palliation, from the acute post-operative pain and suffering of patients undergoing the necessary but unpleasant routine of pulmonary toilet to the chronic pain and suffering of patients with debilitating arthritis. (Patients cannot be expected to "breathe deeply and cough" when pain and fear conspire to make them breathe rapidly and shallowly, or to "get plenty of fresh air and exercise" when every move sets off a cascade of aches.) To the degree that unnecessary pain and suffering impinge on the patient's wholehearted participation in her plan of care, patients—actual and potential—will lose faith in their clinicians' dedication to the healing relationship.

In other words, palliation is an essential component of *any* health care relationship—the fact that its importance is so often ignored notwithstanding. One should not have to abandon palliation if one seeks curative therapy, just as one should not have to abandon—or be abandoned by—conventional medicine when one becomes terminally ill. In short, the conceptual distinctions that have developed on this point between hospice and conventional care do not speak to the reality of the situations in which patients and their clinicians actually find themselves. Rather, we must begin to see these particular conceptual distinctions for what they really are: arbitrary conventions. While there is nothing necessarily wrong with conceptual distinctions, per se, they do merit scrutiny. This is especially the case when they have arisen from and been promulgated by interests and conditions external to the patient/clinician relationship and over which a majority of patients and many clinicians feel they have little, if any, effective voice.

Patients are especially vulnerable in this respect. Far more often than they admit—or their clinicians realize—patients are inordinately influenced by those who care for them. If conditions that are external to the healing relationship between clinicians and patients cause clinicians to represent hospice and conventional medicine as mutually exclusive options, most laypersons will unhappily, but uncritically accept them as such. But, simply because cure is a live option does not mean that palliation can be ignored, and simply because a patient is terminal ill—i.e., that she is imminently dying—does not mean that conventional medicine no longer has a legitimate role to play. We tend to forget—death is an inevitability for all of us; it is just that, at any particular moment in time, it is more imminent for some of us than for others.

The second claim, that "hospice treats patients, and not disease," is more an interesting, if somewhat sloganeered commentary on current attitudes and perceptions here in the states than it is a substantive change of ideals or goals. Presumably, the intimation behind this claim is that conventional medicine treats disease, and not patients. But the fact that conventional medicine has been overly preoccupied with curing disease simply reflects a recent deviation from a long-standing traditional norm that simply cannot be reduced to the technical proficiencies associated with curing disease. Such a deviation is not corrected by adding yet another mutually exclusive technical proficiency that effectively reduces the concept of hospice to an exclusive form of palliative care.

The issue is not whether to treat patients or diseases; one cannot treat a disease without treating the patient whose disease it is! The issue, rather, is how well or badly diseased patients are treated. As we noted in the introductory section of this chapter, there are at least seven broad obligations clinicians have traditionally owed to those who seek out their expertise. Ideally, clinicians need to be mindful of each of those obligations when the treatment they offer cannot satisfy them all. Why should patients be asked to choose between clinicians preoccupied exclusively with disease and cure and clinicians preoccupied exclusively with the palliation of persons (but only so long as they are terminal!)? This claim and the "choice" it represents should be as disquieting to us by what it doesn't say as by what it does say.

The third claim, that "hospice emphasizes quality, rather than quantity of life," represents yet another instance of "black-and-white thinking," a typical reactionary response by a society that has, as yet, been unable to come to grips with one of the inevitable intellectual implications of progress: increased complexity. To be sure, we have come to grips, collectively speaking, with the inevitability of material change. But, our dualistic heritage—that legacy which causes us habitually to separate mind from matter, space from time, science from morals, life from death, to name but a few of those dualisms we uncritically reify and praise—gets in the way. It masks our realization that, for each of us, life is a constant complex balancing act between quality and quantity. Precisely how that balance is weighed will differ significantly between us. To fail to understand this prevents us (both individually and collectively) from coming to grips with the novel ethical responsibilities we increasingly create for others and ourselves as we move from mere observers of the life around us to creative agents of change. To claim that hospice has the corner on quality of life suggests—whether intentionally or not—that conventional medicine's proper concern really ought to be limited to quantity of life. It is a suggestion that ought to concern all of us, certainly as clinicians but perhaps especially as potential patients, because it serves only to reinforce the peripheralization of the role of primary care clinicians in their patients' end of life care.

The fourth claim, that "hospice considers the entire family, not just the patient, the 'unit of care'," is consistent with recent attempts to provide a much needed corrective to our society's current simplistic and overly individualistic interpretation of the concept, autonomy. We have argued elsewhere that individuals are capable of becoming persons—at least in any ethically interesting sense of the term—to the degree that they are able to recognize their existence as dynamically interconnected with the rest of their environments.[8] That is, my entire bio/psycho/social environment affects the person I become just as surely as that environment is affected by me. I cannot even begin to identify myself outside of my interests and relationships—they are who and what make me who I am. Presumably, it should follow that it would be in the best interests of persons to seek homeostatic balance between their own needs and interests and the needs and interests of the rest of their environments. The issue for clinicians has never really been whether to consider things and persons other than the patient in front of them, but how, to what degree and under what conditions it is not only appropriate and justifiable, but also incumbent to do so. Most assuredly, it is an issue neither unique nor applicable only to clinicians working in hospice.

The fifth claim, that "hospice offers help and support to the patient and family on a 24-hour-a-day, seven-days-a-week basis," is most misleading since part of what is entailed in the classic meaning of any profession—but especially the profession of medicine—is accessibility. Anytime physicians are not personally available to their patients they are expected to "sign out" to other clinicians who are qualified to represent them. This is so deeply ingrained an expectation in our society's idea of the patient/physician relationship that those physicians failing to do so immediately open themselves to censure from their peers and potential litigation for "patient abandonment." The problem for traditional medicine is not the lack of accessibility of physician-clinicians, but the lack of accessibility of the *other* members of the health care team. And the problem for traditional physician-clinicians who contemplate hospice care for their patients is the tendency for many hospices to assume complete control of a patient's care, providing very little chance for the continued viability of the relationship between the patient and the physician originating the hospice consult. A good friend and colleague of ours has noted: "I've known physicians who have creatively responded, for example, by contracting with an individual hospice nurse who meets weekly with that physician to review his patients, some of which are signed on to hospice with that nurse as the case manager, others of which that nurse follows as skilled care patients."[9] This may, indeed, be a realistic alternative for some physicians who rarely or occasionally need to resort to this type of response. Nevertheless, it may not be an economically viable option for physicians who are equally dedicated but who have a substantial number of patients that would benefit from hospice care. But even if it were, why should physician-clinicians be singled out to subsidize such an alternative? Do we think nurses should contract with physicians for information about patients? Why should physicians be required to assume all of the burdens associated with preserving the integrity of the clinician health care team/patient relationship?

The claim that patients who need 24-hour care from non-physician health care clinicians ought to receive it is, indeed, an appropriate ethical claim. But, it is so precisely because *all* patients who need 24-hour care ought to receive it irrespective of whether they arbitrarily "qualify" for it or not! As such, it is an ethical claim that demands a social response. This is not something that can be remedied by relying on the voluntary charitable impulse of individual physicians; it is the responsibility of all of us as citizens of a democracy. Frankly, the suggestion that it is "financially impossible" for *all* patients to have the same access to home health services that hospice patients have is a bogus one. Other technologically advanced countries spend less of their respective gross domestic products than we while providing health care services that include much more comprehensive home health services equitably to all of their citizens. Our ethical problem is that we *do* have the means here in this wealthy country—we just don't have the common decency to do so. But, say we really didn't have the means, what is so wrong about the admission, "Okay, so we can't give everything to everybody; but what we *do* decide to make available, we will make available to all who need it, whether they are imminently dying or not"? (For a more extended discussion of such "system errors," see the sections in chapters 2 and 7 that deal with social issues.)

These are, of course, rather brief yet, we think, significant critiques of the claims made by NHO. Yet, because these claims have so thoroughly insinuated themselves into the philosophy and daily practice of hospice clinicians, it is important to realize the extent of their influence on patient/clinician relationships and the divisions they have either induced or exacerbated between hospice and non-hospice clinicians. This is all the more unfortunate, since those aspects of hospice that, at least prima facie, have been the most attractive to the public are not those that tend to be listed prominently in the various pamphlets and brochures created for public information. Rather, the features that have consistently appealed most to laypersons are those they suspect a cure-oriented conventional medicine can no longer provide. These features include:

1. A return to patient-centered care
2. A re-dedication to the importance of palliative issues in patient care assessments
3. The introduction of a more cohesive interdisciplinary approach, i.e., one that has proven to be more effective for marshalling both the expertise and the materials needed to customize and orchestrate a plan of care that is more consistent with the bio/psycho/social needs of each individual patient being treated.

The first feature is seminal, reminding us that hospitals and clinics are not factories and clinicians are not workers on an assembly line—though many clinicians and patients have begun to feel that way. And attitude, while not everything, still matters. It is cause as well as consequence of our beliefs and expectations about each other. It creates the atmosphere within which our daily lives are lived and habits are forged. That is why, when feasible, it is as beneficial for clinicians as it is for patients to keep the central locus of care—physically, psychologically and socially—on the "patient's turf," so to speak. The patient is less likely to be "objectified," and more likely to retain a more active sense of ownership of and responsibility for both her immediate environment and her long-term goals. The clinicians, on the other hand, can assess much more clearly, and with fewer false presumptions, the kinds of interventions that will be most likely to succeed, given the realities of the patient's attitudes, surroundings and lifestyle. Most important, however, whenever terms and conditions of the health care relationship are considered, that consideration will necessarily be defined in terms that are also inclusive of the best interests of patients as well as of others. Any discussion about "efficiency" in the organization or structure of health care, for example, would also have to be considered in terms of its effects on patients.

The importance of the second feature has already been discussed at some length. However, it can hardly be over-emphasized, given the recent spate of articles in the literature since the publication of the now famous "SUPPORT study:"[10] Patients want to retain, for as long as possible, as much control over their lives as possible and they see palliation as one of the major means to that end. And unless a person has some modicum of control over the life she has, the bare biological fact of "being alive"[11] can be, at least, meaningless and, at worst, excessively burdensome. In other words, it is uncontroversial that "being alive" is necessary in order to "have a life." But, for many human beings, when "being alive" is so fraught with pain and suffering that every experience is overwhelmingly negative, it becomes impossible for many persons to appreciate "having a life" in any interesting and meaningful sense of the word.

The last feature is, essentially, the method of delivery and means of coordinating and monitoring the first two. A major deficiency in every area of modern conventional medicine lies in the method of delivery. Since the demise of "house calls," clinicians have had to rely on patient and/or family self-reports as to how well or badly the patient is able to interact and cope with her daily environment. There is relatively little opportunity in the outpatient setting in conventional medicine for the kind of critical, ongoing and dispassionate professional assessment required for efficient monitoring of medical needs and coordination of such care—especially for patients with non-acute and chronic conditions.

The success hospice has achieved thus far has been due, in no small part, to its commitment to create an environment for patients, their significant others and clinicians where open, critical and ongoing discussion about the shared problems of the patient/clinician relationship can occur. These shared problems include misunderstandings and disagreements that arise from unduly narrow, insufficiently critical and reductionistic patterns of thinking. And, again, they concern not only biomedical interventions but those broader issues that continue to engage us as human beings, i.e., what should constitute appropriate care of patients as whole persons, how that should be decided and by whom.

These misunderstandings and disagreements are part of the reason why the average hospice clinician is convinced that conventional medicine cannot routinely offer the same type of closely coordinated, interdisciplinary care as hospice does. But, it is a mistake to conclude simply because something is not routinely offered that it either cannot or should not be routinely offered. But another part of the reason is that health care has become such a complex undertaking. Not only has the "unit of care" expanded to include patients' families and significant others, the sub-specialties of clinicians have proliferated as well. Fewer patients today have—or realize the importance of—a primary care clinician to oversee and co-ordinate the kinds of care they are receiving. Thus, peripheralization of primary care clinicians and fragmentation of care has become pandemic. NHO's emphasis on detailing how hospice differs from conventional care only serves to increase such peripheralization and fragmentation. No wonder many patients are distrustful and clinicians defensive.

3.   THE PATIENT'S "GOOD," THE "GOOD" PATIENT AND THE PITFALLS OF ORCHESTRATING CLINICAL EXPERTISE

One of the most difficult problems all clinicians face, day in and day out, is using their expertise to maximally benefit patients, but doing so in such a way that it respects the patient's best interests—not as, the clinicians see them, but as the patient sees them. As we remarked earlier, the growth of hospice as an alternative methodology and approach to patient care came at a propitious time and has had some unexpected beneficial consequences. It has prompted clinicians to look more critically at the habits of conventional practice, especially the tendencies to focus on the treatment of disease instead of the treatment of patients and to find the technologies of cure so compelling that death has come to be equated with failure. Also, in emphasizing the interdisciplinary nature of health care, it has helped to serve as a reminder that the patient's "good" is not the same thing as the patient's "biomedical good."[12] The patient's biomedical good is the patient's good as the clinician understands it. The patient's good is the patient's good as the patient understands and lives it. Certainly, there are times when these may be complementary or overlapping goods. But they are not the same, and the patient's good cannot be reduced to the patient's biomedical good, whether the latter good is interpreted from the perspective of conventional medicine *or* of hospice. As a result, there will be times when these goods will, in fact, conflict. But, in the course of trying to discover what is in a patient's best interests, it is not unreasonable to consider asking for the patient's perspective on the situation—and as a matter of first, not last resort! And, here, we are admonishing *both* non-hospice *and* hospice clinicians.

Just as the growth of hospice has had some unexpected benefits, it has also had some unexpected negative consequences. As hospice clinicians have become increasingly more experienced caring for terminally ill patients, they are just as apt as their counterparts in conventional medicine to assume a certain perspective about the work they do and to make certain assumptions about the means and ends of their practice. These are a perspective and assumptions that some patients may, in fact, not share about their own particular situation. Such patterns of thinking have encouraged otherwise intelligent people—patients and clinicians alike—to bypass the extremely important process of discussing the appropriateness of medicine's specific means (i.e., biomedical interventions) and ends (i.e., not just the strategic, objective goals of the medical encounter itself, but the wider, more inclusive life-enriching goals of the various participants involved). Adopted in its place are unwarranted assumptions about each other's aims and intentions.

In the case of conventional medicine this kind of thinking is largely responsible for the prevalence of death-denying attitudes and behaviors that discourage frank and thorough communication by all sides. In the hope of maximally benefitting patients by streamlining procedures and establishing more effective and efficient habits of practice, hospice clinicians have made themselves no less vulnerable to the same kind of paternalistic assumptions and practices they sough to counteract in conventional medicine. As a result, unwarranted assumptions about the kinds of means (i.e., interventions) and ends (i.e., goals) appropriate to the hospice encounter has sometimes led to death-oriented (in place of death-denying) attitudes and behaviors that can be equally effective in discouraging frank and thorough communication.

This brings us to the second point of this section, the "good" patient. Patients have a right to make their own decisions regarding the kinds of health care options available to them. They even have a right to make what others might think of as a "wrong" choice about that care so long as they are rational and clearly understand their situation and the implications of such a choice. But being rational is not the same thing as being reasonable. Rationality simply marks the capacity to reason logically about means and ends, to choose means that are appropriate to a given end, irrespective of the "reasonableness" of that end. As clinicians, we may be apprehensive, even exasperated by some patients' choices. But so long as they understand the alternatives and consequences of their choices—and, in pursuing those choices, do not create hazards or undue hardships for others—we have no prima facie justification for revoking that right. This is why it is always a particularly gratuitous and coercive form of paternalism to deny patients key pieces of information about their condition, its consequences, its possible treatments or their consequences. Such a denial may seriously compromise the ability of patients to make choices for themselves that are as authentic, unbiased and well-informed as possible.

The ideology of the "good" patient is a variation on a theme as old as medicine itself. In the Hippocratic tradition physicians were guided by two precepts: (1) "do no harm" (i.e., non-maleficence) and (2) "avoid *hubris*" (i.e., understand the balance of nature and work patiently, intelligently and constructively within her natural constraints). While the "good" patient was expected to follow the physician's instructions regarding health and diet, the physician's role in the relationship was more that of a non-maleficent advisor than that of a beneficent parent. The rise of scientific investigation and the purposive manipulation and testing of the limits of nature, however, shaped the early part of the modern tradition. The idea of working in balance with nature gave way to the "overcoming" or domination of nature. As medicine became more cure-oriented, the patient's good was increasingly more narrowly interpreted in terms of—and often reduced to—the patient's biomedical good. Not surprisingly, our perception of the patient/clinician relationship was, in turn, influenced by the "domination of nature" model of science, and the role of the clinician was attended by an ethic of paternalistic beneficence. The "good" patient—child-like and innocent—was now expected to surrender themselves to the cure-oriented expertise—and the almost priestly devotion—of clinicians.

As some of the less than perfect results of the "domination of nature" model became evident, patients began to lose faith in many of the so-called "miracles" of modern medicine. As the ends and goals of medicine focused increasingly on prolonging life at any cost, patients began to question the wisdom of placing such complete trust in their clinicians' expertise. Increasingly, patients were beginning to see the need for re-asserting their autonomy, the right to make their own decisions about what the ends and goals of their medical encounter should be. But, in its more egregious form, this autonomistic turn, itself, threatens to treat clinicians as little more than external agents—mere means, as it were—for patients to realize their own private goals. Under such circumstances the "good" patient cannot afford to be passive. To flourish she has to develop and practice the virtues of a prudent shopper: she must know what she needs and how to get it. She must have the time to shop around and bargain for the best deal. These are not exactly characteristics that patients, even in their *least* vulnerable moments—much less at the end of life—either do or should find comforting.

It is, of course, undeniable that hospice has been instrumental in getting health care professionals to understand and take seriously the overwhelming need for persons to confront the benefits and burdens of life—including life's end and the choices available to them as that end nears. (It is also undeniable that many of the individual hospice clinicians that we have had the privilege to work with are some of the most selfless and dedicated clinicians we know.) Yet, because patients are especially vulnerable and needy, the fear of alienating those most qualified to help them is very real to them and can inhibit an otherwise careful scrutiny of what might be the most realistic alternatives in that particular person's case. As a result, the "good" hospice patient (or significant other) may feel too intimidated to disagree with or reject the particular death-orientation envisioned and expressed (perhaps even urged?) by the hospice team. When this occurs, the patient is still being defined in terms of a particular health care team's assumptions and tacit expectations about means, ends and behaviors.

Note, for example, what has happened since Kübler-Ross first articulated her now-famous "stages of dying."[1] Clearly, these stages have served as useful guideposts for health care professionals in caring for both the dying and their bereaved. On the other hand, these stages have also, at times, attained the status of mandatory thresholds over which all "good" patients must pass. Not infrequently professional care-givers are convinced that "something is seriously amiss" (if not in the patient, then most assuredly in themselves!) when a patient's behavior does not conform to that now implicit standard.[13] Indeed, some patients may wish to end their lives quietly, allowing events to take their own course and requesting that nothing be done to intervene. According to the ideological paradigm that threatens to overwhelm hospice today, these are "good" hospice patients. However, there are others who may not wish to "go gentle into that good night,"[14] but may, for any number of reasons they find compelling, wish to continue this particular battle and delay the inevitable just a bit longer. Because such patients do not fit the ideological paradigm described above, they will not be considered "good" hospice patients. As a result, it is highly unlikely that they will receive the expert palliative care that, presently, only hospices can currently provide. Unfortunately, rigid ideologies have a way of blinding health care professionals to the need for keeping options flexible, for providing gentle support when needed and intelligent guidance when requested—central features of humane and scientific patient-centered care.

The economically driven alternative that hospice now offers patients today—namely, a choice between life-extending care and terminal palliation—does little to resolve these problematic issues about decision-making and the nature of the patient/clinician relationship. It merely says to the shopper that she now has two, pre-packaged and mutually exclusive choices. But, because of the way in which these alternatives have been pre-packaged, they function less as means to be crafted to the patient's ends or goals and more as ready-made ends or goals in themselves. In either case, to the degree that the patient does not actively participate in the construction of her ends or goals, she exercises the formal, but not the effective, autonomy required to make a truly authentic choice. And the types of intrusions made by third party players who, until relatively recently, were external (at least, biomedically!) to the relationship—e.g., insurance companies and managed care organizations—have only exacerbated the problem. Under these conditions, the "good" patient must be more than a prudent shopper, she must be good at betting the odds as well, for finding and keeping a good health care plan today assumes the proportions of a Nietzschean crap-shoot.

Forcing hospices to maintain a myopic dedication only to end of life palliation unwittingly contributes to the creation of a serious false dichotomy in medical care. It results in patients being urged to choose between cure-oriented and palliation-oriented interventions—as though cure and palliation were ready-made, free-standing and mutually exclusive Platonic forms just waiting to be "applied" like cookie-cutters to shapeless dough. Current reimbursement schemes only serve to exacerbate the problem as, increasingly, patients are forced to structure their choices solely on the basis of economic considerations between palliative and curative interventions—again, as though they are ready-made, free-standing and mutually exclusive. The very meaning of "choice" presupposes that one has a realistic means of securing the alternatives between which one is choosing. To argue that, in principle, patients may still choose otherwise when, in reality, they do not have the means to do so is, at the very least, ethically insensitive, if not downright patronizing.

It bears remembering that a theme figuring prominently in rekindling interest in hospice in the first place was a desire to orchestrate medical care around the particular needs, issues, interests and goals of each patient as a unique person. Such orchestration has to proceed in a manner that respects and attempts to restore, rather than further compromise, the irreducible bio/psycho/social integrity of the patient.[8] In this respect, hospice has proven, up to now, every bit as time-consuming, labor-intensive and restrictive as the conventional practice of medicine it seeks to complement and/or replace. This is so because a patient's bio/psycho/social integrity is hardly an easy notion to get at, even under the best of circumstances. It is not static, eternal or fixed, but dynamic, temporal and evolving. And, as with any complex mechanism, any attempt to help restore its balance requires an appreciation of its unique contextual details. These details include the entire myriad antecedent, current, and continuing conditions and intercurrent and interdependent relationships that contribute to making that particular patient the unique person he or she is. In the same sense that persons cannot be reduced simply to their biochemical substrate, caring for patients cannot be reduced simply to a narrowly focused, one-goal-fits-all set of biomedical interventions, whether those interventions take the form of life-extending or terminal care.

When health care professionals, for whatever rationale, permit reflective inquiry (and the open, critical and ongoing dialogue with patients and their significant others it entails) to be overshadowed or supplanted by some generic, ready-made and free-standing set of assumptions, expectations or strategic plans of care, they have begun engaging in a particularly domineering form of paternalism. Why? Because their loyalty and focus begin to shift from the ideals of medicine as embodied by the unique patient in front of them to improving upon an intricate set of strategically efficient routines and practices geared to a "universal" patient who simply doesn't exist. When this occurs, patients begin to feel confused and disenfranchised—and well they should.

Ideally, patients ought to feel that their end of life complements rather than clashes with their vision of themselves (see also chapter 2). Realistically speaking, there simply is no inherent conflict between palliation and therapies that are aimed at prolongation of life or cure. Indeed, both kinds of interventions can and should be complementary means by which the larger issues that affect the health care relationship can be more adequately addressed. The problem lies elsewhere: it lies in our failure, individually and as a society, to recognize that critical thinking is also an intervention; it is, in fact, the pre-eminent form of "doing something." We must pursue critical inquiry into the roots of this alleged disparity between various kinds of interventions by means of an on-going, public dialogue about what values, goals and expectations should characterize medicine as a social institution. As consensus evolves—it is, after all, an on-going critical commentary on a dynamic and on-going process—the disparity and conflict that invariably results from reactive, oppositional thinking will be minimized, the richness and complexity of issues will be better understood and medical interventions will cease being treated as ready-made ends. But, as we have argued, this process requires reflective inquiry as a method of intelligence. As such, it requires time and space (which, of course, in today's climate, is money)...but also the ethical and political commitment that we can make it happen

As originally conceived, hospice can—and properly should—form an integral part of orchestrating the end of life. Today, hospice serves an important function for some patients while putting others—like the donkey who starves between two equally attractive piles of hay—into an impossible quandary of choosing between life prolonging and palliative care. This need not be the case and appears to be largely an artifact of the way hospice is financed. What has happened in hospice is what so very often has happened in capitalist societies: a rigid ideology was created to serve funding instead of funding being created to underwrite a growing and developing idea. From the beginning, through the middle and finally during the end of life a smooth transition of options and services should serve to support patients' goals and ends. What we currently have are uneven, unevenly distributed and disconnected sets of services that mold patients into a preconceived notion of what is needed. Hospice most certainly can (and does, albeit in limited respects today) help create such a process.

ENDNOTES AND REFERENCES

1. Elisabeth Kübler-Ross, *On Death and Dying* (N.Y.: Macmillan Publishing Company), 1969.
2. Miscellaneous statistical information culled from the National Hospice Organization's "The History of the National Hospice Organization: 1978-1988."
3. "NHO Hospice Fact Sheet," a two-page summary of the most recent statistics available from the National Hospice Organization (Spring, 1999).
4. *Dorland's Illustrated Medical Dictionary*, 27th ed., (Philadelphia: W.B. Saunders, Inc.), 1988.
5. "The Basics of Hospice," brochure # 711135, copyright by the National Hospice Organization, 1996.
6. The methodological flaws in research done in North America have been noted in a number of articles, two of which we cite here: EK Wilkinson, *et al*, "Patient and Carer Preference for, and Satisfaction with, Specialist Models of Palliative Care: A Systematic Literature Review," *Palliative Medicine*, May 13, 1999; (3):197-216; J. Corner, "Is There a Research Paradigm for Palliative Care?" *Palliative Medicine*, July 10,1996; (3): 201-8.
7. *The Compact Edition of the Oxford English Dictionary* (Oxford: Oxford University Press), 1971.
8. For a fuller discussion of the idea of bio/psycho/social integrity, see Roberta Springer Loewy, *Integrity and Personhood: Looking at Patients from a Bio/psycho/social Perspective* (NY: Kluwer Academic/Plenum Publishing), 2000. Bio/psycho/social integrity, in turn, is based on the notion of homeostatic balance developed by Erich H. Loewy in *Freedom and Community: The Ethics of Interdependence* (NY: State University of New York Press), 1993.
9. From e-mail conversations with our friend and colleague, Anita Tarzian, Ph.D.
10. "A Controlled Trial to Improve Care for Seriously Ill Hospitalized Patients: The Study to Understand Prognoses and Preferences for Outcomes and Risks of Treatment (SUPPORT)," by the SUPPORT Principal Investigators, *JAMA*, 22/29 November, 1995, 274; 20:1591-8.
11. The Greek distinction between "zoe" ("being alive") and "bios" ("having a life") was first discussed in the medical ethics literature by Thomasine Kushner in an article entitled "Having a life versus Being Alive." *Journal of Medical Ethics*, 1984, 1:5-8.
12. For a more complete discussion of the variety of "goods" connected to patients, see Edmund D. Pellegrino and David C. Thomasma, *For the Patient's Good: The Restoration of Beneficence in Health Care* (NY: Oxford University Press), 1988.

13. For similar criticisms of how Kübler-Ross' stages have been misappropriated, see Erich H. Loewy, idem, chap. 9: "Care of the Terminally Ill," pp. 161-206, esp. pp. 162-7 and Larry R. Churchill, "Interpretation of Dying: Ethical Implications for Patient Care," *Ethics, Science and Medicine* 1979; 6(4): 211-22.
14. From the poetry of Dylan Thomas.

Chapter 8

Challenges for Tomorrow: Where Do We Go from Here?

If we are to deal effectively with the end of life we need, above all, to turn our attention to two issues: providing the necessary education in the skill of orchestrating the end of life to all health care professionals and creating a social context in which good end of life care for all is integrated into the totality of their lives. To do these things well we have, first of all, to admit to ourselves that the overall care of patients at the end of their lives leaves much to be desired. Nowhere are these skills taught in a systematic and coherent manner.[1] We also need to admit that our society fails to provide an even minimally acceptable context of dignity—not simply at the end of life but throughout life.[2] Only by recognizing our deficiencies as educators, as professionals and ultimately as a society can we begin to address the questions of implementing changes.

1. EDUCATING HEALTH CARE PROFESSIONALS

One of the problems in proper orchestration is education. Our education in medical and other health care professional schools and colleges is largely geared to acute interventions. Problems of public health or prevention are not dealt with in depth nor are students routinely exposed to clinical experience in these areas. Likewise, problems at the end of life are not dealt with in a systematic manner. If they are at all addressed, they are addressed in an elective course that a student may or may not choose to take. It is generally those students most sensitive to the issues and most interested in acquiring the skills who elect such courses. Students who have little interest in the subject or who believe that it is something that each health care professional

153

just intuitively knows how to do without further training fail to take these courses. These are the very students who, if they are to become good and compassionate professionals, should take such courses.

Even when students are exposed to palliative or end of life care, such exposure is generally in the context of acute care. Moreover, when it comes to pain control—students are taught about such issues in an acute setting and with little attention paid to any but the pharmacological interventions necessary to deal with pain. Little attention is paid as well to the question of suffering (as distinct from pain) as an area of important and legitimate study and understanding. In general, students pay little attention to the notion of suffering,[3] are ill prepared to recognize or deal with it and are woefully ignorant of the resources needed and/or available so that end of life care can be managed in systematic, efficient and humane manner.

Acute interventions are frequently aimed at particular organs or organ systems. Often there has been overemphasis on a particular disease, a myopic view that sees a patient as a set of separate and separable pathologies and as separate and separable organ systems instead of as an integrated whole whose function cannot be reduced to its physical components. A classic example of this is the septic patient with renal, cardiac and pulmonary failure, each pathology and organ system being studiously supervised by a particular specialist. Each specialist is convinced that the particular organ failure might be successfully dealt with: a supposition which out of the context of this particular patient (who may be 94 years old and have a number of coexisting conditions) might be quite correct but which, in this particular patient, is not. Each specialist sets his or her own particular goals and leaves the others to set theirs. And that would be bad enough: but often these goals are set in a manner which fails to appreciate that what is being dealt with is a person afflicted by a terrible combination of conditions with a personal history and prior life. The overall life goals of such a patient may be quite incompatible with the separate organ system goals set by each specialist. What is missing is the realization that there happens to be a patient wrapped around the disease and that this patient has goals and values which may not be supported by the narrower purely physically oriented notion of "his medical" goals. Even when lip service is paid to the fact that one is dealing with a patient who has a disease process and not merely a disease process with a patient, little is generally known about the social setting, the values, hopes and fears of particular patients. This attitude is, unfortunately, not confined to physicians—frequently nurses know little if any more. Most certainly one would not wish to speak against aggressive attempts to cure patients. However, these efforts need to be coordinated and aimed at common, patient-selected goals. Orchestrating the end of life is more than selecting technical means to a variety of narrowly predetermined ends—especially when the patient is left out of the conversation! Orchestrating is an interdisciplinary task and one deserving its own theoretical and practical foundations, its own body of literature and its rightful place in the curriculum.

Medical education does not emphasize or indeed pay more than lip service to the skill of orchestrating the end of life. Indeed no medical or nursing colleges in the United States or abroad offers a disciplined and required course that might teach physicians and nurses such a skill. The concept "physician" or "nurse" raises in our minds, among other things, a set of abilities we presume that such persons must possess: health care professionals (at least our image of health care professionals) are persons who know some anatomy, some physiology, some medicine, etc. For a physician (or a nurse) these are essential abilities. Managing end of life care well is likewise essential. The concept physician or nurse should, in our view, also include the capacity to know something about orchestrating the end of life and doing it well.

Orchestrating end of life care is a skill which, like all other medical skills, needs to be taught and learned. It is a skill that in today's medical or academic world should form a coherent whole and not something left to the caprice of individual instructors or to a "catch-as-catch-can" approach. When such instruction is given on one of today's existing medical school clerkships, it is often given without adequate preparation. That is, it lacks a theoretical and conceptual foundation and is, therefore, less useful than it might otherwise be. Such instruction is liable to be given by an instructor coming from a particular discipline and informed by a particular set of personal beliefs, experiences, attitudes and biases. When learning about orchestrating death is left to a "catch-as-catch-can" elective basis, it is apt to miss the point. Students who are interested and, in general, already sensitive to the issue will certainly profit. But students who are unaware of the issue or who believe it to be unimportant—and who are the very students for whom such a course would be the most profitable—will leave medical school grossly deficient in the basic knowledge necessary for the task.

In medical schools, it is a task whose theoretical underpinnings might best be taught in the first years when issues of cultural diversity, psychology, religious attitudes, etc. need to be introduced. Such a course could be part of a public health offering or might well be integrated into other disciplines. In any event, an interdisciplinary group, section or department, who would then be responsible for both its content and co-ordination, would optimally, work out the curricular plan. In the clinical years, a two or three week rotation during one or more of the clinical clerkships specifically aimed at demonstrating this skill in a variety of clinical setting would enable students to understand and get practice in applying what had been taught before. Here, of particular importance is the work of role models who can show how a variety of disciplines can be smoothly and respectfully integrated and brought to bear on the problem at hand. An elective offering in the senior year for those who either may want to deepen their understanding or are contemplating a career in such a field should be available. What is essential is that teaching end of life care must have a definite and recognized place in the curriculum.

There are many possible ways in which such a place in the curriculum could be secured and there is not necessarily one "best" way. Whether such a task is accomplished by the creation of yet another department or yet another section within an existing department is irrelevant. What is important is that an interdisciplinary team teaches the necessary skills. In other words, orchestrating the teaching effort is critical to the enterprise. It requires a leader, someone who has the responsibility and the authority to assemble a team of players and then to conduct a performance. Since the task of orchestrating the end of life is clearly multidisciplinary, students must be taught by a variety of persons coming from a variety of disciplines and skills. Introducing any course into the medical curriculum necessarily means that the curriculum as a whole needs to be restructured to accommodate it. One cannot add more to an already bulging curriculum unless one is prepared to modify what is currently being taught or how it is currently being taught.

In colleges of nursing similar courses tailored to the needs of the nurse need to be created. Such courses—just like those in colleges of medicine—need to be taught by a team able to draw upon the expertise of various disciplines. Just as courses in colleges of medicine need instructors from a variety of disciplines outside of medicine, such courses taught in colleges of nursing should draw upon the expertise of persons other than nurses. Since most nurses do not receive post-graduate (other than "on the job") training, it is especially important to train graduates to take their rightful place as major players in the orchestra. The skills—social, psychological, communicative, cultural as well as medical—taught throughout nursing education should include material specifically aimed at integrating the graduate into a successful team.

Orchestrating the end of life is not a task that starts with hospice. Hospice is at one end of the scale. Certainly hospice is one of the chief players, but hospice needs to be integrated into an effort that properly starts long before a patient's terminal phase is reached. Preferably continuity of care but, at least, continuity of information necessary to such care must (as was pointed out in chapter 3) start much earlier than at the time a diagnosis of a potentially fatal disease is made. It is necessary for all persons who deal with patients to be familiar with the process and, therefore, be able to prepare the soil on which good orchestration can then proceed. It is not only the physician or nurse who must be taught: it is, likewise, the patient who must come to understand what eventually can be offered. Ultimately, it is the community that must be educated so as to enable it to play its crucial role in supporting such care.

When we set educational goals for health care professionals we try to equip fledgling clinicians with the skills needed to take care of a variety of patients in a variety of settings and with a variety of conditions. The aim, for example, in medical school, we would suggest, should not be to produce a good physician—this is premature. The aim should be to educate students so that they will be good interns or junior residents who can profit from the education offered during that year. It should be the task of internship to produce a good resident and the task of residency finally to mold a good physician whose habits of thinking and of self-education have been acquired throughout this long training process. The term "good" needs clarification: by a good intern, resident or physician we mean one whose knowledge and skills are appropriate to the task at hand and who is prepared to continue to grow throughout the next level of experience. Clearly, physicians at all levels have a role in the care of patients at the end of their lives. They must be able to speak with and relate to such patients and their significant others. Thus, they need to be conversant with the medical, social and ethical problems which such patients present.

What is taught in medical school should form the theoretical and conceptual foundations and provide the necessary practice with skills which graduates need to benefit professionally as well as humanly from their postgraduate experience. What is taught in the college of medicine needs to be reinforced and expanded throughout post-graduate training and needs to be made appropriate to the particular discipline chosen by the student.

2.   SOCIAL PROBLEMS, MEDICINE AND GAINING ACCESS

An article in the New England Journal of Medicine argues persuasively that while, in the United States, a constitutional right to physician help in dying may not exist, a constitutional right to palliative care well may.[4] But to take such a right seriously is incoherent absent a right to access to comprehensive health care for all. It makes eminent sense to include equal access to palliative care when equal access to basic health care is assured. When, however, access to palliation is assured but access to prior care—especially prior preventive care—is ridiculous. One now has access to good palliation for the metastases of one's prostate cancer—which is now advanced precisely because one lacked the opportunity for having that cancer investigated and treated at a time when the possibility for cure or long term benefit was still present! It has also been forcefully argued that all should have a right to a death "with dignity." But just as the right to palliative care makes sense only in the context of a right to comprehensive health care, a right to a death with dignity can make sense only in a social setting in which all have a real—as opposed to merely theoretical—opportunity to a life of dignity. A death with dignity absent a life with dignity—or palliative care absent preventive or curative care—inverts the pyramid; it makes death and palliation more important than life and health.

We need, therefore, to turn to some social concerns. Physicians who are practicing medicine are primarily concerned (and legitimately so) with the problems of their individual patients. The care a physician can give to an individual patient depends, however, upon the context and framework within which such care takes place. If nothing else, managed care and the problems with patient care within such a context has taught us that. If physicians are truly concerned with good care to individual patients they cannot refrain from becoming a part of building a "patient-friendly" instead of an "industry-friendly" context in which to practice. The institutional settings in which physicians practice not only determine how physicians shall practice but, in turn, are an expression of concerns and decisions made in the wider social arena. The problems of patient care, the problems of institutional structure and the problems of social existence are not separate or separable.

We shall presume (for here is not the place to argue the point) that, at the very least, everyone is entitled to access to basic health care.[5] Virtually all industrialized nations (save the United States) have accepted this premise and all persons have access to at least basic health care. However, life with dignity means more than universal access to health care: health care is not the most important social good.[6] Within the context of other social goods, health care is but one—and not the most important—good. In the United States, the number of uninsured and inadequately insured continues to rise, hunger is not infrequent and homelessness is rampant. The primary and secondary school system—acceptable (at times excellent) in wealthy suburbs, barely acceptable in many middle class areas, progressively less effective in the lower income areas and utterly terrible in the poverty areas—is not what it ought or could be. Colleges are less and less accessible to those from poorer homes and tuition plus living expenses are well beyond the reach of the average lower income family. Such conditions do not promote the opportunity for a life with dignity. Offering persons who have been reduced to poverty the possibility of a death with dignity might make those who are well off feel better, more virtuous and more kindly. However, it does little or nothing for the poor, the underprivileged or the destitute. It can, in fact, be looked upon as a secular variation of quieting the masses by promising the solace of heaven in the hereafter. The statement "be patient, once you are dying the chance for good palliative care will be yours," is not too dissimilar from the promise of eternal bliss after a life of misery on earth! The opportunity for a death with dignity is as meaningless to the person living in squalor as the opportunity to speak freely is to the starving.

Long ago Virchow (the father of pathology as well as one of the architects of social medicine) wrote that physicians are the proper advocates of the poor. He made this claim because of the intimate association between poverty and disease. If we truly wish to promote good palliative care that smoothly interconnects with curative and life prolonging care and, if we wish to secure for all the opportunity for a death with dignity, we have yet another reason to become "advocates of the poor." In general and for the most part our ethics has been an ethics of the strong, of the powerful and of the healthy. At best, it has and in a relatively condescending fashion, been an ethics for the weak, for the poor and for the sick. It is time that we, as a democracy, avoided such an essentially divisive point of view. It is time we began to craft not so much an ethic *for* the weak, *for* the poor or *for* the sick as an ethic *with* the poor, *with* the sick and *with* the weak—an ethic which includes their legitimate concerns as co-equal members of our community and society. A society's standing among civilized nations has often been measured by how well it takes care of the weakest members of its society. We would, beyond this, suggest, likewise, that this is determined by how much such a society does to empower its weakest members and to truly include them in their notion of what constitutes "us."

Creating an ethic with the weak, the poor and the sick of course implies a reconstruction of our social structures so as to make them consistent with devotion to a real democracy and to those changes necessary to create, maintain and sustain it. True democracy is no more the rule of the powerful than it can be the rule of the weak. It is a working together of all for the common good, of dividing the world not into "them" (the weak, poor and sick) and "us" (the strong, well-off and healthy) but seeing the world as a "we." To accomplish this, as John Dewey pointed out long ago[7], political democracy (the kind we usually refer to when we say "democracy") must be underpinned by at least three pre-conditions. These pre-conditions include:

1. Personal democracy—a state of affairs in which we respectfully listen to and consider each others concerns
2. Economic democracy—a state of affairs in which basic necessities for all are met, where none starve, go homeless or without health care
3. Educational democracy—a state of affairs in which all have equal access to an equal quality and quantity of education.

Without such underpinnings, political democracy becomes a sham controlled by private interest and big power groups—one in which citizens are no longer confronted with real choices. To be able to see the less fortunate as part of a greater "we" requires curiosity and imagination. It requires enough curiosity to wonder how it would be to live in a ghetto, how it would be to exist without health insurance or how it would be to be truly hungry or riddled with cancer. It requires enough imagination to draw from our common and inevitable store of common human experience sufficient nourishment to go at least a few steps towards answering the question curiosity has posed. Curiosity and imagination, like empathy and the power to reason, are essential to ethics as well as to the functioning of a democracy concerned with the interests of all its members.[8]

3.   AN ILLUSTRATIVE CASE WITH COMMENTS

In choosing a particular case to demonstrate what we have been discussing we must be aware that, given our fragmented social and health care system, the variations are infinite. First of all, end of life care is hardly limited to malignancies. Dying can be initiated by many things: emphysema, cerebral accidents, progressive heart failure to name but a few. The orchestration of the care of each of these varied patho-physiological conditions presents unique problems which affect the types of instruments chosen as well as the music. The common denominator is the attempt to make this stage of life one which is more tolerable and perhaps (one might hope) one that is still filled with activity and satisfaction. The dying process in ancient times could provide a certain satisfaction to the patient, to the family and to the community. Hopefully, orchestrating the end of life may help restore some of this lost opportunity.

But variations are not merely due to differences in disease process. Whatever the disease process, variations in the way we die often start with the question of initial access to proper care and develop throughout the case depending not only on cultural or personal factors but also on economic, social and structural factors. Thus an almost infinite number of pathways for any patient are conceivable and only a few can be discussed here. The case is meant to demonstrate not only an approach to a particular case but how such an approach is shaped (some of us would say distorted) by the particular social setting and circumstances in which it occurs. Let us start with the "bare bones" scenario of a lady found to have breast cancer: "Mrs. Jones is a 59 year old married lady."

Here we come to the first problem of access: already the term "found to have breast cancer" depends upon the social circumstances of the patient. If Mrs. Jones has a job at minimum pay and without insurance her access to health care will vary from some charity care for a variety of health problems to care only being available only after severe illness to the point of interfering with daily activities develops. Let us say that Mrs. Jones grew up in a setting in which family structure and values may not have supported the attempt to secure the training needed for a better position. Opportunities (except for the very lucky and very talented) were few. Access to medical care (except for the occasion when she has become acutely ill) is extremely limited. Her chance of getting a routine check-up is remote. It is more likely (but highly dependent upon particular circumstances) that she might have gained access at one of the charity clinics had she found a lump in her breast. However, this already assumes that she could have afforded either the cost of transportation, missing work or the lengthy waiting period common in such a setting. In that event, Mrs. Jones would most likely have finally gained access to medical care when her cancer was far advanced, would then most likely have been biopsied and given appropriate treatment for a condition which very likely would be beyond cure. Her progress to end of life care would then have been rapid. Her opportunity to receive good palliative care would have been limited by her economic circumstances, her social setting and by what was available to a charity or public aid patient. Even if good medical palliative care were technically available, a social setting of poverty does not lend itself to making optimal use of such care. Often living in at least sub-optimal settings and often in squalor, having obligations towards her family which she could not meet and constantly worried about her and her families daily bare existence would severely limit the type and effect of palliative care possible.

Had Mrs. Jones been on Medicaid (and depending upon her state of residence) she may or may not in fact have had access to the kind of care in which routine mammography was done. If she did and, again, depending upon the variables of access in each state, she would then have been entitled to full care. Once beyond cure, however, and entered into a hospice program her economic circumstances and social setting would still have been a severely limiting factor in the type of palliative care possible. As we have seen, hospice care in the United States is largely outpatient and, therefore, its quality and effectiveness is very much dependent on the social milieu. For example, one of three criteria for access to hospice care (at least through government supported funding) stipulates the availability of a "primary care giver" in the home. If her family, due to threat of loss of employment, cannot guarantee the availability of such a primary care giver, Mrs. Jones could not meet the hospice benefit criteria.

Let us change the scenario:

Mrs. Smith is also 59 year old married lady. She has health insurance both through her husband's and her own job but of a type that fails to provide for routine office visits, mammography or prescription drugs. She has two teen-age children in high school and living at home. With the patient's income, the family has managed to "get by" but has no savings or other outside sources of income.

In many ways, Mrs. Smith is in a similar position as our non-medicaid Mrs. Jones. Although access will be easier for her (both she and her husband work at jobs that at least carry some insurance) she will still fail to get prophylactic care and, therefore, her disease is apt to be discovered late. Once it is, her problems in dealing with palliative care will again be modified by the family's economic circumstances which with the patient's salary gone are—at the same time as expenses escalate—considerably worse. Her ability to obtain her medications is limited by her ability to pay for them—it has been estimated that even the bill for an average dose of morphine which cancer patients may require is in the range of $ 7,500 per year![9] Insurance which fails to cover out-patent visits, laboratory or x-ray tests or prescription drugs leaves patients in some respects equally badly off as the uninsured. Since once they agree to enter hospice their overall care will usually be covered, such patients may be forced to give up life-prolonging treatment and enter a hospice program (and "refuse" life-sustaining treatment) far sooner then they might otherwise choose.

Let us look at yet another scenario in this particular disease:

Mrs. Swerdl is a 64 year old married lady. She was found to have a positive mammogram on a yearly routine check-up. Subsequent biopsy revealed breast cancer. Her husband has worked for a local factory for many years, is a foreman and carries reasonably complete health insurance. The patient has two children: one is in graduate school and the other has a good position with a local bank.

Not infrequently, the story starts with the positive mammogram, the biopsy and the diagnosis of breast cancer. If we assume that this patient is adequately (that is relatively fully) insured, we now face the question of when orchestrating the end of life should begin. On the one hand beginning when a diagnosis of a potentially fatal illness is first made may be optimal; on the other hand starting here may be seen as overly pessimistic and perceived by both patient and physician as burdensome. This, we think, demonstrates the fallacy in trying to divide the ongoing care of patients in such a way. End of life care seen as separate and separable from care throughout life is an artifact. Good overall care at the end of life is most meaningful when integrated into good overall care and acceptable socio-economic circumstances throughout life.

End of life care and the patient's wishes are matters that should have been discussed with her health care providers long ago. As patients are asked about past history they should be involved in conversations about future plans and options. Physicians and other health care professionals should seek to understand their patients' values, wishes, plans and fears at least as well as they understand the patients' prior illnesses. If this has not been done before, it is at this point that the possibility of executing an advance directive should be discussed and details fully discussed with patients and friends. Some patients may (for a variety of reasons) not wish to execute an advance directive. However, one should be clear who the patient would like to have as decision-maker should decisional capacity be lost. In today's world, both the past and the future are properly the health care professionals concern. Values, wishes, plans and fears, furthermore, change as experience grows, as patients age and as particular illnesses or disabilities are really experienced rather than merely contemplated. A patient's values, wishes, plans and fears cannot simply be recorded and then never again discussed. Proper discussion should be ongoing. Today, patients and physicians unfortunately only rarely have relationships that extend over many years and decades. Recording a patient's values, wishes, plans and fears and transmitting them to physicians caring for the patient is, therefore, as essential a part of the medical record as is the recording of blood pressure or weight.

If such a discussion had been one which was not new to the patient (i.e., if it is one that this patient had had with her physician and other health care providers in an ongoing manner), it is easy to see how such a new diagnosis can easily lead into a re-examination of the patient's current values, wishes, plans, fears and prior advance directives without unduly disturbing the patient. Not only is it less burdensome to the patient to again take up such a discussion than it would be to start the discussion at this point in time, it is much easier for health care professionals who can build upon a firm foundation of wishes expressed and values understood. Patients who once begin to think about and discuss such issues are more ready to include such thinking into their overall medical plans.

If no such conversation had taken place before the diagnosis was made, a lot of time will have to be set aside by health care professionals to deal both with the strictly "medical" and the social and ethical choices which must be made. Such a conversation is best not one held all at once. A diagnosis of cancer and the options of treatment (or non-treatment) are quite enough and perhaps more than a patient should be asked to process in a single day. Furthermore, it is prudent to hold these conversations together with other members of the family whom the patient selects. It is (see chapter 3) most helpful if these conversations are recorded on tape and the tape given to the patient and family to listen to at home. Patients (and families) often hear what is being said incompletely and through a personal filter of values, hopes, fears and expectations—and, therefore, each may take away something quite different from that conversation. The ability to revisit the conversation helps patients (a) to understand what has been said, (b) to ask coherent questions,

(c) to discuss the implications of what has been said with family and friends, and (d) to participate, as fully as they are able to in future conversations. Such strategies are an essential part of orchestration.

Throughout these conversations other health care professionals (the players in the orchestra) must be fully appraised of what has and what is being said and may be well advised to also listen to some of the tapes. In this way all "get their acts together," a critical accomplishment if one is to prevent different information from being presented by different players at different times. It is not so much that different persons are apt to convey different "facts." It is more likely that the same facts are conveyed in a manner that, to the listener, makes them seem different. Just as it is important for the musicians of a great orchestra to understand what the particular interpretation of the conductor is all about and to add their own particular reading to that of the conductor, it is important to have key players participate in important conversations.

Mrs. Swerdl is now offered a choice of a variety of treatment and non-treatment options. Physicians are, of course, expected to fully explain options and outcomes to the best of their ability. But explaining options and outcomes and then asking the patient to choose does not exhaust the obligations which health care professionals have. Patients turn to health care professionals not merely because of their greater technical knowledge; they turn to them because of their greater experience with such problems and to seek their advice. It is true—physicians should not "stack the cards" so that the choice the patient will make is all but foreordained; but neither should they assume a stance of neutrality that, to the patient, may indicate abandonment and a lack of concern. Abandoning patients to their autonomy is no more ethically defensible then depriving them of it. Physicians and other health care professionals are well advised not only to offer choices and options but also to advise patients of what course of action they themselves deem best and why it is that they think it so. The patient may well make another choice, more commensurate with their own values and goals; but they will feel that, in the very act of subjectively approaching the problem (of putting themselves into their patients shoes) physicians will have behaved as more than mere technical experts. Rather, they will have shown by their interest and empathy that they very much care about the choices a patient may make and, therefore, about the patient him or herself.

Other health care professionals, again, are advised to consult and inform each other and where possible to participate or listen to the conversation. This, of course, may seem time consuming. In their busy lives, health care professionals are often pushed to the limit of their capacity. Nevertheless, integrating such an approach into overall patient care, into team conferences and case-management sessions may, in the longer run, save considerable time lost when people work (or seem to the patient to work) at cross purposes.

When Mrs. Swerdl makes a choice, it may be for a modified radical, for a lumpectomy or for a variety of other options. Unless her choice is non-treatment, the outcome will remain uncertain. Social and psychological support of the patient and the family should start with the first diagnosis and continue throughout the future course. This means that from the very first her care-givers must be aware of more than her "medical" diagnosis, prognosis and choices for treatment: they must be equally alert to her particular background and values as well as her psycho-social needs. When the patient enters the hospital for surgery it would be advisable to establish brief contact with social services, with persons trained in psychological care of such patients and, if it is commensurate with the patients values and wishes, her spiritual adviser or clergyperson. In other words, the orchestra here may be seen as rehearsing and as tuning their instruments for the performance of a particular anticipated piece of music.

It may be that Mrs. Swerdl remains free of disease for many years or perhaps for life. Surgery and recovery may go smoothly. Cancer may not resurface and the patient may be pronounced "cured." But it will be many years before this is known—years that will be worrisome and stressful for her and her family and which may well change her values and outlook. The time will inevitably leave its mark on her quite differently from what it would have without the diagnosis and its consequent uncertainty. Her attitude towards future illnesses will change depending in good measure on the competence and compassion with which this period is handled. For what has been cured has been the disease and not the illness itself. Moreover, such a diagnosis, the trauma of the treatment and with it the prolonged period of uncertainty inevitably leave its mark not only on the patient but likewise on the family, on the relationships of the various members and, therefore, on the social context. During this time, once again, pets may be most helpful. If a pet does not already exist, suggesting one at this point may introduce a dimension of immense psychological but, likewise, (there is some literature to substantiate this) of physical value.[10]

If patients are so inclined, they may profit from support groups. On the other hand, such groups may cause patients to focus their attention on their disease and not prove to be beneficial at all. Sometimes patients might profit a lot more from a mixed support group, one in which patients with advanced emphysema, cancer, heart disease and cerebral accidents help support and learn from one another that, all things considered, there are others worse off. Such decisions depend upon the patient's personality and world-view. The conductor, in studying the score and in communicating with the patient (and, therefore, the music), must try to select the correct approach to a given patient at a given time. Likewise, the help of clergy may be, most or not at all, appropriate. In the view of the authors, physicians themselves are not entitled to proselytize to patients or to attempt to influence their religious beliefs—doing so is, in our view, a gross abuse of power. Even if the physician and the patient are fellow churchgoers, we feel that it would be ethically inappropriate for the physician to be the one to initiate such activities. Patients, by definition, are already compromised by their illness; they do not need to be further coerced (or embarrassed) by their physician about non-medical issues. When, however, patients freely (and without having been manipulated into doing so) request, for example, that their physician pray with them and if the physician feels comfortable doing so, it may very well be appropriate.

If the patient remains disease free for some years—and breast cancer is notorious for being able to metastasize years later—and the disease then recurs, careful follow-up is needed. Along with that follow-up there may be some intermission in the actual performance. The instruments have been tuned and the initial score has been studied. Now the task is to maintain an ongoing dialogue and careful communication with the patient as well as with those closest to him or her—measures that may offer clues as to changes in the patient's values, fears, hopes and wishes. This is why listening—always much more important than talking at any point along the line—is so important. It is not only what patients say or do not say (often just as important) to the health care professionals involved, but also how the dialogue among patient and family proceeds. Listening to patients and families talk often will yield a lot of otherwise missed information. If, for example, Mrs. Swerdl is found to be totally dominated by her husband or if she uses her disease to dominate him, early help with family counseling may become part of the way the music is orchestrated. At this point it is important that health care professionals do not superimpose their own vision of what a "correct" relationship ought to be on persons who have willingly established and mutually continue to nurture what is, for them, a comfortable relationship—even if that relationship is perceived by others as "atypical" or even "dysfunctional."

On the other hand, things may not go that smoothly. Nodal involvement may suggest a worsening prognosis and a course of adjuvant chemotherapy. At this point the level of fear is higher, the need for support and understanding is not only greater, but may well begin to involve more and different players. The more the clinical facts denote a worsening of prognosis, the more important, immediate and involved orchestration becomes. The worse the prognosis, the more certain it seems that we have moved from tuning and rehearsal to beginning the first (and hopefully long and satisfying) movement which must establish a thematic whole with the movements to come.

The conductor of the orchestra will here need to exercise the skills he or she has learned. In learning the values, aims and goals of the patient, the conductor begins to understand the type of music appropriate for the occasion and will be alert, as time goes on, as themes develop, change and yet remain connected one to another. The score needs to be inspected so that players appropriate to the proposed musical offering can be properly chosen and so that they can begin to play together smoothly blending themes and movements. The conductor begins to understand the type of players needed, will be able to select an appropriate team and begin to anticipate what players will need to be involved and can begin the discussion with the members. It is crucial that all accept the process of orchestration as a team effort and not an individual effort. This requires frequent consultations among all team members, respectful listening to the suggestions and concern of others and a resolution of problems to which all can (even when sometimes not wholeheartedly) subscribe. But it also requires more; it requires that, when possible, patients, their families and others close to the patient (and, when not possible, patients families and those close to the patient) be drawn into this conversation. A "top-down" strategy, in which the conductor fails to consult and take seriously the musicians suggestions and in which the decision made by the team are conveyed but not jointly made with patient, family and friends is grossly paternalistic and needs to be studiously avoided. Good orchestration should be seen as a species of democratic process.

As much as possible, a patient's ability to make and carry out decisions must be supported. Mrs. Swerdl may well, under the burden of her illness, become more and more dependent upon her health care providers, her family and her context. As the disease progresses, this is probably inevitable. However, there are ways in which her decision making can be affirmed and the freedom of her will supported. There are many small things that can be done. A patient who loves puttering in her garden, for example, may have a wheel chair fitted with devices enabling her to do this. A patient who becomes progressively weaker and finds stairs increasingly difficult to negotiate, might be able to have his bedroom relocated so that he can move freely in and out. Translating willing into acting can be made much easier if what it takes to act is commensurate with the patient's capacity to do so. Likewise, the judicious, rather than exuberant, use of analgesics and sedatives is important. Patients should—whenever possible and if they wish—be kept pain free or as pain free as possible. But often, decision-making capacity and autonomy must be balanced with pain control. Generally, though not always, good pain control can be achieved without a significant loss of autonomy. On occasion, it can actually increase the overall ability to be and act autonomously. It is here that close collaboration with pain specialists is most helpful. The degree to which patients are willing to sacrifice clarity for pain control will vary with patient, circumstance and time and determining the patients choice requires astute listening and careful adjustments. Often, as has been pointed out, as patients grow weaker the gap between ability to freely choose and the capacity to freely act widens. Physicians, and with them other health care professionals, can do a lot to preserve a patients sense of dignity by helping them express choices and by helping to translate their willing into acting. Simple things like turning first to patients and not primarily to families when decisions must be made, arranging for physical aids to weakened limbs and providing readily accessible, convenient and above all private toilet facilities can all be a great help.

As, at this point inevitably, Mrs. Swerdl deteriorates in her physical condition she will be increasingly in need of medical and social support. It is at this point that hospice becomes an important option. Hospice, the way it is constituted today, is not for all patients. If Mrs. Swerdl decides to enter a hospice program it is essential that her previous clinicians continue to be meaningfully involved. They must not be relegated to the sidelines where they are made to feel like tolerated spectators; rather they must continue to play a central role in the patient's care. Throughout her illness, relationships have developed. These are valuable supports and maintaining this continuity is essential to the patients overall care. Speaking frankly with the patient, neither painting an unwarrantedly rosy picture or degenerating into dark gloom is helpful. Patients can maintain hope—not for cure, but for social support and for their last weeks or days still carrying within them the possibility of satisfaction.

It is immensely important that persons share food and drink with one another. The symbolic and social value that such sharing has had in all cultures and societies must not be forgotten or neglected. As long as we eat and drink together, we share a common humanity with one another; when we stop partaking of food and drink with one another we tend to feel isolated from our group, our family, our community. We pay too much attention to the caloric and nutritional and not enough to the social value which food and drink have. All efforts should be made to have patients continue to participate in family meals and especially in social events in which food and drink are shared. If patients are, despite our efforts to make this possible, unable to come to the table, sharing food and drink with them at the bedside assumes immense importance. At all costs patents must be kept members of the human community, members who feel not only taken care of and secure but who also feel that their presence enhances rather than burdens the lives of others. Honesty here is critical: as she becomes sicker and weaker, Mrs. Swerdl will feel that she is a burden and that her contributions to the family and to social life are diminishing or no longer present. Honesty is especially important here. To pretend falsely that she is no burden at all is a polite lie aimed at avoiding reality and making everyone feel better. It is far better to be forthright, to tell her, for example, that, of course, she requires time and attention but that in the every act of giving that attention and spending such time much benefit is also experienced by family and friends. To speak of such things in the language of shared responsibilities and commitments (of the responsibilities friends, family and even stranger implicitly share with one another in a well functioning social unit) is far more fruitful and far more realistic than speaking of burdens. Solidarity in a community does not come about when people are ready to share only good times, but comes about when people are ready to share the bad times as well.

As the disease progresses and as physicians and all else concerned continue to work with and support the patient and the family a time may be reached when patients no longer can be cared for by the family in a home situation. Often, if orchestration has been done well and with sufficient foresight and hospice has been involved well and early, care can be given at home. However it is very emotionally and financially exhausting for everyone when families must so totally disrupt their lives and work. That is, not only may such a course of action demolish the future lives of the care givers, it will generally burden the patient who must helplessly watch as her condition forces such disruption on her loved ones. In some nations generous leaves of absence are granted by employers to employees caring for such a patient and, in some countries, the state will, in addition, pay them a modest stipend. This is not presently the case in the United States and, therefore, more realistic arrangements must be made. Families go on long after patients die and their lives are no less important than are patients. Care givers—who sometimes see themselves merely as advocates of a particular patient at a particular moment in time—should be careful to take such facts into consideration.

Eventually, the time comes when a patient loses the "will to live." Such a point comes at different stages in every patient's decline. Not all—perhaps not even most—are entirely willing to go "gently into that good night" but many, in fact, are. At this point the support of physicians and other members of the orchestra as well as of the family is crucial. It is, first of all, necessary to determine whether the loss of a will to live has come about because of a remediable situation—Intolerable pain, nausea, immobility, or the feeling of having been abandoned or of being a burden. Sometimes some simple adjustment may restore such a patient's will to live. Patients may suffer from organic depression that, with judicious medication, can often be alleviated. Situational depression is, of course, quite normal (after all, if patients were elated at this point one would seriously question their contact with reality!). It must not be forgotten that those left behind have lost one person—a person of great importance to them—but not their whole world. The dying patient is losing everything they have ever held dear. Often, when the will to continue living has been truly lost, patients fear that their dying will burden others—that it will let family and health care team down. Giving them direct "permission" to die by saying "we will miss you terribly, but we will get along; it is all right to die." may come as a great relief to patients. This is the case for many patients who have been holding on against their will because they have been reared in a society in which death has, in various ways, been seen as a moral failing.

Some patients will die a more or less terrible death and some, towards the end of the symphony, may wish to walk out. It is at this point, after all that can has been done to improve the performance, that physician assisted suicide or euthanasia may become a tenable option. But that should happen rarely.

While the patient dies—and this is something which may happen relatively suddenly or be protracted—support must be given to those left behind. Not only will they lose the patient, they are with that death losing an occupation which, as time-consuming and nerve-racking as it was, has nevertheless come to fill a central role in their lives. In one sense they will feel relieved—and may feel guilty about feeling relieved. This is something that needs to be addressed head on during discussions before the event. In another sense, they often feel that they have lost a valuable purpose and may, in a sense, feel at sea. Taking note of such situations, supporting in a more than pro forma manner those who are now left behind, is a task that should legitimately be a part of orchestration. If we are truly concerned to support Mrs. Swerdl's interests and to make her final time on earth tolerable we should not forget that part of her interest is the welfare of her husband and loved ones. Re-assuring her that they will receive the support of a team they have come to rely upon is an important task. Losing one;s loved one should not occur simultaneously with losing a trusted group of people one has come to rely upon.

4.   SUMMING UP

The current emphasis on end of life concerns provides us with some glorious opportunities. It gives us the opportunity to work for meaningful training and procedures that can enable an overall skill in orchestrating the end of life while avoiding undue emphasis on physician assisted dying. Even those who oppose physician assisted dying are concerned about all the other aspects of "orchestrating the end of life." We, who are likewise concerned, ought not to alienate those who in many respects and on many issues are our natural allies by placing an undue emphasis on physician assisted dying. The latter is a potentially legitimate part of orchestration, but it is clearly only part of that process and one that persons of good will can disagree about. We have the opportunity to work for including the teaching of the skill necessary to orchestrate the end of life efficiently and well in the training of all health care professionals and to augment it by necessary laws.

Likewise, we have the opportunity of avoiding the "quick fix" approach: while emphasizing the need for good pain control we should do so only within the context of proper orchestration; while leaving the option of physician assisted dying open, we emphasize instead the primary desire for physician assisted living. We have the opportunity for doing all of this within the context of sensitivity to and recognition of larger social issues. Addressing the concerns of those who die today or who will die tomorrow and addressing the social concerns of our entire population must not be viewed either as mutually exclusive propositions or as unrelated goals. On the contrary: they are inexorably intertwined and necessarily mutually complementary. Society cannot successfully address one without concerning itself about the other. Physicians must play their part in the discussion not only as it pertains to the immediate and more narrow issue of proper procedure and training but also as it concerns the wider social issues in which these narrower issues are inevitably embedded. A life filled with dignity, but an end that looms with horror is neither socially desirable nor calculated to enhance that life. However, a death with dignity embedded in a life in which the opportunity for dignity was not a reality until the very end, is a tragic and cynical joke.

In this book we have tried to discuss some of the ethical issues which end of life care raises. The message we have tried to convey is clear: the end of life is neither a separate nor a separable stage from the rest of that life. If health care professionals take their task seriously, then dealing with and orchestrating the end of life becomes a part of their overall task. Likewise, if health care professionals take their task seriously and find themselves constrained by the institutions and systems in which they must work, they must play their proper part in attempting to change the system itself. Beyond this, the care given to patients at the end of life and the attempt to create a more congenial and a more just system will influence society in many explicit—and, perhaps more importantly—subtle ways. We can hope that, as our attitudes as a society towards death and dying shift and as our ideas of community slowly change towards one of greater solidarity, health care professionals can play their proper roles. Individual effort exists in a community which shapes the realm of the possible and which, in turn, is shaped by the effort made.

ENDNOTES AND REFERENCES

1. See, among others, an excellent recent summary of the problem by J.A. Billings and S. Block, "Palliative Care in Undergraduate Medical Education: Staus Report and Future Directions," *Journal of the American Medical Association*, 1997; 278(9): 733-738.

2. E.H. Loewy, "Physician Assisted Dying and Death with Dignity: Missed Opportunities and Prior Neglected Conditions," *Medicine, Health Care and Philosophy*, 1999; (2): 189-194.

3. For the interrelationship between pain and suffering and the differentiation of these concepts in a clinical setting, see E.J. Cassell, "The Nature of Suffering and the Goals of Medicine," *New England Journal of Medicine*, 1982; 306(1): 639- 645; E.J. Cassell, "The Relief of Suffering," *Archives of Internal Medicine*, 1983; 143: 522-523; and E.J. Cassell, "Recognizing Suffering," *Hastings Center Report*, 1991; 21(3): 24-31.

4. In a recent article Burt argues eloquently and persuasively that a constitutional right to palliative care might exist. See: R.A. Burt, "The Supreme Court Speaks—Not Assisted Suicide but a Constitutional Right to Palliative Care," *New England Journal of Medicine*, 1997; 337(17): 1234-1236.

5. A "right" is conceived somewhat differently in law than it is in ethics. In law a right is something which is legally fixed—it becomes "right" only after a legislature or a court declares it to be. In ethics the term is used in a number of different senses ranging from a "natural law" to a "law" crafted and fashioned by and in community with one another. It is, perhaps, better not to speak of "rights" but rather to look upon the whole concept of "rights" as being a matter of more or less justifiable or justified claims. See L.R. Churchill, and J.J. Siman, "Abortion and the Rhetoric of Individual Rights," *Hastings Center Report*, 1982; 12: 9-12.

6. Rawl's "veil of ignorance" can, despite its drawbacks, serve as a heuristic device in making important social choices—see J. Rawls, *A Theory of Justice* (Cambridge, MA: Harvard University Press), 1971. Imagine yourself behind a Rawlsian veil of ignorance which would not have you know who you are, how old, how well or unwell you might be, what race, what gender or what income group you belong to. You are told only that you will have to choose among three different social goods, only two of which would be guaranteed to you -- the third would be up to luck and your own devices. These three would be (a) all biological necessities would be guaranteed; (b) a full education to develop your interests and talents would be yours for the asking; and (c) health care would be fully supplied in case of illness. It is likely that most prudent choosers would choose to forego guaranteed health care in favor of the other two.

7. John Dewey eloquently speaks to the problem of democracy in more than its political sense. See: J. Dewey, *The Public and its Problems* in *John Dewey: The Later Works, 1925-1953*, ed. by J.A. Boydston (Carbondale, IL: Southern Illinois University Press), 1988 and J. Dewey, "Creative Democracy: The Task before Us," in *John Dewey: The Later Works, 1939-1951*, ed. by J.A. Boydston (Carbondale, IL: Southern Illinois University Press), 1991. As concerns contemporary problems, we have taken Dewey's ideas and applied them to some of the situations today. See Loewy E.H. Loewy, *Moral Strangers, Moral Acquaintance and Moral Friends: Connectedness and its Conditions* (Albany, NY: State University of New York Press), 1997 and R.S. Loewy, *Integrity and Personhood: Looking at Patients from a Bio/psycho/social Perspective* (NY: Kluwer Academic/Plenum Publishing), 2000.

8. E.H. Loewy: "Curiosity, Imagination, Compassion, Science and Ethics: Do Curiosity and Imagination Serve a Central Function?" *Health Care Analysis*, 1998; (6): 286-294.

9.   K. Foley, "Competent Care for the Dying Instead of Physician Assisted Suicide," *New England Journal of Medicine*, 1997; 336: 54-58.

10. The prolongation of life in cancer patients with pets seems to be a very real thing.

Index